W9-CUA-624

# Deconstructing Dignity

# Deconstructing Dignity

*A Critique of the Right-to-Die Debate*

SCOTT CUTLER SHERSHOW

The University of Chicago Press

CHICAGO AND LONDON

SCOTT CUTLER SHERSHOW is professor of English at the
University of California, Davis. He is the author of *Puppets and "Popular" Culture*
and *The Work and the Gift*, the latter published by the University of
Chicago Press, and is also coeditor of *Marxist Shakespeares*.

The University of Chicago Press, Chicago 60637
The University of Chicago Press, Ltd., London
© 2014 by The University of Chicago
All rights reserved. Published 2014.
Printed in the United States of America

23 22 21 20 19 18 17 16 15 14     1 2 3 4 5

ISBN-13: 978-0-226-08812-9 (cloth)
ISBN-13: 978-0-226-08826-6 (e-book)
DOI: 10.7208/chicago/9780226088266.001.0001 (e-book)

Library of Congress Cataloging-in-Publication Data
Shershow, Scott Cutler, 1953– author.
Deconstructing dignity : a critique of the right-to-die debate /
Scott Cutler Shershow.
pages ; cm
Includes bibliographical references and index.
ISBN 978-0-226-08812-9 (cloth : alkaline paper) —
ISBN 978-0-226-08826-6 (e-book)
1. Right to die. 2. Dignity. I. Title.
R726.S54 2014
179.7—dc23
2013017717

♾ This paper meets the requirements of
ANSI/NISO Z39.48-1992 (Permanence of Paper).

*For Frances—*
*"The heart of the singular being* is *that which is not totally his,*
*but it is thus that it is* his *heart."*

# Contents

# Preface: The Sacred Part

> Let me ask you this: if everything that ever lived is dead, and everything alive
> is going to die, where does the sacred part come in?
>
> GEORGE CARLIN

About a "right to die" there is obviously not yet any legal, political, or ethical consensus. But has the very *question* of such a right been formulated clearly? Despite a long philosophic tradition addressing the question of suicide itself and, more recently, a half-century of legal decisions, a growing library of scholarly studies across multiple disciplines, and a steady outpouring of polemic from advocacy groups, the debate about a right to die remains marked by contradictions and misrecognitions on every side—if one can even speak of the "sides" of a debate whose warring positions often seem secretly complicit with one another. Something still seems to impede our access to a vexed set of decisions about the end of (human) life—decisions that have never been easy, and that will not become easy even when all the common arguments so far brought to them have been deconstructed, assuming such a thing is possible.

My preface title, which already takes from my epigraph a hint of the comic, also gives homage to Georges Bataille's *La Part Maudite*—the "cursed part" or, as Robert Hurley translates it, *The Accursed Share*—to invoke the "burst of laughter" with which (in Derrida's memorable summary) Bataille responds to the very work of philosophy under its privileged name of Hegel. This laughter, which emerges from or perhaps *constitutes* a certain relation between the finite being and death, seems at once to be the very thing always at stake in this debate, and the very thing that remains entirely unthought within it. I also intend an oblique reminder that what is called deconstruction, as Derrida acknowledges in an early interview, is often "situated *explicitly* in relation to Bataille" (*Positions* 105-6n35). Derrida's texts, both early and late, often force us to confront a strange relation of incalculability and calculation (or what Bataille termed "general" and "restricted" economy) that emerges in a wide variety of discourse and thought—including, as I suggest here, the debate about a right to die.

My preface title also more distantly echoes a term at the center of another theoretical debate, this one between Derrida and Jean-Luc Nancy, about the *partage*: a word that in French can mean both joining and division—as we glimpsed above with *part*, a noun that similarly means, in French, either "part" or "share." As J. Hillis Miller suggests, *partage* might be taken either as "sharing" or as "shearing" (252). I invoke this term here because death itself, or at least any conceivable way to think a certain "right" to death, is the very instance and limit of *partage* in each of its senses. *Partage* thus figures, so to speak, that irreducible *spacing of time* that makes possible a "*sharing* of singularities" (Nancy, *Experience of Freedom* 70): a sharing that must, accordingly, *always* involve "at once partition and participation" (Derrida, *Rogues* 45). For any hypothetical *right* to die, as we shall see, would necessarily involve a certain (social, legal, or political) sharing of the one thing (death) that can never be shared, and a certain process of division, distribution, and calculation that, however, finally undoes itself by being so shared.

In this book, I approach the debate about a right to die as a whole, and my focus may therefore seem at once too large and too small: too large because I will be summarizing a voluminous debate, a debate both ancient and contemporary, only selectively and schematically; and too small, because I offer no final, specific resolution and for the most part refrain from taking sides. Perhaps the latter will seem especially paradoxical, since what it is always at stake in the question of a hypothetical right to die are life-and-death *decisions* in the most literal sense of the word: decisions to which individuals, families, doctors, judges, and lawmakers are all alike called, and yet about which it remains today unclear precisely what person, or what principle, is or should be sovereign. But, as Derrida has repeatedly argued, the structure of any decision, and therefore any possibility of justice, rights, or responsibility, also involves this strange relation of calculation and incalculability. As he writes, "a decision has to be prepared by reflection and knowledge"—and hence by calculation—"but the moment of the decision, and thus the moment of responsibility, supposes a rupture with knowledge, and therefore an opening to the incalculable" (Derrida and Ferraris, *Taste* 61). This aporia or interpretive dilemma, necessarily involved in the structure of any decision, will guide my critique of this vexed question of a right to die.

In the first chapter of this book, I begin with some broad methodological observations—though the term "method," as I acknowledge, cannot really be employed—about the strategy and protocol of deconstruction, observations that will guide my readings throughout. Readers more specifically interested in the political and bioethical questions otherwise central to the book are invited to move past this introductory discussion, which involves a relatively detailed foray into the texts of Jacques Derrida. The first few chapters that follow provide a selective genealogy of the key concept underlying the whole question of a right to die: "human dignity." I consider the shifting historical and semantic structure that underlies this term, especially its relationship to two other equally difficult concepts—"sanctity" and "sovereignty." For dignity is often, in various discursive contexts, set in specific *opposition* to either one or the other of these two, even as its own semantic structure also forces it into a certain near-identity with both. Across its whole history, and in a variety of different ways, *dignity* seems always to denote the worth and value of humanity as a strange relation of calculable and incalculable value, in a manner that conceals a certain internal gap or fissure in its own concept. The strange groundlessness of the concept of human dignity proves to be particularly pertinent in considering the modern debate about a "right to die," as I do in the second half of the book. To consider this debate schematically or structurally will be to bring to light how, here again, a certain *relation* of calculation and incalculability structures not only arguments on both sides of the issue, but also the debate as a whole.

I then contextualize this modern debate by considering a few outstanding examples of the philosophic approach to suicide itself. From Plato to Kant, a theological and ethical *prohibition* of suicide proves always to be troubled by a certain signal exception: the figure of self-sacrifice. Such an insight, in its turn, allows me to return to the contemporary debate, whose shared economy then reveals itself, similarly, as one of *sacrificial calculation*. But is not sacrifice, some may already object, the very thing that is *not* at stake in the question of a (legal and political) *right* to die? In fact, is not sacrifice the very thing that is, in principle, beyond all calculation? Such questions, which will animate the discussion that follows, already perhaps evoke a faint irony, or a burst of laughter, that in pursuing these arguments I have often, despite their solemnity, found impossible to repress.

Indeed, considered as a whole, the contemporary debate about the right to die appears at once (to appropriate Derrida's description of Heidegger's text) "horribly dangerous and wildly funny, certainly grave and a bit comical" (*Of Spirit* 68). The gravity and danger of this debate are obvious.

Perhaps no issue involves so many confusingly entwined political, legal, and theological issues, nor forces so intimate a confrontation with the spatial and temporal conditions and limits of bodily life. Today, even to name or describe the thing itself is to enter a field of controversy. Does the right to die mean the right to decide the time, place, and circumstances of one's own death, the right to take one's own life under *any* circumstances, the right to be assisted in dying, or the right of some to decide on the death of others? Are we speaking of *euthanasia* (a word with its own vexed history, and that merely elides the question of what might constitute a "good" death), of "physician-assisted suicide," "death on demand," "death with dignity," or even, as some have claimed, of "judicial murder"? By each of these definitions and names, a debate about the right to die would demand a different set of arguments and interpretive protocols; yet in no case would the question of such a right become any easier to decide.

The comic note that attends the question of a right to die is, by contrast, subtle, convoluted, and oblique: evoked as much by certain structural or historical contradictions marking the debate as a whole as by any of its specific articulations, and conditioned by a certain embarrassment about its own emergence in a context otherwise so grave. For one thing, can one really conceive of a *right* to that which comes inescapably to all whether they like it or not? Can the political and legal concepts of "right" or "freedom" apply to something that, so to speak, marks the very limit of all rights and all freedom? The very idea of death is obviously and absolutely inseparable from the fundamental question of temporality itself—and also, therefore, from what Martin Hägglund calls (in his important reading of Derrida), the *time of life*, the fundamental "space-time," or *spacing of time*, which is the absolute condition of possibility for mortal being itself. Certain questions of time and history, of evolution or degeneration, have accordingly been among the most contentious in the debate about a right to die, and but one of many examples of a symmetry in which its opposed positions often seem to join.

Consider, to begin with, how both the proponents and opponents of a right to die often envision the whole debate as a linear or narrative history. For both, the same succession of watershed events—for example, the cases of Karen Quinlan (1975-85), Nancy Cruzan (1983-90), and Terri Schiavo (1990-2005)[1]; the legalization of physician-assisted suicide in the Netherlands (2002) and in the American states of Oregon (1994) and Washington (2008); the career and eventual conviction for assisting suicide of Dr. Jack Kevorkian (1999)—are understood as historical signposts of either emancipatory progress or moral and social decline. Moreover, proponents of a right to die commonly inscribe their cause within an assumed history of technoscientific progress. For example, it is often claimed by proponents of a right to die that recent advances in medical technology, especially techniques for prolonging the biological life of elderly and severely ill patients, have, as Derek Humphrey puts it, "pushed the assisted death issue to the forefront" (Humphrey and Clement 15; cf. Glick 14). William H. Colby (who had served as the attorney for Nancy Cruzan) declares that "the hard questions raised by a case like Terri Schiavo's are blindingly new for humankind" (Colby, *Unplugged* 95). A right to die is thus not merely a right newly added to the list of those considered indispensible, but a right that only recently emerged as necessary. Such an argument, however, seems to predetermine its own symmetrical refutation, by which one argues (as opponents of the right to die commonly do) that *precisely because of* this rapidly changing technoscientific landscape, as Charles Colson puts it, "bioethical reasoning based on the meaning and value of human beings must precede and guide biotechnology" (Colson 17).

Now, there can be no doubt that new technologies for prolonging life have created many more cases in which *decisions* about the end of life seem inescapably to present themselves. A treatment may be accepted even if it hastens death; another treatment might be refused although it might prolong life. Medical technology has also created (if this word is the right one, given that such a development appears entirely inadvertent) many more cases in which patients survive in comatose or "vegetative" states, viewed in the popular imagination as a kind of "living death" and understood within a certain theory of biopower as a paradigmatic instance of the "bare life" to which it is the destiny of sovereign power to reduce us all (Agamben 186). American jurisprudence, while not yet recognizing any absolute right to suicide or to have assistance in committing suicide, has moved towards recognizing a partial or implicit "right to die" by affirming an individual's right to refuse treatment (and to record his or her wishes to this effect in "living wills" or "advance directives"). Yet as E. J. Emmanuel suggests, the major *philosophic* positions in this debate have not changed significantly since Samuel D. Williams' essay "Euthanasia" of 1870, commonly identified as the first published text to advocate unequivocally what we would call today physician-assisted suicide (793). Moreover, a debate about suicide in general goes back as far as ancient Greece: to take just the most notable example, the Stoic philosophers believed (citing R. S. Guernsey's summary), that it is "essential to the dignity" of a human being "that he should regard

death without dismay, and that he has a right to hasten it if he desires"
(Guernsey 11). And as Ian Dowbiggin and Shai J. Lavi have shown, the possibility of legalizing some forms of euthanasia was already being debated
by doctors, philosophers, and legislators in the early years of the twentieth century, long before the invention of the respirator or the nasogastric
tube.[2]

Thus the question of a right to die somehow both is and is not techno-
logically determined, and both does and does not evolve progressively. But
if this debate as a whole cannot finally be understood as a simple narrative
of progress, still less can it be understood in terms of decadence or decline.
Yet opponents of a right to die today doggedly repeat the same fundamental
claim: that "modern culture is going" toward a new "philosophy of 'human
life' that reduces the stature, the worth, and the irreplaceable uniqueness of
the individual person" (Ramsey, "Indignity" 61); that a "culture of death . . .
has enveloped our medical and moral world during the last generation"
(Smith, *Culture of Death* 238); and that "contemporary liberal political theory abets the culture of death" by "justifying and defending euthanasia"
(George, *Clash* 39-40). In the face of such claims about some allegedly new
"culture of death," one can only rub one's eyes in astonishment and wonder
exactly when or where some contrasting "culture of life" ever prevailed.
Is it even necessary to name the brute facts of the past few centuries of
American or world history that suffice to expose the hollowness of such
claims? To take just the most proximate example, the Nazi programs of
involuntary euthanasia and racial eugenics—the cautionary example commonly cited by opponents of a right to die as the likely consequence of any
change in the laws regarding assisted suicide—were inspired and influenced
by a whole range of discourse, legislation, experimentation, and political
activism in early twentieth-century America.[3] Would it be in those years
that one should look for a model of the "culture of life"?

In all this, and as we will see in other ways throughout, the symmetry
with which the two sides of this debate confront one another and sometimes seem secretly complicit provokes an inescapable laughter that seems
to gather itself, in any case, around the very possibility of *deciding about* or
even *deciding on* death. In his early nightclub comedy, Woody Allen used to
joke about majoring in philosophy in college, when, he says, he had taken
courses such as "Truth," "Beauty," "Intermediate Truth and Beauty"—and,
finally, "Death 101." In the recorded version of this performance, it is the
final possibility that gets the biggest laugh. It would seem that the laughter
here confronts our sense that death itself, whatever else that might be said
or thought about it, and however much it must always compel our attention

and our decisions, somehow remains singular and secret, something that in its totality cannot be organized into a syllabus or subjected to the universality of academic reason. I have spoken already of a laughter that, for Bataille, is perhaps "the ultimate given" of philosophy and thought (Gemerchak 209) even as it escapes the latter's incessant aspiration to complete itself, "to include within itself and anticipate all the figures of its beyond, all the forms and resources of its exterior" (Derrida, "From Restricted to General Economy" 252). To be sure, as Mikkel Borch-Jacobsen suggests, in Bataille "there is no theory of laughter" (742). What is referred to as laughter in his fragmentary texts often seems a furtive and ungraspable concept—especially since, indeed, it is *not* finally a concept or even an object to be theorized but, rather, a kind of *experience*, yet one that never presents itself in a manner that might be grasped in the form of conceptuality.

Nevertheless, let me venture to speak of two laughters, or of what I will call here a *comedy* and a *laughter*. My terms, although perhaps not quite consistent with Bataille's own shifting deployment of them, can be broadly associated with his theoretical opposition of "restricted" and "general" economies.[4] The restricted economy, in its rhythm of investment and return, of deferral and profit, pertains to finite beings defined by their insufficiency and need. Such restricted beings are bound to necessity, to a daily task of supplying their bodily requirements; and their task thus has the shape of *comedy*: a sowing followed by a reaping, a planting leading to a fruition, a dispersal or dissemination completed by reconciliation or regathering. This comedy would also designate what Bataille describes in *Inner Experience* as the impossible aspiration of *"ipse* seeking to become everything" (89), of the human being seeking to overcome his insufficiency by struggling up to a "summit" where his being might be whole and complete: *sovereign* both in the sense of supreme and as *sufficient* unto itself. Comedy is also Bataille's name for the evasion or subterfuge constituted by the ritual sacrifice, a mechanism by which, he argues, humanity manages to find a way to witness its own death, to *die* while actually continuing to live. Since the comic resolution by which *ipse* would indeed become all in all, attaining an absolute sovereignty beyond need, could only really be possible in death,

> death itself would have to become (self-) consciousness at the very moment that it annihilates the conscious being. In a sense, this is what takes place (what at least is on the point of taking place, or which takes place in a fugitive, ungraspable manner) by means of a subterfuge. In the sacrifice, the sacrificer identifies himself with the animal that is struck down dead. And so he dies in seeing himself die, and even, in a certain way, by his own will, one in spirit with the sacrificial weapon. (Bataille, "Hegel, Death and Sacrifice" 19)

Death, the very instance of the moment that can never be brought to light, that appears only by disappearing, here parades itself in the broad light of day and even enjoys its own aftermath: thus conscious being finds a way to give itself death by its own will and hand, and yet remain alive. But this performance, Bataille declares immediately after, "is a comedy!"

Accordingly, the exclamation point that concludes this well-known passage itself marks where a certain laughter escapes the completion of this comic movement. The "burst of laughter from Bataille" that follows this sacrificial subterfuge is the same one, in Derrida's reading of Bataille, provoked by Hegel's "lord" who similarly undertakes an absolute risk of death within a philosophic schema in which he is always-already certain to remain alive. This laughter, Derrida writes, "bursts out only on the basis of an absolute renunciation of meaning, an absolute risking of death, what Hegel calls abstract negativity" ("From Restricted to General Economy" 255–56); and laughs at the Hegelian dialectic when it, on the contrary, "reappropriates all negativity for itself, as it works the 'putting at stake' into an *investment*, as it *amortizes* absolute expenditure; and as it gives meaning to death" (257). This laughter thus gestures toward the impossible experience of Bataille's general economy: senseless expenditure, loss without return, the absolute sovereignty which "has little to do with the sovereignty of states" (*Accursed Share* 2:197). For the singular being, such sovereignty could be realized only in death, for it could only be the property of being as a whole (cf. Borch-Jacobsen 744–45). Indeed, *ipse* at the summit has in this supremacy stranded himself in a place where no one else could arrive and nothing could happen (cf. Derrida, *Rogues* 152): sovereignty's absolute self-realization is the revelation of an absolute insufficiency that makes it (as Bataille writes in *Inner Experience*) "tragic . . . in its own eyes," but in every other way "laughable" (89). In the same book, similarly, Bataille writes of "the comedy—which *tragedy* is—and vice-versa," and of "the sacrifice, the comedy which demands that a sole individual die in the place of all the others" (98). Figures of sovereignty—such as the Hegelian lord who claims to master all negativity in philosophic speculation, or the man Bataille describes in an early essay who, "ready to call to mind the grandeurs of his nation, is stopped in mid-flight by an atrocious pain in his big toe," and whose "viscera, in more or less incessant inflation and upheaval, brusquely put an end to his dignity" (*Visions of Excess* 22)—become the very things at which this (sovereign) laughter laughs. Such laughter thus responds or opens to a contestation or transgression so powerful that it can only be grasped as affirmation, or in other words, as a kind of sovereignty against sovereignty, a sovereignty defined by its impossible suspension at the very limit *of* sovereignty.

Such a laughter, as that final quotation indicates, also laughs at *dignity* itself, which, as I will suggest in a variety of ways throughout, is a concept always locked in a strange relation with sovereignty, and which might finally be considered the name that humanity gives itself in the very moment of its attainment of the summit, just before the belittling burst of laughter. This point shifts our attention to Kant, who inevitably figures in debates about a right to die and whom we will consider twice in the pages that follow. To briefly cite here a few lines of a famous passage from the *Groundwork of the Metaphysic of Morals* to which we will return, Kant contrasts "price" and "dignity" as two forms of value:

> What has a price can be replaced by something else as its *equivalent*; what on the other hand is raised above all price and therefore admits of no equivalent has a dignity. (4:434)[5]

Kant makes this distinction, of course, in order to argue that "morality, and humanity insofar as it is capable of morality, is that which alone has dignity" (4:435). Kant's humanity is thus constituted by a double economic structure in which two forms of value are joined in a strange relation, and about which one might suggest at least a distant analogy to Bataille's economic opposition of restricted and general economies. In both cases, two economies or value-forms divide in terms of an apparent opposition of calculation and incalculability. Therefore, on the one hand, human beings possess a "natural" or animal life, a life bound to a rhythm of ingestion and growth, and whose limited or contingent value stems from its ability to produce itself: both in this literally bodily manner and by working to fulfill what Kant calls "general human inclinations and needs" (4:434). This natural life with its calculable value or price would seem to correspond to Bataille's "restricted economy," the economy of circulation and deferral, of labor and need, of investment and return. On the other hand, human beings, insofar as they are capable of reason and moral choice, are also the bearers of an incalculable value (dignity), a value transcending their specific works and all utility of any kind. Dignity in this sense, as an attempt to designate a value beyond price, a value that cannot be calculated, might seem to correspond to Bataille's general economy: the economy of the "world" or the "universe" grasped in their greatest possible generality. Or at any rate, in both of these quite heterogeneous schemas, a realm of calculable value and a realm of incalculability are set against one another in a relation that, however, is not one of simple opposition, since in each case it might conceivably be said that the term of incalculability does not merely *reverse* its counterpart but, rather, opens it, loosens it up, or even explodes it into a new and wider horizon of possibility.

Even to suggest this correspondence, however, is to instantaneously reveal its untenability as a reading of either Kant or Bataille, and to illuminate with peculiar vividness the parameters of Bataille's "Copernican revolution" in ethics.[6] As I have argued elsewhere, Bataille was trying above all to articulate the relation between an individual being, who remains bound to the law of scarcity, and the "general" sphere of existence in which value and energy are limitless.[7] For Kant, dignity is finally still a mode of *elevation,* and thus a kind of *achievement*—that is, to recall the semantic root of the latter term, a coming-to-a-head (*a chief venir*). Thus human dignity, at least in any convincing reading of Bataille (who once declared himself to be "violently opposed to all dignity" [*Oeuvres* 7:460]), must remain under the horizon of the restricted economy: the economy of individual being and of project, achievement, investment, and return. And, by the same token, it could be only the sovereign whole, the common or community that, beyond or beneath all dignity, might open to the limitlessness of the general economy—*either* to death as joyously absolute negativity, *or* to "life" as a whole: that "general existence whose resources are in excess and for which death has no meaning" (*Accursed Share* 1:39).

Therefore, as will be apparent in various ways throughout this book, the laughter that pervades the debate about a right to die, despite the latter's obvious gravity and danger, pertains above all to the strange concept of "dignity" that so informs it on every side. And why not? Dignity has always been a privileged target of every sort of laughter, in more than one of its senses. If we laugh at the discomfiture of a would-be gentleman or at the unexpected dignity of a tramp, we also laugh more generally at "this vain animal / Who is so proud of being rational."[8] Even in all the serious and dangerous contexts in which it figures today, dignity can seem to be at once everywhere and nowhere: a sort of semantic trickster that at one moment refers to an inalienable human essence (what the International Declaration of Human Rights calls "the inherent dignity . . . of all members of the human family" [Brownlie and Goodwin-Gill 24], at another moment to something that one can put on or take off ("he behaved with great dignity"), and at still another moment to something that can be stripped away by violence or coercion (e.g., the "outrages upon personal dignity" prohibited in the Geneva Conventions [Roberts and Guelff 245]). In the discourse surrounding the right to die—so often understood, of course, as being about "death with dignity"—the concept plays a similarly devious part. To very briefly consider one initial example among innumerable possibilities, the liberal Protestant theologian and cleric Leslie Weatherhead writes (in 1965):

> I sincerely believe that those who come after us will wonder why on earth we kept a human being alive against his own will, when all the *dignity*, beauty and meaning of life had vanished; . . . I for one would be willing to give a patient the Holy Communion and stay with him while a doctor, whose responsibility I should thus share, allowed him to lay down his useless body and pass in *dignity* and peace into the next phase of being. (cited Downing 14, emphases added)

Weatherhead makes clear in his own rhetoric that the very occasion in which a right to die would be exercised is often one in which "all the dignity . . . of life had vanished." In other words, a right to die *with* dignity is justified by the *loss* of dignity. Here again, so paradoxical an argument seems to mark out in advance its own symmetrical refutation, which is indeed commonly put forward by opponents. For example, Paul Ramsey argues (in an essay from 1974) that "there is nobility and dignity in caring for the dying, but not in dying itself." Therefore, Ramsey suggests, the very idea of a death with dignity is a fatal contradiction in terms, because "to deny the indignity of death requires that the dignity of man be refused also" ("Indignity" 48, 56). Thus, even the "with" of the crucial phrase "death *with* dignity" can only mark a space of controversy and question: it names a condition in which a certain crucial yet indefinable form of value seems always at once, and in multiply contradictory ways, both present and absent.

It might be said of the debate I consider here, to risk one final pun on my own preface title, that on both sides death itself is envisioned as a kind of *sacred partage*: a sharing that is *religious* even when understood, as it sometimes is, in wholly secular terms, because it would always involve a re-binding (*re-ligare*) of singular beings in terms of some determination of their being. That is, both sides approach the possibility of decision with regard to death by predetermining it (in one direction or another) in terms of an immanent and inalienable value or characteristic of humanity (a sanctity or dignity of human life). If I do not finally take sides in the debate as currently constituted, I do join Derrida and others in understanding that such a strategy makes a truly ethical decision impossible. As Derrida puts it, "pure ethics, if there is any, begins with the respectable dignity of the other as the absolute *unlike*, recognized as nonrecognizable, indeed as unrecognizable, beyond all knowledge, all cognition, and all recognition; far from being the beginning of pure ethics, the neighbor as like or as resembling, as looking like, spells the end or the ruin of such an ethics" (*Rogues* 60). The lines I have just cited appear in a context in which Derrida is formulating a sympathetic critique of Nancy for, among other things, a certain overreliance on the concept or figure of *fraternity*.[9] Without rehearsing the details of that critique any further here, I might add a similar caveat about Derrida's own use of the word "dignity" in the passage above. To be sure, Derrida uses the word only to transform it, in that he identifies "the absolute *unlike*" as the ground or origin of "the respectable dignity of the other." This alone might be a sufficiently large conclusion in the face of a debate whose central concepts of the "dignity" or "sanctity" of (human) life are by contrast always grounded in some category of likeness, resemblance, or recognition that, at the very least, lifts us above all other natural creatures and then supposedly invites or guarantees our mutual respect. Even then, however, it might still remain to be questioned whether the word and concept of dignity can indeed be wrested successfully from the anthropological and metaphysical determinations that so obviously condition its meaning and use. Without, obviously, being somehow *against* human dignity, or opposed to the emancipatory project so often conducted in its name, one must still subject it to "a rational deconstruction that will endlessly question [its] limits and presuppositions, the interests and calculations that order [its] deployment" (*Rogues* 151). In the pages that follow, I take some tentative steps toward tracing this strategic, adventurous, and unfinishable project.

# *Acknowledgments*

Portions of this book were published as "'A Triangle Open on Its Fourth Side': On the Strategy, Protocol, and 'Justice' of Deconstruction," *Derrida Today* 2 (2011), and as "The Sacred Part: Deconstruction and the Right to Die," *CR: New Centennial Review* 12:3 (2012). Thanks to the editors and reviewers of these journals for their queries and comments; and also to Alan Thomas, Elizabeth Branch Dyson, Russell Damian, Mary Corrado, and their colleagues at the University of Chicago Press. David E. Johnson and one other anonymous reviewer for the press provided a wealth of helpful suggestions on the final manuscript.

I especially want to acknowledge Margaret W. Ferguson, Martin Hägglund, and Gerhard Richter for reading and commenting on the essay that became the first chapter of this book. Although I found their suggestions invaluable, whatever problems may remain in these pages are, of course, solely my own. To my once and future collaborator, Scott Michaelsen, I owe thanks for conversations over many years that profoundly shaped my understanding of the texts of Derrida and others. Nathan Brown directed my attention to the texts by Eric. L. Santner and John Protevi that I consider in chapter 7; and Karen Embry and Mindi McMann read drafts of the book and assisted with my research. Special thanks go to Lester Stephens for double-checking my Latin citations. Thanks also to Christopher Schaberg and his colleagues at Loyola University New Orleans, and to my colleagues at the University of California, Davis, who listened to me read some of these pages just as I was finishing the manuscript, and helped me refine it with their rigorous questions.

Thanks, finally, to Jean-Luc Nancy, whom I do not have the honor to know personally, for providing the words (in his essay "Shattered Love") with which I dedicate this book to Frances E. Dolan—who read the whole manuscript with meticulous attention just before I allowed myself to call it finished, and for whose infinite generosity and daily companionship I remain always incalculably grateful.

## CHAPTER ONE

# Methodological Introduction: A Strategy and Protocol of Deconstruction

"Learning to live," observes Jacques Derrida (in a now-famous interview conducted just weeks before his own death in 2004),

> should mean learning to die, learning to take into account, so as to accept, absolute mortality (that is, without salvation, resurrection, or redemption—neither for oneself nor for the other). That's been the old philosophical injunction since Plato: to philosophize is to learn to die.

And yet, he goes on to concede,

> I have never learned to accept it, accept death, that is. We are all survivors who have been granted a temporary reprieve. (*Learning* 24)

Derrida's words, inescapably privileged by their context and occasion, will serve as an vivid reminder that deconstruction remains, both first and last, a thought of what Martin Hägglund calls, with eloquent simplicity, *the time of life*. The idea of a hypothetical "right to die" is all-too-obviously inseparable from the difficult questions of mortality and survival of which Derrida speaks above; indeed, one might venture to suggest that what is envisioned under this phrase is no more and no less than a specific and practical version of the ancient philosophic challenge to learn how to die. It is equally obvious that the idea of a right to die might be approached via almost any mode of philosophy and thought. A right to die might be (and often has been) considered as a question of law, of religion, of psychoanalysis, or of the emergent fields today referred to as bioethics or biopolitics. I will argue here, however, that only deconstruction can be adequate to unfold the knot of unexamined assumptions remaining to be unfolded at the heart of this vexed question, assumptions that invisibly join both sides of this contemporary debate in a secret complicity.

Because, as Hägglund exhaustively demonstrates in his important reading of Derrida, *Radical Atheism*, deconstruction always involves "an unconditional affirmation of survival" (Hägglund 2), one might initially suspect that deconstruction should *oppose* any conceivable possibility of *choosing death*. Derrida himself, in the remarks he composed to be read at his own funeral, enjoins us to "always prefer life" (Peeters 541). Such suspicions would be all the more paradoxical in that deconstruction is sometimes denounced (and often precisely by the kind of thinkers otherwise opposed to any right to die) as a pernicious nihilism or ethical relativism, or at best a sort of quietism concerned with merely linguistic or semantic questions. But in fact, as Hägglund argues, deconstruction's affirmation of survival is actually an affirmation of finitude as (practical) possibility, and a thought of that fundamental *spacing of time* that makes possible all that could be encompassed under the name of "life." Deconstruction is a thought of the time of life *and* of death: of time as limit and as limiting condition, yet also of time as the condition of possibility for anything and everything like experience, meaning, or thought itself. What Derrida means by survival is something that, as he writes, "structures every instant in a kind of irreducible torsion, that of a retrospective anticipation that introduces the untimely moment and the posthumous into what is most living in the living present" (*Aporias* 55). The problem of a hypothetical right to die, therefore, is finally one and the same as the problem or problems of finitude itself: problems that are infinite, as Derrida puts it in a different context, not only because "they are infinitely numerous, nor because they are rooted in the infinity of memories and cultures (religious, philosophical, juridical, and so forth) that we shall never master," but also because "they are infinite, if one may say so, *in themselves*" ("Force of Law" 244). Deconstruction is necessary in the face of these limitless questions, therefore, because what one finally refers to under this term is a commitment to a perpetually renewed interrogation of the axioms, assumptions, and norms that govern our theories and our practices—and also, by the same token, our lives and our deaths.

Even if all this be granted, however, another possible objection interposes itself in the face of my claim to be "deconstructing" a contemporary debate whose roots so obviously go so deep into this infinity of history and thought. It would be this: does deconstruction provide in any sense a "method" that might be followed or put into practice as I seem to be promising? More broadly, does this so-called deconstruction, often associated with merely linguistic questions and, indeed, sometimes said to be already superseded by more recent theoretical paradigms, provide any tools or insights that can be brought to bear on an urgently practical question, such as the question of a hypothetical right to die? In this chapter I thus attempt to outline what will be called, for particular reasons, a strategy or protocol of deconstruction, and also a distinctively deconstructive thought of justice, that will guide the readings that follow in the rest of this book. This double responsibility necessitates a relatively detailed venture into the texts of Derrida. As I briefly mentioned in the preface, readers who would prefer to go straight to the practical and political questions primarily at stake in this book are invited to go on to the second chapter.

In response to this initial question—is deconstruction a "method"?—even undergraduates could today be expected to cite one or more of the well-known passages where Derrida repeatedly insists that deconstruction is neither a method, nor a mode of analysis, nor "a set of rules and transposable procedures," nor "even an act or an operation." Rather, deconstruction merely "takes place," in the absence of any subject, and each time with the absolute singularity of an "idiom or a signature" (Derrida, "Letter" 4). As Rodolphe Gasché observes, in the course of a detailed attempt to assess a deconstructive methodology, a *method* is commonly understood to be "an instrument for representing a given field, and it is applied to that field from the outside" (Gasché 121); but deconstruction "does not apply itself . . . to anything from the outside," for it is something that a text "does itself, by itself, on itself" (Derrida, "Force of Law" 264). Deconstruction thus cannot even be definitively linked to some specific history or period such as that of modernity (or, still less, any so-called postmodernity), for it takes place in what can only be described as an "'epoch' of being-in-deconstruction, of a being-in-deconstruction that manifests or dissimulates itself at one and the same time in other 'epochs'" (Derrida, "Letter" 4-5).

Such stipulations are now entirely familiar. But doesn't one more or less assume that they will always be followed by the antithesis that I have now duly attached to them? In fact, don't such assertions sometimes approach, as Derrida puts it in another context, "very close to that at which laughter laughs" ("From Restricted to General Economy" 252). Won't someone (perhaps the undergraduate imagined above) always observe that even the lines just cited appear in essays and books that were composed, translated, printed, and so forth, and that a whole mechanism of practices, productions, and operations do attend, even if they do not exactly constitute, whatever could possibly be meant by deconstruction? And even if such material questions are dismissed, couldn't one further suggest that even to think or write about deconstruction must be to project, at least hypothetically, some procedure or method or operation in at least the sense of a course of action or a path set down to be followed? "Différance plays neither the role of a 'concept,' nor simply of a 'word,'" Derrida told an interviewer in 1971, but went on to concede that "this does not prevent it from producing conceptual effects" (*Positions* 40). Jean Wahl, introducing the discussion that followed Derrida's original presentation of the lecture that became the essay "Différance," put it like this: "It was said that *différance* with an *a* could not be spoken of, and yet, in the most fascinating way, we have heard *différance* with an *a* discussed for over an hour" (Wood and Bernasconi 83).

Nevertheless, to speak this way is by no means simply to subject deconstruction, if there is any such thing, to a belittling reduction. Rather, such questions touch unmistakably on that laughter that, as Derrida argues in his reading of Bataille, "alone exceeds dialectics" and the recuperative work of meaning ("From Restricted to General Economy" 256), and whose advent marks the very place at which all method or discipline finally exceeds and dislocates itself. Therefore, to continue this terminological play whose necessity we have begun to glimpse not despite but in the faintly comic note that attends it, one will first conclude that deconstruction could never be a method, procedure, or operation because such terms appear to be inextricably linked to questions of progress and profit, to philosophic "work" and therapeutic intervention. Here, I explore two other terminological possibilities, suggesting that, for Derrida, deconstruction involves a certain *strategy* and a certain *protocol*. Although neither term could somehow master the whole field of what is called deconstruction (for the reasons briefly touched on above and for others that further consideration of these terms will bring out), they serve as part of that open, non-taxonomical collage of terms with which a field of deconstruction can be, if not defined, then at least demarcated. I go on to suggest that Derrida's early critique of logocentrism and his later audacious claim that "deconstruction is justice" ("Force of Law" 243) share—if I may be permitted already to put these terms in play—a fundamentally similar protocol and strategy. In my view, a certain structural similarity of all of Derrida's arguments both early and late is part of what gives the later ones so urgent a claim on our attention. Although one would never wish to say simply that the method is the message, one should surely notice that the questions of "method" addressed here by no means pertain to a kind of envelope or package in which some issue or question (such as the right to die) can simply be fitted. But these methodological questions, however carefully we must bracket them, prove to be the very place where deconstruction proves itself to be *practical:* to be, that is, a thought that can be brought to bear on practices, textual, philosophic, and political. As Gasché suggests, if there is something about a deconstructive methodology that limits "the intervention of its strategic dimension to only one particular discursive space and time," then such a limitation is precisely what gives deconstruction a particular power to intervene "in historically specified contexts" (Gasché 154).

In Derrida's own text, both terms proposed for consideration here seem both to designate a certain process, a way of proceeding, and to serve as an example of that process. That is, both terms are themselves subjected to something like the semantic displacement given to other well-known deconstructive "terms" such as trace, supplement, mark, and so forth (a process that itself has some claim to be understood as the methodology of deconstruction). Derrida's explicit invocation of the figure of strategy is perhaps almost as familiar as his renunciation of method. "In the delineation [*le tracé*] of différance," Derrida famously writes in the essay of that name, "everything is strategic and adventurous" ("Différance" 7). The two words here invoked would usually be understood as near opposites, since strategy (which descends from the Greek *strategos*, a general or military commander) conventionally refers to a calculated plan that governs specific actions (or "tactics"). To formulate a strategy is to envision the future in advance so as to minimize the role of chance and avoid unexpected adventures. The "delineation" or tracing-out of *différance*, however, is both strategic *and* adventurous, for, as Derrida describes it, it involves a strategy that is "blind," that cannot master its field, and that cannot even orient "tactics according to a final goal." Derrida even suggests that this process of delineation is strategic not despite, but *because* "no transcendent truth present outside the field of writing can govern theologically the totality of the field" ("Différance" 7). How are we to understand such a point, which seems to turn the word *strategy* inside out? It can only be that, in the absence of any governing power to command the field, what emerges in the field, or in the tracing of the play that constitutes the field, is a kind of sovereignty without sovereignty: a governing power that can exercise itself only by abandoning itself in a sovereign manner to what Derrida elsewhere calls, "the *seminal* adventure of the trace" ("Structure, Sign and Play" 292).

As such formulations perhaps already will indicate, deconstruction could be said to resemble the "sovereign operation" evoked by Georges Bataille in which, as Derrida summarizes, one pursues a particular method (what Bataille called a "méthode de meditation") that finally and essentially "breaks with method" and "seeks neither to be applied nor propagated" (Derrida, "From Restricted to General Economy" 269). In early interviews, Derrida also describes himself explicitly as pursuing "a 'general economy,' a kind of *general strategy of deconstruction*" and speaks, similarly, of the necessity to elaborate "a general, theoretical, and systematic strategy of philosophical deconstruction" (*Positions* 41, 68). The strategy of deconstruction is called "general" to acknowledge its link to Bataille's "general economy": an economy of loss and excess which is opposed to a "restricted economy" of investment and profit, and intended, above all, to displace the philosophic privilege of the Hegelian "speculative" dialectic.

In multiple ways, therefore, Derrida's deployment of the term *strategy* is itself strategic insofar as the term, beyond or before any more specific meaning, indicates and responds to a terminological problem. "We must elaborate," Derrida writes, "a *strategy* of the textual work which at every instance borrows an old word from philosophy in order immediately to demarcate it" (*Positions* 59, emphasis added). The theoretical exigency outlined here always redoubles because, as soon as one declares the "'strategic' necessity that requires the occasional maintenance of an old name in order to launch a new concept," one must also, by the very same necessity, ask "why do we still call strategic an operation that in the last analysis refuses to be governed by a teleo-eschatological horizon"? (*Positions* 71). Just as, above, Derrida pulls the notion of strategy to its semantic limit and beyond by evoking an "adventurous" strategy, so here again he transmutes the term by making it refer "to the play of the stratagem rather than to the hierarchical organization of the means and the ends" (*Positions* 71)—the latter being how one would more commonly understand strategy itself.

Thus the formulations cited here associate strategy both with conservation, a calculated economy of borrowing and "maintenance," and, via Bataille, with a "general" economy of limitless excess that opens itself to the play of chance and innovation. The figure of strategy thus embodies or indicates in itself what Derrida famously and repeatedly describes as the "double gesture," "double writing," and "double science" of deconstruction ("Outwork" 4). In the final pages of "The Ends of Man" (1972), Derrida suggests that any attempt to critique or rethink the foundational concepts of Western thought faces an apparent choice between "two strategies" which are also "two forms of deconstruction":

a. To attempt an exit and a deconstruction without changing terrain, by repeating what is implicit in the founding concepts and the original problematic, by using against the edifice the instruments or stones available in the house, that is, equally, in language. . . .

b. To decide to change terrain, in a discontinuous and irruptive fashion, by brutally placing oneself outside, and by affirming an absolute break and difference. (135)

But this opposition of two "strategies" again opens up a fissure in this term, for the choice Derrida describes here is also one between (1) a *strategy* conceived narrowly as a calculable plan, as calculation itself: strategy as the calculated decision to make do with whatever is available; and (2) an *adventure*: that is, an abandonment to the incalculable chance of whatever may come (*ad-venture, ad-venire*) after the absolute break with or interruption of (*ir-rumpere*) these foundational concepts. As is well known, Derrida repeatedly formulates versions of this same double gesture throughout his career. In "Force of Law," for example, and we will come back to this, he evokes Walter Benjamin's "two sorts of general strikes, some destined to replace the order of one state with another (general political strike), the other to abolish the state (general proletarian strike)," and adds that these are "In sum, the two temptations of deconstruction" ("Force of Law" 271). Even more simply, in "The Villanova Roundtable," he describes deconstruction as essentially constituted by a "tension between memory, fidelity, the preservation of something that has been given to us, and, at the same time, heterogeneity, something absolutely new, and a break" (6).

As Derrida often reminds us, notably in "Structure, Sign and Play in the Discourse of the Human Sciences," such apparent oppositions neither designate a simple choice nor are open to any simple mediation and synthesis. As Derrida observes here, Claude Levi-Strauss's structural anthropology encounters what it calls a "scandal," for its own observations reveal that the fundamental opposition of nature and culture (on which the whole project of anthropology is founded) cannot be maintained rigorously. But Levi-Strauss's method, like the procedure labeled (a) above, "consists in conserving all these old concepts within the domain of empirical discovery while here and there denouncing their limits, treating them as tools which can still be used." Such concepts, neither true nor false, would then be "employed to destroy the old machinery to which they belong and of which they themselves are pieces" ("Structure, Sign and Play" 284). Such a description seems to resemble the *first* of deconstruction's two possible strategies as summarized above. But Derrida repeatedly contrasts Levi-Strauss' method to another which, in this essay, is not named: one whose "quality and fecundity . . . are perhaps measured by the critical rigor with which this relation to . . . inherited concepts is thought" (282), and in which, as a "first action," one would "question systematically and rigorously the history of these concepts" so as to "deconstitute" them (284). What seems to be envisioned here, once again, is a kind of process or mode of proceeding (that must be grasped, however, structurally rather than temporally), by which the critical interrogation of inherited concepts is joined to their absolute deconstitution. To do both at once, he says, is then itself "a problem of *economy* and *strategy*" (282). In "The Ends of Man," similarly, the common ground between two "strategies"—each of which, as Derrida carefully stipulates, has its own potentially fatal risks as a mode of theoretical intervention or critique—would be what he calls the "strategic bet" (135): that is, a "strategy" rethought as I summarized above, as the common ground of the strategic and the adventurous, a mode of proceeding neither wholly abandoned to chance nor so predetermined that it closes off the possibility of the future.[1]

As for *protocol*, Derrida here again sometimes uses the word in more or less its conventional sense as a set of rules, guidelines, or procedures intended to guide and govern the actions that follow them. He sometimes speaks, for example, of "protocols of translation" (Derrida and Ferraris 16) in the sense of basic assumptions intended to guide a practice. Similarly, while discussing psychoanalysis, he denies that there can be any "final, inviolate protocol absolutely given as guaranteed by science" (*Positions* 113n46). During an interview with Jean-Louis Houdebine and Guy Scarpetta from 1971, Derrida was asked about his failure, up to that time, to engage with the texts of Marx. Those texts, like all others, Derrida suggests in reply,

> are not to be read according to a hermeneutical or exegetical method that would seek out a finished signified beneath a textual surface. Reading is transformational. . . . But this transformation cannot be executed however one wishes. It requires *protocols* of reading. Why not say it bluntly: I have not yet found any that satisfy me. (*Positions* 63, emphasis added)[2]

Note how, in these initial examples, protocol retains in large part its conventional meaning as something preliminary: that is, as something preceding the threshold of a practice for which it sets down in advance an agenda or a set of rules. Yet it would seem that a certain supplementary sense is already being implicitly added to the term. For as Derrida describes it, a protocol for reading both limits freedom (one cannot read "however one wishes"), and yet enables the realization of reading's "transformational" potential. By the same token, Derrida sometimes seems to offer a set of protocols in place of a more detailed discussion which he does not yet have the time or space to address adequately. In the first pages of "Force of Law," originally delivered as the keynote address to a conference at Cardozo Law School in 1989, Derrida offers a whole series of preliminary points "even before I begin" (233), and stipulates repeatedly, as these opening points multiply, that he has "not yet begun" (237). Some fifteen pages into the essay (perhaps nearly an hour into the original "keynote" lecture), and just after he directly asserts the inextricable connection of deconstruction and justice (the central argument of the essay as a whole), Derrida claims yet again that

> I have not yet begun. Perhaps I will never begin and perhaps this colloquium will have to do without a "keynote." Yet I have already begun. I authorize myself—but by what right?—to multiply protocols and detours. (243)

Here again, an unmistakable note of the comic seems to play about this evocation of a protocol that, instead of preceding and governing the course of a reading from outside its threshold, presents itself instead as always-already a *detour* by which one is detained within.[3]

The lines just cited also recall the argument of "Outwork, prefacing" (1972), where Derrida considers the "strange warp of both time and space" (Barbara Johnson xxxii) constituted by the literary preface. The opening pages of this essay also briefly outline something that one will again be tempted to call a method. Specifically, Derrida asks about the "historical and strategic function [that] should henceforth be assigned to the quotation marks . . . which still make the deconstruction of philosophy into a 'philosophical discourse.'" (Or, as it might be put in the present context, why does the deconstructive critique of method still obstinately seem to involve *something* like a "method"?) Such questions concern what Derrida calls the "structure of the double mark . . . in a binary opposition" in which "one of the terms retains its old name so as to destroy the opposition to which it no longer quite belongs" ("Outwork" 4). We have been seeing a version of this with *strategy*, whose own implicit permutation in Derrida's texts, as I've already suggested, both mirrors and exemplifies the "general" strategy of deconstruction itself. The preeminent example, however, and the one I will use as a reference from now on, would obviously be the celebrated critique of logocentrism developed across all of Derrida's early texts. As is now very well known, Derrida shows how a whole range of Western thought tends to privilege a "living speech," the bearer of self-presence, against a "writing" seen as secondary, contaminated, dangerously supplementary. This argument necessarily involves a terminological problem of the kind we have been following, so that, in "Outwork," Derrida suggests that "we will try to determine the law which compels us to apply the name 'writing' to that which critiques, deconstructs, wrenches apart the traditional, hierarchical opposition between writing and speech" (4). In other words, in treating all such classical oppositions, one faces the same choice outlined above: on the one hand, one can "put the old names to work" or at least "leave them in circulation," which risks "regressing into the system" being deconstructed; or, on the other hand, one can "claim to do away immediately with previous marks and to cross over, by decree, by a simple leap, into the outside of the classical oppositions," which risks obscuring that the original opposition was always a dissymmetric and violent hierarchy "whose closure is constantly being traversed by the forces . . . that it represses" (5). Deconstruction thus must somehow navigate between these two alternatives, each with its own transformational potential *and* its own potentially fatal risks, in the process of discovering their common ground and *différance*.

To that end, one must apparently proceed in a particular way that is summarized in these difficult pages, and also, a little more clearly, in a well-known passage from *Positions*. In the latter text, Derrida describes deconstruction as involving

> a double gesture . . . On the one hand, we must traverse a phase of overturning. To do justice to this necessity is to recognize that in a classical philosophical opposition we are not dealing with the peaceful coexistence of a vis-à-vis, but rather with a violent hierarchy. One of the two terms governs the other (axiologically, logically, etc.), or has the upper hand. To deconstruct the opposition, first of all, is to overturn the hierarchy at a given moment. To overlook this phase of overturning is to forget the conflictual and subordinating structure of opposition. Therefore one might proceed too quickly to a neutralization that in practice would leave the previous field untouched, leaving one no hold on the previous opposition, thereby preventing any means of intervening in the field effectively. . . . That being said—and on the other hand—to remain in this phase is still to operate on the terrain of and from within the deconstructed system. . . . we must also mark the interval between inversion, which brings low what was high, and the irruptive emergence of a new "concept," a concept that can no longer be, and never could be, included in the previous regime. (*Positions* 41–42)

Thus, to return to Derrida's most famous argument: deconstruction discovers an apparent opposition between speech and writing in which speech is everyway privileged, so that this apparently symmetrical opposition is really a "violent hierarchy." To overturn this hierarchy is to show how all signification of any kind is in fact a form of "writing." Such an insight then evacuates or displaces the original opposition, and indicates or delineates a new "concept"—which in this case would be the trace, différance, or "arche-writing," which represent what Hägglund, for example, calls an "ultra-transcendental" condition of possibility for everything else indicated by the original opposition. As Hägglund writes, *différance*, the spacing of time, "has an ultratranscendental status because it is the . . . condition not only for everything that can be cognized and experienced, but also for everything that can be thought and desired" (19). Not only every kind of signification and communication, but even anything like experience or subjectivity, are wholly constituted in and by the strange economy of the trace or arche-trace.

As outlined so far, we seem to have three terms in play: the original dyad and the new "concept" whose "irruptive emergence" marks the interruption and displacement of the classical hierarchy. There also appears to be a kind of implicit link or connection between the second, less privileged term of the original dyad and this irruptive new term. Here, the concept of "writing" in its literal sense, following the phase of inversion revealing that all signification relies on some mechanism of trace and inscription, is displaced by "arche-writing," with the quotation marks indicating that the place of emergence is not a new concept in its own right, but the mark of a displacement that exceeds the original system. To return to "Outwork," we can now see how and why Derrida opposes the preface to the protocol, in an argument that will proceed in the same way as this now-familiar argument about speech and writing. As he suggests, in part through a reading of the preface to Hegel's *Phenomenology of Spirit*, a preface both precedes its text and claims to answer for it, to double it and represent it in advance; thus, the preface "recreates an intention-to-say after the fact," and presents the text itself

> as something written—a past—which, under the false appearance of a present, a hidden omnipotent author (in full mastery of his product) is presenting to the reader as his future. . . . The *pre* of the preface makes the future present, represents it, draws it closer, breathes it in, and in going ahead of it puts it ahead. The *pre* reduces the future to the form of manifest presence. (7)

To this classical preface, Derrida here interposes (deliberately playing with the tense at issue) "a certain protocol" that "will have—destroying this future perfect—taken up the pre-occupying place of the preface" (24). In this opposition or hierarchy between preface and protocol, the preface plays the role of speech, for it (allegedly) governs, controls, and "speaks for" the writing that follows it and over which it claims to be sovereign, giving to the sovereign author the "form of manifest presence." Correspondingly, Derrida suggests, referring to the etymology of the word, the protocol takes the place of writing, because

> In place of this discursive anticipation [of the preface], the notion of "proto-col" substitutes a textual monument: the first (*proto-*) page *glued* (*kollon*) over the opening—the first page—of a register or set of records. In all contexts in which it intervenes, the protocol comprises the meanings of priority, formula . . . and writing: pre-inscription. And through its "collage," the *protokollon* divides and undoes the inaugural pretention of the first page, as of any incipit. (8n11)

This opposition of preface and protocol must then traverse a first phase of overturning. Above, the phase of overturning revealed that "speech," like all signification, is always-already "writing." Here, similarly, it is revealed that there is finally no such thing as a preface as classically determined. Instead, there are only protocols and "outworks" that, as Derrida puts it at the end of this text, serve as a "kick off" (*coup d'envoi*) for the text to which they are joined without re-presenting or pre-determining it from some imagined moment of present-past or present-future. But, again, one cannot or must not stop here, for "if the protocol itself amounted to the gluing in of a simple sheet . . . it could become a preface again" (8n11). What, then, is the irrup-tive new "concept" that emerges in the second phase of the deconstructive strategy, and after the displacement of the original opposition or hierarchy? As a terminological matter, the answer in this case is difficult, and Derrida himself stipulates only that "if one insists on fixing this protocol in a repre-sentation . . . it has the structure of a *magic slate*" (8n11): that is, as Derrida considers the figure in his early essay on Freud, it would have the ability at once to *retain* an imprint and yet remain *open* to be imprinted anew. Perhaps therefore one can only retain the name "protocol," using quotation marks or other precautions to indicate a protocol that no longer determines, represents, or "speaks" the text to come in the "soothing order of the fu-ture perfect" (21)—and that, like the deconstructive strategy or "strategic wager," implies "a certain way of giving ourselves over to not-knowing, to the incalculable" (Derrida and Ferraris 13). Just as the self-presence always dreamed of in Western philosophy finds itself divided and interrupted by the spacing of time that Derrida calls différance, so the "inaugural preten-tion" of the preface is divided and undone by the protocol as recast within the strategy of deconstruction.

It must of course be stipulated, as Derrida goes on to do, that this apparent triangular structure (in which a dyad is overturned and then displaced, making possible the irruption of a new "concept") is by no means a dialectical triad, but rather, a schema intended quite precisely to displace the authority of dialectical speculation. In deconstruction, the apparent "third" term emerges only via the displacement of an original dyad that is revealed as such as nonsymmetrical and nondialectical—as is further indicated by the implicit link between the second, nonprivileged term of the original dyad and the emergent new term. As Derrida puts it, in deconstruction (or, as he calls it here, "dissemination")

> it is no longer possible to count by ones, by twos, or by threes; in which everything starts with the dyad. The dual opposition . . . organizes a conflictual hierarchically structured field which can be neither reduced to unity, nor derived from a primary simplicity, nor dialectically sublated or internalized into a third term. The "three" will no longer give us the ideality of the speculative solution but rather the effect of a *strategic re-mark* [emphasis added], a mark which, by phase and by simulacrum, refers to that absolute otherness which was marked—once again—in the exposé of *différance* [*sic*]. . . . Dissemination displaces the three of ontotheology along the angle of a certain re-folding [re-ploiement]. ("Outwork" 25)

In this difficult passage, Derrida describes a deconstructive strategy that is pointedly distinguished from the Hegelian dialectic. It is because deconstruction takes place only by means of "a certain re-folding," or displacement, because this process does not "produce" anything but comes only to interrupt itself (as *différance*, the spacing of time, interrupts all determinations of being as presence), that deconstruction can claim to displace and, indeed, (as Derrida is about to put it) "destroy the Trinitarian horizon" (25) of ontotheological authority and presence. The process by which a classical opposition allows itself to be strategically re-marked is correspondingly what Derrida is about to call a "loosening-up," an exposure to an "otherness" that the original dyad had at once expelled and retained as its most intimate condition of possibility.

These "strategic re-marks," Derrida immediately goes on to say—that is, the irruptive new "concepts" made possible by the inversion and displacement of the original dyad—"add a fourth term the more or the less" (25). What does this enigmatic phrase mean? The process we've been following, and however careful we are to indicate our various precautions with quotation marks, seems to involve three "terms." Thus the "fourth term" of which Derrida speaks here must finally be grasped, quite precisely, as *nothing* and as *not*. In the case of the "speculative" Hegelian dialectic, as Derrida famously argues via his reading of Bataille, the process of *aufhebung* conserves all the value of the original dyad and produces a new profit via synthesis: this is why Hegel is "the best speculator," for the system fore-closes from the beginning any possibility of loss. In the strategy and proto-col of deconstruction, by contrast, at stake above all would be an opening to a certain "general economy" that misses its profit. What emerges from the strategic re-marking and displacement of the classical opposition of speech and writing is a *"différance"* that is "neither a word nor a concept," that is neither sensible nor intelligible, and that is, therefore, in or as itself, noth-ing more than the condition of possibility for all signification or conceptual-ity, all sensibility or intelligibility.

The schema in question here is therefore what Derrida calls "a triangle open on its fourth side" (25). Although here again we come close to some-thing at which laughter might laugh, Derrida's strange figure is more than a joke or a quibble: it is the emblem or mark of a strategy that "loosens up the obsidionality of the triangle and the circle which in their ternary rhythm (Oedipus, Trinity, Dialectics) have always governed metaphysics" (25)[4]—and, as we might add, with an eye on his parenthetical examples, not only metaphysics, but also everything that might be called lives, communi-ties, and histories.

Apart from such hints, however, Derrida does not always make it easy to see the continuity between his early texts and the more explicitly politi-cal arguments of his later career. In "Force of Law," as we have partially seen, Derrida seems to call attention to certain organizational difficulties in his text and even, despite the seriousness of the topic, to invite oblique laughter. He grants himself the "right" to multiply detours and protocols even as, in the very midst of such textual circumlocutions (and therefore in a certain sense contradicting them), he asserts a set of audacious proposi-tions about deconstruction and justice. But Derrida approaches this ques-tion indirectly, via the titular opposition between force (sovereignty) and law. Derrida argues for a foundational connection between force and law that "goes beyond a conventionalist or utilitarian relativism, beyond a ni-hilism ancient or modern" (240-41), and beyond even the necessary and useful work of contemporary "critical legal theory," any of which tend to reduce the law by understanding it as no more than a passive instrument of political and economic power, however constituted. Beyond or before all these, Derrida suggests, would always be a "more intrinsic structure" by which the very constitution of law always involves a *"coup de force"* (241), a "violence without ground" (242). It is not merely that laws need to be "enforced," a word whose efficiency in English Derrida allows himself briefly to admire, but that law and force share a more originary connection, a constitutive relation.

If, then, it is sovereignty and law that join in an irreducible opposition, then a first move in its deconstruction would be revealing it as a violent hierarchy. But which side of the opposition will appear as privileged? With regard to signification, the answer seems inevitable, for as Derrida's own work establishes, more or less every major figure of Western thought tends to privilege speech as a vehicle or figure of self-presence and truth. But with regard to the opposition of sovereignty and law, the political *decision* versus the juridical *code*, one can cite multiple traditions of thought in which each side appears to be privileged. The existence of these contrasting discourses means that the triangle of law, sovereignty, and justice offers itself for deconstruction in at least two different ways. One must therefore wager twice, so to speak.

On the one hand, a range of otherwise heterogeneous discourses may be said to privilege the determinative role of force and sovereignty over law in the field of the political. Among many other possibilities, one might cite: (1) a tradition of absolutist monarchism for which "kings were the authors and makers of the laws, and not the laws of the kings" (James I, c3r); (2) a certain "decisionism" today associated above all with Carl Schmitt, for whom "the sovereign exception" remains an unsurpassable horizon of all political practice; and (3) contemporary theories of a "unitary executive" for which the essence of sovereignty is similarly said to lie in its power to "address emergencies which, almost by definition, cannot be addressed by existing laws" (Yoo 119–20). As Derrida implicitly signals in the early pages of the essay, however, one would have to add to this list any relativist, utilitarian, or nihilist critiques of the law, including though not limited to those on the "left," for whom law could never in principle be anything but the exercise and maintenance of a (political or economic) power originating elsewhere, and from which law is radically dissociable, at least theoretically ("Force of Law" 241). In these varied and heterogeneous discourses, a certain force or sovereignty is understood—whether as a normative ideal or as an object of critique and resistance—to govern or have the upper hand in the whole juridico-political field.

One is all the more persuaded to adapt such a protocol and follow this strategy in that the opposition of force and law, when understood like this, parallels that of speech and writing. Speech, as envisioned in logocentric terms, is in every way semantically and historically linked to the concepts of force and sovereignty, for all these are envisioned as privileged expressions of a certain free will and autonomy, of "freedom as force, as mastery or sovereignty, as the sovereign power over oneself" (Derrida, *Rogues* 43; cf. David E. Johnson 279–80). In his early essay "Force and Signification," Derrida uses the word "force" to denote a kind of agency and freedom that resists and irreducibly opposes structure (and therefore structuralist analysis). By contrast, law, like writing, can be "itself" only if it also functions as a mark: as document, record, or inscription, whether oral or written. Even in Plato, the thinker of logocentrism par excellence, the one exception to the philosophic privilege otherwise accorded to speech is the power of writing to ensure the permanence of legal codes and guarantee "the means of returning at will, as often as necessary, to that ideal object called the law" (Derrida, "Plato's Pharmacy" 113). The opposition of force and law (in which force has the upper hand) thus reveals itself to be broadly analogous to the opposition of speech and writing; in both, a mode of alleged sovereign self-presence is believed to relate hierarchically to something else that expresses, represents, or supplements it on another level.

Now, in Derrida's most familiar argument, the violent hierarchy of speech and writing is overturned, and the alleged self-presence of speech reveals itself as always-already interrupted by the strange economy of the mark and the trace—in other words, by "writing" conceived as the spacing of time. The same thing happens when we put our second opposition into play with "force" taken as privileged. In the phase of overturning, one would have to entertain the possibility that both force and law are in some sense forms of "law." Law becomes the name for the recognition that every "act," every "decision," every possible manifestation of sovereignty, is always-already haunted by iterability and the mark, by a *différance* which here denotes, so to speak, the inevitable becoming-law of force (cf. "Force of Law" 277–78). Sovereignty, envisioned in its classical form as a kind of inviolable supremacy, one and indivisible, cannot exercise itself at all without compromising and dividing itself. As Hägglund explains,

> if there were such a sovereign instance, nothing could ever happen to it since it would be completely given in itself. The concept of sovereignty is thus predicated on the exclusion of time. (29)

And as Michael Nass observes, similarly, "As soon as sovereignty tries to extend its empire in space, to maintain itself over time, to protect itself by justifying and providing reasons for itself, it opens itself up to law and to language . . . and so begins to undo itself" (Nass 127; cf. David E. Johnson 287). Sovereignty too, then, is compromised essentially by its exposure to the spacing of time in a manner precisely analogous to the interruption of speech by writing.

Despite the fact that it can be couched in these familiar "deconstructive" terms, it would appear that the argument at this phase tilts towards a kind of classical "enlightenment" liberalism that looks to law as the last and best hope for human emancipation, and for which "justice" manifests itself precisely when, and insofar as, sovereignty and force are interrupted by law. That deconstruction could at any one of its moments find itself in tune with a kind of liberalism would probably surprise only those liberals who have sometimes, far too hastily, dismissed deconstruction as mere nihilism or quietism. As Derrida writes, at the end of the first half of "Force of Law": "Nothing seems to me less outdated than the classical emancipatory ideal" (258).

But so far one would have deconstructed the opposition of law and sovereignty from only one of its aspects. It remains necessary, as Derrida goes on in the passage cited just above, "to re-elaborate, without renouncing, the concept of emancipation, enfranchisement, or liberation while taking into account the strange structures we have been describing" ("Force of Law" 258). One now necessarily observes that many other significant traditions of Western political thought begin by inverting the strategy just outlined, and privileging the law as the master concept of the political field. One might now reference, among many other possibilities, (1) a "Whig" history celebrating the ongoing struggle, from Magna Carta to the "Glorious Revolution" and beyond, by which law seeks to "tame the sovereigns" and consolidate itself in a popular law-making body[5]; (2) a still-nascent project of international law that aspires to transcend state sovereignty and guarantee "human rights" on a global basis; (3) a contemporary "legal liberalism" that sees the law as at least potentially perfectible, and looks to the juridical as the key site of social and political progress. In ideological terms, this second general approach to force and law appears to be the one to which all modern states nominally give homage, proclaiming themselves above all to be "nations of laws"—even if, in coldly practical terms, the political sphere seems all too obviously still in thrall to sovereign power and the state system. This would also be the position associated with the general "Western" tradition of enlightenment and emancipation whose continuing relevance Derrida acknowledges above. Nevertheless, our second wager requires us to entertain the possibility that, even within such legalist discourses, force was always-already the most intimate source and essence of the law, which law therefore repressed and expelled as its "other." This is the argument Derrida entertains in the first part of the essay, suggesting that any legal order is always constituted by a *coup de force* that is neither just nor unjust. This also appears to be the inner logic or driving force of the "anti-parliamentary and anti-'Aufklarung' wave" of the 1920s and 1930s in Germany ("Force of Law" 259) that Derrida examines in part two of "Force of Law" via a close reading of Walter Benjamin's "Critique of Violence," an essay for which Carl Schmitt expressed his admiration. As we have seen, the first deconstruction seems to risk falling back onto a classical liberalism, or at least, with its emphasis on law as code and mark, to risk reducing the inevitable play of decision and force. This second deconstruction seems correspondingly, at least hypothetically, to pose political risks of the kind (today unavoidably gathered under the signifier "fascism") warned of by deconstruction's most bitter critics. Nevertheless, this deconstruction also enfolds both a radical critique of the law's use of force (both the violence that attended its founding and the force it exercises to preserve itself via such things as the police and military); *and* Schmitt's analysis of the "sovereign exception" as an inescapable horizon of all political practice that law can never overcome once and for all. As Derrida writes, "without this category of exception, we cannot understand the concept of sovereignty" (Derrida and Roudinesco 91).

It should be acknowledged that what I've been considering here is not deconstruction itself, if such a phrase has any meaning, but only a kind of schema of it. Dealing with the open triangle of law, force, and justice also turned out to be, as Derrida predicted, dealing with a circle. When each of the two specific sets of discourses is revealed as really governed by its "other"—when force was shown to be inseparable from an order of law, and when law was shown to be always-already dependent upon force—the double inversion might be thought merely to reinstate the original opposition in reverse, so that we would still have before us an opposition or hierarchy of law and force. Or, momentarily laying aside even the specificity of these terms, we also seem to have simply reformulated the inner tension of those two strategies that, as we saw above, Derrida always defines as characteristic of deconstruction. As we recall, in the second part of "Force of Law," Derrida reads Benjamin's "Critique of Violence," and focuses on Benjamin's opposition of "two sorts of general strikes, some destined to replace the order of one state with another (general *political* strike), the other to abolish the state (general *proletarian* strike)." These are "in sum," Derrida asserts, "the two temptations of deconstruction." Accordingly, the strategy here itself constitutes an implicit opposition of two "deconstructions": (1) one (apparently the primary one because it resembles structurally the deconstruction of speech and writing) in which law interrupts force; and (2) a second one in which force interrupts the law. Each of these does what it does in the name of a certain "justice": the first seemingly in the name of *law as justice* or *justice as law*; the second in the name of that justice that *exceeds the law*. In the first case, therefore, we attempted "an exit and a deconstruction without changing terrain, by repeating what is implicit in the founding concept"; while in the second case, we changed terrain "in a discontinuous and *irruptive* fashion" (emphasis added). But then, this new opposition of two deconstructions obviously itself constitutes an irreducible opposition, which as such calls for its own displacement, and *différance*. How are we to think such a thing, which irresistibly reminds us of the point that Derrida marks explicitly as "of greatest obscurity" and "the very enigma of *différance*," in which one has to think the relation of a *différance* as "the economic detour" (which therefore always returns to its origin) and a *différance* that "misses its profit," and abandons itself to dissemination without return ("Différance" 19)?

It appears that our second deconstruction (in which force interrupts law) now plays the part of the less privileged term that, as one might put it, somehow announces the irruptive new "concept" of justice that interrupts and displaces this new oppositional system. This would therefore seem to be a "justice" conceived, this time, as a mode of incalculability that always and absolutely exceeds the law, and that therefore encompasses a kind of force or sovereignty just as the "arche-trace" encompasses the disseminative and supplementary qualities ascribed to writing in a logocentric model of signification. Indeed, when we read further in the pages from "Force of Law" from which this invocation of twin temptations is taken, doesn't Derrida seem to be, if I can put it this way, *especially* tempted by the second one, by the possibility of a deconstruction that wholly destroys the conceptual system from which it comes? He asks, putting our two original terms of method into play again:

> Can what we are doing here resemble a general strike or a revolution, with regard to models and structures, but also modes of readability of political action? Is that what deconstruction is? Is it a general strike, or a strategy of rupture? Yes and no. Yes, to the extent that it assumes the right to contest, and not only

theoretically, constitutional protocols, the very charter that governs reading in our culture and especially in the academy. No, at least to the extent that it is in the academy that it has been developed (and let us not forget, if we do not wish to sink into ridicule or indecency, that we are comfortably installed here on Fifth Avenue—only a few blocks away from the inferno of injustice). (272)

The radicality of deconstruction—and even perhaps the "deconstructive affirmation" itself (298)—is only partial ("yes and no"). Indeed, when Derrida says that deconstruction could claim only partially to be a "strategy of rupture," this curious phrase enfolds one more level of mediation by yoking together both of deconstruction's temptations. The general *political* strike (for example, a union striking for better wages) would seem to be *strategic*, at least in the conventional sense of the word: one asks for so much and no more, and the calculation of this "so much" is centrally important. By contrast, the general *proletarian* strike—which rejects "every kind of program, of utopia—in a word, of lawmaking" (Benjamin 292)—must in some crucial sense *abandon* all calculation, to break with all preexisting protocols and strategies, since it cannot in principle be specified in advance what will follow its radical break with law and the order of the state. In passing, one might also ask: is the very idea of *rupture* tied inextricably to the singular event, or can one pursue or continue what Derrida calls above a "strategy of rupture" *over time*? Derrida seems to give an example of the latter by using the phrase to refer to the legal strategies pursued by Jacques Vergès, the French lawyer famed for representing accused terrorists, in which the accused "appears only to testify (without testifying) of his opposition to the law" (267).

But in any case, as Derrida also concedes, deconstruction has only a mediated relationship to even such already-mediated forms of revolutionary political and legal practice. For one thing, deconstruction largely remains, as the saying goes, merely academic, always vulnerable to the belittling reduction of the "ivory tower." If, in this book, I am finally challenging such a reduction by bringing deconstruction to bear on an urgently practical question, the right to die, I can intervene in this debate only in what Derrida also calls a "mediated way":

> Not to change things in the no doubt rather naïve sense of calculated, deliberate and strategically controlled intervention, but in the sense of maximum intensification of a transformation in progress. (236)

But Derrida's point overflows such stipulations about the mediatedness of theory, however necessary they always remain. He implicitly suggests that a deconstructive protocol might "kick-off" either a specific reading of laws *within* a constitutional order that otherwise remains in place, or a more fundamental interruption and break with the "inaugural pretensions" on which a whole order has been founded. But deconstruction, as Derrida writes, is also finally the demand to think the *"differential contamination* between these two," which are at once dissociable and irreducible ("Force of Law" 272). To contest constitutional protocols is, so to speak, both more *and* less than to contest the constitution. The law, however conceived, must always be pursued to its limit via the methods or strategies that are called "practical." But a radical contestation of the founding assumptions of the law (the state, the citizen) remains all the more necessary, in order to pre-serve an opening not only to all those originally excluded from the consti-tutional order, but also to whoever and whatever may someday arrive to strain its limits once again.

Correspondingly, Derrida's reading of Benjamin finally becomes what might be called a cautionary tale or object lesson. Benjamin, in effect, wholly succumbs to the temptation of interruption and rupture by envision-ing a messianic, law-destroying violence as "the only secure foundation" for a critique of violence. He envisions a situation in which a "rotten" law had somehow infected the whole field of the political, monopolizing a force that served it on both sides, by making *or* by preserving law—or even both at once, as happens with the modern police force. Suggesting that "all violence as a means is either lawmaking or law-preserving" (287), Benjamin finally denounces both of these as "pernicious" in order to envision a violence of *ends*: a divine, law-destroying, "violent manifestation of violence that . . . would not be a means toward an end" (287). Benjamin's strategy is thus precisely not a deconstructive one: it cuts through and effaces (instead of deconstructing) the opposition whose play has been at issue, envisioning the emergence at every point of the system of what Benjamin calls, in his final sentence, "sovereign force." This is where Benjamin's text, closing the triangle, shows itself potentially complicit with "the very thing against which one must act and think, do and speak" (298).

All this indicates that the formulation briefly outlined above, in which sovereignty or force is regarded as the less privileged term of the original op-position (and therefore the ghostly augur of the irruptive "concept"), can be entertained only with important qualifications. It might be objected that the irruptive quasi-concept cannot be associated, even in this partial or oblique way, with sovereignty or force, for Derrida in his late works seeks above all to "dissociate *unconditionality* and *sovereignty*" ("Of Forgiveness" 59).

That is, more precisely, he submits for discussion "a certain inseparability between, on the one hand, the exigency of sovereignty in general (not only but including political sovereignty . . . ) and, on the other hand, the unconditional exigency of the unconditioned" (*Rogues* 141). But this argument, I suggest, is related to but distinct from that of "Force of Law." In this case, Derrida is in effect splitting the classical concept of sovereignty in two, and opposing (while insisting on their inseparability) an "ipsocentric" or "ipsocratic" sovereignty (*Rogues* 17), the sovereignty of a subject, that is hence essentially conditional and calculative, to the sovereignty that, "especially in its modern political forms, as understood by Bodin, Rousseau, or Schmitt, [is] precisely unconditional, absolute, and especially, as a result, indivisible" (*Rogues* 141). When law is opposed to and privileged against sovereignty, as in the second of the two deconstructions outlined above, sovereignty there plays precisely the role of the unconditional as opposed to law as "the element of calculation" ("Force of Law" 244). But because the opposition of law and sovereignty offers itself to deconstruction in two different ways, it puts into play two "deconstructions" and thus demands that we think, yet again, their "common ground and *différance*" ("Structure, Sign and Play"). One might therefore understand this opposition of two "deconstructions" as one between *justice as law* (that is, justice as the law that interrupts force, justice as the exercise of calculation) and *justice as sovereignty* (that is, justice as the force that interrupts law, justice as a kind of absolute incalculability that overflows the calculations of law). Deconstruction is tempted by both of these, just as it is tempted by the analogous opposition between the "political strike," the strategy in which one remains on the ground of whatever one resists, fighting it with its own weapons and seeking only to replace its laws and orders with new ones (calculation); and the "general proletarian strike," the strategy of interruption and rupture (which must exceed calculation). Without some possibility of law, code, or institution, the justice of "sovereign force" risks what we witnessed with Benjamin; but without some opening to the unavoidable play of decision and force, the emancipatory hopes invested in the law dwindle into a mere legalism that is unable to think (and hence always vulnerable to) the sovereign "exception." What then is the emergent and interruptive quasi-concept indicated by the deconstruction of this meta-opposition of two deconstructions, its *différance* or common ground? If law is the element of calculation then, correspondingly, "justice is incalculable, it demands that one calculate with the incalculable" ("Force of Law" 244).

But the justice Derrida refers to here, the justice that calculates with the incalculable, cannot simply be incalculability itself, so to speak. Rather, this justice emerges, if it can be put that way, from a kind of strange differential relation between calculation and incalculability that in effect requires us to think (retaining the old word so as to make possible an intervention within particular discursive and political fields) a sovereignty without sovereignty, a kind of "weak" force. With reference to Benjamin's contrary formulation above, one might also perhaps call this emergent "concept" *sovereign justice*—provided, however, one grasps it neither as a traditional transcendental Idea nor as some normative or Kantian regulative ideal but only as a kind of interruption or invocation (a "burst of laughter") that governs nothing even as it alone makes possible (by inspiring, leading, or simply making sense of) the very *projects* of law or politics. This justice or sovereignty is weak because it is never fully present in itself, and yet, just as the coming of time is also nothing in itself and yet is the condition of possibility for anything like signification, communication, or experience, so this sovereign justice is the unconditional condition of possibility for any act or event that might in any sense of the word be considered "just." As Derrida writes, "what is at issue is precisely another thought of the possible (of power, of the masterly and sovereign 'I can,' of ipseity itself)" (*Rogues* 143); and therefore,

> What must be thought . . . is this inconceivable and unknowable thing, a freedom that would no longer be the power of a subject, a freedom without autonomy, a heteronomy without servitude, in short, something like a passive decision. (*Rogues* 152)

In the violent hierarchy of sovereignty and law, as I conceded above, it appears at first that an "ipsocentric" sovereignty plays the role of speech as the originally privileged term. Therefore, it is precisely the necessity of also restaging this structure in reverse—so that even "the classical emancipatory ideal" may open to deconstruction—that indicates how the emergent figure of an unconditionality without power always remains in a certain sense a figure of "sovereignty," although only the sovereignty that, as Derrida puts it in his reading of Bataille, "*is always in question*," a sovereignty that "has no identity, is not *self, for itself, toward itself, near itself*" ("From Restricted to General Economy" 265).

This almost unnamable, irruptive, and inaugural openness must be grasped as the result, or more precisely the *remainder*, of the deconstructive play of calculation and incalculability that seems to be at work in all of Derrida's signature arguments, both early and late. In the famous final paragraphs of "Structure, Sign and Play," Derrida opposes, as "two interpretations of interpretation," the saddened, *negative*, nostalgic, guilty, Rousseauistic side of the thinking of play whose other side would be the Nietzschean *affirmation*, that is the joyous affirmation of a world of signs without fault, without truth, and without origin which is offered to an active interpretation. . . . There are thus two interpretations of interpretation, of structure, of sign, of play. The one seeks to decipher, dreams of deciphering a truth or an origin which escapes play and the order of the sign, and which lives the necessity of interpretation as an exile. The other, which is no longer turned toward the origin, affirms play, and tries to pass beyond man and humanism. (292)

Although Derrida obviously appears to be, if I can once again put it this way, more "tempted" by the second "interpretation," to the point that he has sometimes been read as simply affirming and celebrating it, he also clearly indicates: (1) there is no question of *"choosing"* between these two interpretations of interpretation because (and this is the formulation that has guided our discussion here) "we must first try to conceive of the common ground and the *différance* of the irreducible difference" (293), and (2) the practice of Levi-Strauss, as Derrida has deconstructed it in the essay, also partakes of both interpretations in a manner that lacks the "rigor" or "fecundity" (282) that might attend some other way of working from within the "strange economy" (293) of this two-fold relation. Levi-Strauss *aspires* to pursue the second interpretation, to abandon his intellectual practice to the play of signs, affirming repeatedly that his own "book on myths is itself a kind of myth" (Levi-Strauss 6, 12), and suggesting that "it is in the last resort immaterial whether in this book the thought processes of the South American Indians take shape through the medium of my thought, or whether mine takes place through the medium of theirs" (Levi-Strauss 13). But such assertions, whose audacity remains admirable, reveal themselves as untenable even *within* a discourse that, wishing to "present itself as scientific," constantly falls back on a kind of naïve empiricism (288) and even, as is "well known," on "an ethic of archaic and natural innocence" (292).

To ask about the common ground of these two interpretations of interpretation will obviously return us to the methodological questions broached at the beginning of this chapter. For to say that deconstruction is not a method, or to unfold the strange methodological blindness in the practice of Levi-Strauss or another, is by no means to say that nothing can be done. With regard to intellectual (or political) practice, one would therefore have to think (and put into action) a "strategy" that is not a strategy insofar as it remains in tension with a *"genetic* indetermination" ("Structure, Sign and Play" 291), neither governing any field absolutely nor abandoning the game wholly to chance; and a "protocol" that "divides and undoes the inaugural pretention of the first page, as of any *incipit*" ("Outwork" 8n11), and yet, precisely as such, unlocks the transformative potential of what is read or thought. Both of these, if not quite in themselves what could be called "practical" (in the sense of providing a ready-made guide to action), pertain above all to the *possibilities* of practice. In the original violent hierarchy of sovereignty and law, deconstructed according to the first strategy above, the displacement of the hierarchy reveals that classical ipsocentric sovereignty, were it even to realize its impossible dream of complete immunity, would find itself unable to open to any event, unable even to *act*. Sovereign justice, by contrast, is never present in itself, but it "*presses* urgently here and now" (Derrida and Ferraris 23).[6]

In other late works, similarly, as is very well known, Derrida entertains what he calls a series of "unconditionalities without power": for example, the figures of unconditional hospitality, gift, or forgiveness. As he summarizes in *Rogues*, Derrida writes of

> an *unconditional hospitality* that exposes itself without limit to the coming of the other, beyond rights and laws, beyond a hospitality conditioned by the right of asylum, by the right to immigration, by citizenship. . . . Only an unconditional hospitality can give meaning and practical rationality to a concept of hospitality. (149)

This argument thus places a kind of "law" (a hospitality by duty and right) in the privileged first position and a kind of "sovereignty" (an unlimited or unconditional hospitality) in the second position. It might once again be objected that the irruptive "concept" is simply the latter, as Derrida seems perhaps to suggest in the lines just cited. But to claim this would be to remain at the phase of inversion without proceeding to the displacement of the original binary. By contrast, Derrida clearly argues that unconditional hospitality is neither possible nor even desirable. The very possibility of hospitality requires a certain *ipseity*, a certain sovereignty over the *oikos*: if there were no doors or borders at all, no boundaries of "one" and "the other," no hospitality could henceforward ever be offered. Hospitality as an unconditional ideal is also, precisely *in* its unconditionality, always subject to perversion, as Derrida suggests in his brief concluding evocation of the Biblical story of Lot, who sends his daughters to be raped by a mob rather than infringe the hospitality offered to his guests (*Of Hospitality* 153–55). In the passage above, Derrida also makes clear that what is at stake above all is that which "happens or arrives," which is to say the very possibility of the event or the arrival. What arrives or remains from the deconstructive play of conditionality and unconditionality in this instance can perhaps only be called "the hospitality to come," a hospitality that retains, as it were, some *trace* of unconditionality, even as it responds to the demands of a "practical rationality." After all, even though unconditional hospitality is impossible, anyone who ever offers a concrete act of hospitality must still embrace the unconditional. No matter how many conditions I impose, any Other whom I allow through my door could prove to be my enemy; no matter how many barriers I erect, someone might always break through them; and even were my defenses perfect and inviolable, I would then have done no more than wall myself off in an absolute self-sovereignty in which nothing could ever happen and no one could ever arrive (cf. David E. Johnson 287).

Derrida makes broadly similar arguments about other figures of unconditionality, as he again summarizes:

> Another example would be the unconditionality of the *gift* or of *forgiveness*. I have tried to show elsewhere exactly where the unconditionality required by the purity of such concepts leads us. A gift without calculable exchange, a gift worthy of this name, would not even appear *as such* to the donor or donee without the risk of reconstituting, through phenomenality and thus through its phenomenology, a circle of economic reappropriation that would just as soon annul its event. Similarly, forgiveness can be given *to* the other or come *from* the other only beyond calculation, beyond apologies, amnesia, or amnesty, beyond acquittal or prescription, even beyond any asking for forgiveness, and thus beyond any transformative repentance, which is most often the stipulated condition for forgiveness, at least in what is most *predominant* in the tradition of the Abrahamic religions. (*Rogues* 149)

A forgiveness offered on the condition of repentance and restitution, or a gift offered in an economy of recompense and reciprocation, are "predominant" or privileged figures against which must be interposed the impossible figure of a pure, absolute, or unconditional forgiveness or gift (which, Derrida implies in passing, is occasionally glimpsed, as a simple inversion of the binary, from within even the Abrahamic tradition). And, he adds, he has shown where "the purity of such concepts leads us." A pure gift could not even appear as such without reconstituting in its very appearance "a circle of economic reappropriation," and a pure forgiveness, correspondingly, "In order to have its own meaning, must have no 'meaning,' no finality, even no intelligibility. It is a madness of the impossible ("Of Forgiveness" 45). One might even venture to suggest, somewhat incongruously, that Derrida's complex critique of Abrahamic theology (the predominant source for the prevailing concepts of such things as gift, forgiveness, hospitality, and the like) resembles analogically his much earlier critique of the intellectual practice of Levi-Strauss. In broadly similar terms, this theology is marked by a

> tension . . . between *on the one side,* . . . a demand for the *unconditional,* gracious infinite aneconomic forgiveness . . . and *on the other side* . . . a conditional forgiveness proportionate to the recognition of the fault, to repentance. ("Of Forgiveness" 34–35)

In this case again, one might say that Abrahamic religion *aspires* to the unconditional, only to fall back, both in theory and in practice, on a concept of "transformative repentance." In this case once again, therefore, one must not simply *invert* the theological formula but rather, think a different relation *between* conditionality and unconditionality. As Derrida puts it:

> if one wants, and it is necessary, forgiveness to become effective, concrete, historic; if one wants it to arrive, to happen by changing things, it is necessary that this purity engage itself in a series of conditions of all kinds (psychological, sociological, political, etc.). ("Of Forgiveness" 44–45)

That which comes, the future itself, the chance of what Derrida repeatedly calls "progress" (e.g., "Force of Law" 242; "Of Forgiveness" 51), is thus precisely what is at stake in anything that might be called deconstruction, which always aspires above all "to *change* things, and to intervene in an efficient and responsible (though always of course in a mediated) way not only in the profession, but in what one calls the city, the *pólis,* and more generally the world" ("Force of Law" 236).

To be sure, in these cases we seem to have no name for the irruptive new "concept" that might emerge as the *différance* and common ground of this engagement of the conditional and the unconditional, and must resort to formulations such as "just forgiveness" or "the hospitality to come." Such formulations thus perhaps risk appearing merely tautological, or (as Derrida concedes in *Rogues*) as normative or Kantian regulative ideals. They can be used at all only with circumspection and with the fundamental qualification that there are no preexisting criteria by which one might define, determine, or anticipate such things in advance. To return one last time to "Structure, Sign and Play," we recall how Derrida leaves us with two interpretations of interpretation between which we are unable to choose. To adapt Derrida's words from a different but analogous context, between these two interpretations we remain "torn," and yet "without power, desire, or need to decide" ("Of Forgiveness" 51). In "Structure, Sign and Play," however, Derrida also refers famously to the common ground that might emerge between these two as "the yet unnameable that is proclaiming itself," acknowledging that it presents itself to us as a "monstrosity," something before which we turn away our eyes (293). Many years later, he would similarly observe the "monstrous, unpresentable character, demonstrable *as un-monstrable*" of "the event," that which "must . . . announce itself without calling in advance" (*Rogues* 144).

In the pages that follow, the *event* we shall be anticipating via the arguments that surround it is not simply *death* itself (which, in the situations anticipated in this context is often difficult to consider an event precisely because it announces itself so far in advance or defers itself for so long) but, rather, the hypothetical establishment of a possible "right" to *decide for death*. Such an event might well also be, and often is, imagined as monstrous and unthinkable. But to bid welcome to the unpresentable and the unrepresentable—which is also to say, far more simply, in order to give, to be hospitable, to decide justly (including about dying and death, one's own or another's)—no fixed or predetermined *method* could in principle ever present itself. But all this, to put the thing precisely, *remains* our responsibility, both "now" and *henceforward*.[7] Deconstruction itself is finally no more and no less than a name for this infinite and unfinishable task.

## CHAPTER TWO

# Dignity and Sanctity

In the cacophony of voices in which two basic positions about the right to die, for and against, take shape today, it often seems as though one is dealing with a clash of two abstractions, *dignity* and *sanctity*. The phrase "death with dignity" has become the standard slogan for those in favor of a right to die, and is now formally enshrined as the title of the assisted-suicide laws in the states of Oregon and Washington. The phrase "sanctity of life" plays a similar rhetorical role for those opposed to both abortion and euthanasia. As many have already observed, however, obvious questions about either term emerge even before any specific consideration of the practices defended or attacked in their name.

It is obvious, to begin with, that the word and concept of dignity, like more or less any abstraction of its caliber, is at best imprecise. In these initial observations, I join other thinkers who, even as they also seek to reclaim dignity in one or more of the meanings that emerge across its long history, begin by observing the irreducible polysemy of the word. Michael Rosen, for example, observes "significant distinct strands in the meaning of dignity, strands that come together and move apart at different times" (Rosen 8). Patrick Lee and Robert P. George begin their account of the word by distinguishing between two ways of understanding dignity: (1) that "all human beings have a special type of *dignity*," which means they must be treated in certain ways; and (2) that "only some human beings, because of their possession of certain characteristics . . . have full moral worth" (Lee and George 173).

Even in its colloquial deployment today, the word *dignity* obviously unites several different shades of meaning, and the momentous legal and political senses with which the term is now invested further complicate any process of definition. Although I will often be observing the vagueness or imprecision that attends the concept of dignity, this is by no means the only question that must be raised. One might even ask: is the contemporary concept of dignity too small (not yet precise enough) or too large (unable to master the enormous constellation of theological, philosophic, and political meaning entrusted to it)? Is *dignity* merely a floating signifier that means something different in each of the many different contexts in which it is deployed? To claim to be observing, in any simple, "empirical" way, how the word *dignity* is deployed today would be especially tricky because the whole concept of dignity, in any conceivable sense, seems to mark a certain limit of the empirical as a register of *value*. Alan Gerwith argues, for example, that the word dignity unites an "empirical" sense, by which it refers to "a kind of gravity or decorum or self-respect," and an "inherent" sense, by which it refers to "a kind of intrinsic worth that belongs equally to all human beings as such" (Gerwith 12). Such a schema, however persuasive as a map of contemporary parlance, seems perhaps to assume in advance the very thing that must be interrogated: namely, a metaphysical structure embodied in the word, by which dignity seems to name the expressive relationship between an inside and an outside, an essence and a manifestation. If dignity is something that is at once "inherent" in human beings, *and* a kind of self-presentation, a gravity or decorum, then are these two modes of dignity mutually dependent upon one another? Or, on the contrary, is one subordinate to the other as its condition of possibility—and if so, which one?

For much of the tradition, the common strategy would be to envision dignity as a fundamentally intrinsic value—Kant would call it an "inner worth"—that, however, ought to and usually does manifest itself in certain kinds of behavior. To envision a kind of metaphysical correspondence between the substance and its emanation, between the inner worth and the outer expression of that worth, is always to concede the possibility that such correspondence could be lacking. Similarly, one might understand dignity (in something like the Althusserian or Foucauldian manner) not as the *source* but as the *product* of normalizing behaviors imposed on social subjects via complex discursive processes and dynamics of power in which some of the texts I read here obviously participate. The contemporary concept of dignity also obviously splits, as Gerwith's schema suggests only implicitly, between particular and general meanings, between (1) dignity as a quality or characteristic of an individual human being, and 2) dignity as a definitive quality or characteristic of humanity. A closer analysis reveals that this division of the general and the specific does not simply correspond to the metaphysical opposition of outside and inside, extrinsic and intrinsic, empirical and inherent; but rather, that both its general and particular meanings already divide themselves in precisely this way.

The modern English word descends from the Latin *dignus* and *dignitas*: the former an adjective denoting, as the Oxford Latin Dictionary (OLD) has it, "appropriate, suitable, worthy, deserving;" the latter a noun with four interrelated meanings:

1  Fitness for a task, etc. . . . suitability, worthiness.
2  The quality of being worthy, excellence. b visual impressiveness or distinction. c impressiveness, dignity (of style, gesture, etc.).
3  Rank, status b a position conferring rank, etc., office c (pl., meton) persons of high rank or position.
4  Standing, esteem, importance. b a condition in which one enjoys one's own and others' esteem, honour.

There appears, however, to be both an overlap and a potential disjunction between meanings 1 and 2 and meanings 3 and 4. "Worthiness" and "fitness" (meaning 1), and "the quality of being worthy" (meaning 2), are all closely related; and although one can distinguish between a particular "fitness" and a general "worthiness," these two are both qualities that would be immanent or inherent in a being, as opposed to a "visual impressiveness" or a "dignity of style and gesture," which are extrinsic conditions or qualities. Similarly, rank, status, and office (meaning 3) would usually also be conditions of honor in which one would enjoy "one's own and others' esteem" (meaning 4)—though it remains always possible in practice that a person possessing high rank might not be *deemed* worthy of such esteem. The four senses defined here thus appear to be reducible to a triangular semantic structure, by which *dignitas* unites (or, as it were, *aspires* to unite) three related but distinct things: (1) intrinsic worth, fitness, or value; (2) rank or status; and (3) an impressiveness or distinction of style, gesture, bearing, and comportment.

All three of these senses also remain familiar in contemporary English usage. The Wordnet lexical database at Princeton University, developed to facilitate "natural language" processing in computer applications, gives dignity more or less this same triangular structure of three fundamental senses:

• self-respect, self-regard, self-worth (the quality of being worthy of esteem or respect): "it was beneath his dignity to cheat"; "he showed his true dignity when under pressure."

- (high office or rank or station): "he respected the dignity of the emissaries"
- lordliness, gravitas (formality in bearing and appearance): "he behaved with great dignity."[1]

It is notable that these definitions, which clearly show the persistence of the semantic triangle of worth, status, and bearing, substitute the idea of self-respect or self-worth for the classical ideal of worthiness, and entirely omit the universal or inherent idea of "human dignity." It is also remarkable to observe how many of the exemplary locutions cited above are either actually or potentially negative in their sense. The locution "it was beneath his dignity to cheat" might be said either of someone who did or of someone who did not actually cheat. Similarly, to say of someone that he "showed his true dignity under pressure" is to concede, at least, a certain potential failure to show such dignity. The same is true even if one rephrases such locutions in positive form, as in the last example above: "he behaved with great dignity." If we truly believed, not simply as an ideal or an aspiration, but as an empirical fact, that human beings were, simply as such, the possessors of dignity, would not such a locution be a kind of tautology? In this sense, dignity presents itself as the very fulcrum of that strange axis by which humanism has always been a thought of the Other. For example, one can praise someone for having great dignity just as one might for having great "humanity." But is it really possible for a being to have, as it were, *more* of the definitive essence that also necessarily binds him categorically to his fellow beings? One way or the other, the word dignity today continues to be deployed in a manner that always threatens to expose such invisible (and at times nearly laughable) contradictions.

In any case, the concept of "human dignity" in the general or universal sense (which, as we will soon see, appears in classical Latin only in a single passage in Cicero) merely recapitulates on a higher level the same semantic triangle of worth, status, and bearing. This three-fold structure of meaning seems to persist in dignity throughout its long and difficult genealogy, whether it is understood in terms of a Stoic, classical, or humanist vision of man as the measure of all things, or the Judeo-Christian vision of the godlikeness of humanity, or, in Kantian terms, as the incalculable "inner worth" of the human person. In any of these determinations, human dignity always designates, first and foremost, an absolute worth and value of humanity as such, calculated quantitatively as well as qualitatively. Thus, at least in the wide tradition of medieval and early-modern thought from which the concept of dignity originally emerges, humanity is placed upon a "chain of being" at a level (as the familiar slight mistranslation of Psalm 8 has it) "a little lower than the angels." Within this widespread tradition of thought, human dignity necessarily names humanity's exceptional status among all other living creatures. Even beyond so literal a vision of ontological hierarchy, a general philosophical humanism similarly elevates humanity over what Derrida calls "animality in general . . . as if there were only a single 'animal' structure that could be opposed to the human" (Derrida, "Economimesis" 5). Finally, human dignity is also typically associated with a kind of literal and figural "uprightness" that itself has long been construed as a distinctively human characteristic. What Jean-Luc Nancy calls the "erect stance of the body of the biped" (*Creation* 96) is understood to embody the divine likeness (humanity is, writes Milton, "Godlike erect"), and also, more generally, to express or manifest the ethical ideals of fortitude, courage, temperance, and the like. Both English and French usage confirms how dignity as *droiture*, moral rightness and up-rightness, is as such construed as the ground or source of *droit*, legal and political right(s).

It would therefore be only with difficulty that the *relation* of these two analogous semantic triangles (that is, between dignity in its particular and its general sense) could be construed as an opposition of the empirical or extrinsic and the inherent or intrinsic. Dignity as a property of individual human beings can be understood as an inner worthiness, fitness, or self-esteem, or as a bearing, style, or comportment. Dignity as the inherent worthiness and incalculable value of humanity is similarly figured as a corporeal uprightness, and also, as we will see, always limited in practice to certain kinds of behavior as opposed to others. This insight is already indicated in colloquial English in a variety of ways: from the common use of the participial *dignified* (by which dignity becomes a quality apparently capable of being applied, assumed, or put on like a costume), to the revealing formulation by which a certain action can be said to be "beneath" one's dignity. The inner division in the concept of dignity thus embodies a relation of calculation and incalculability, of the conditional and the unconditional. One set of meanings, all having to do with esteem, bearing, appearance, comportment, and behavior, pertains to a being's conditions of existence. For example, in April 2005 as part of an ongoing debate about the future of Social Security, President Bush praised the program as one that had "ensured *dignity* . . . to millions of Americans in retirement" (Stevenson and Bumiller). This familiar formulation betrays the dependence of dignity, in a literal or practical sense, on a certain level of financial and material welfare, which is to say on certain *conditions* which could, or indeed must, be *calculated*. But it is also clear that human dignity in its universal sense, whether understood in the Judeo-Christian manner as the sanctity or godlikeness of humanity, or in terms of the Kantian vision of humanity's priceless "inner worth," is always to be understood as something incalculably and unconditionally valuable. Dignity in its contemporary deployment must therefore encompass a whole spectrum of senses at once absolutely conditional and absolutely unconditional, inscribing in a single concept a strange relation of calculable and incalculable value and worth. This strange relation cannot be reduced to an opposition of extrinsic and intrinsic, of expression and essence; and neither dignity as something conditional (a gravity or decorum of bearing, a corporeal and mental soundness, a social or personal status that is worthy of esteem) nor dignity as the priceless value inherent in all human beings can finally be understood to be the cause, source, or ground of the other.

Still, can we not conclude, at least, that the phrase "human dignity" in modern human rights discourse serves as a performative utterance by which human beings accord one another their mutual esteem by declaring their own worthiness to receive such esteem? The question would be whether the concept of dignity can transcend the figural and semantic economies that have ordered its deployment for so long. It is obvious that the universal political sense of dignity has in effect *added on* to an earlier semantic chain in which dignity was, by contrast, aristocratic, hierarchical, and exclusive; so that one might even summarize the word's history as paralleling the history of democracy itself. For example, the well-known bioethicist Leon R. Kass (who will be cited several more times in the course of this book) suggests that "dignity is not something which, like a nose or a navel, is to be expected or found in every living human being" (246), but also expresses his hope that dignity can be ever-further "democratized"—that is, that more and more people will *deserve* the term provided they receive "proper models, proper rearing and proper encouragement" (248). Similarly, Ron Bontekoe suggests, in his study of the concept, that we should concern ourselves with "that form of dignity that we find exhibited in the behavior of a certain kind of morally superior individual," because "bad and even just morally mediocre people *cannot* possess dignity to any significant degree" (43–44). In other words, dignity must always be grasped as an "achievement" (1).

Such formulations, however, cannot fail to indicate how dignity continues to be widely understood as, so to speak, a coming to the head (*a chief venir*): a rising-up to rights and up-rightness. Here again, therefore, an actual or potential *gap* opens up between dignity as an intrinsic quality of humanity, however that may be defined, and dignity as it may, or may not, be embodied in practice by individual human beings. Thus human dignity, the incalculable value we claim to accord to each other, presents itself at once as something absolutely unconditional and absolutely conditional. In this crucial word and concept certain practical or material qualities or conditions (status, rank, bearing, visual impressiveness, deportment) claim to represent or express certain moral or ethical qualities (worthiness, self-esteem); and then, this whole precarious semantic combination is further yoked to a metaphysical or ontotheological assessment of the universal value and worth of humanity as such.

As for the "sanctity of life," one obviously has to begin by asking whether such a concept can even be rigorously distinguished from the concept of "human dignity" that it sometimes seems to oppose. In contemporary political discourse, *dignity* and *sanctity* are commonly used as virtual synonyms, or at least as mutually supplementary concepts. For example, on January 20, 2006, President George W. Bush proclaimed the anniversary of the *Roe v. Wade* decision (that legalized abortion) as National Sanctity of Life Day. In his official statement, however, Bush declared "our Nation was founded on the belief that every human being has rights, *dignity*, and value" (Bush, "National Sanctity"). The paragraph in the 2008 Republican Party platform that addresses abortion and euthanasia is entitled "Maintaining the Sanctity and Dignity of Human Life" (Republican National Committee). But even if such formulations are dismissed as mere polemic, a fundamental theological, philosophic, and semantic interconnection of dignity and sanctity would be easy to demonstrate. Here, it will perhaps suffice to recall how Kant himself, perhaps the single greatest influence on the contemporary concept of "human dignity," envisions such dignity as something so "infinitely above all price" that "it cannot be brought into comparison or competition at all without, as it were, assaulting its *holiness*" (4:435). It would be quite difficult to formulate any adequate definition of either term without some recourse to the ideas of inviolability, intrinsic value, absolute worth, and so forth.

But if dignity and sanctity can neither be reduced into simple identity nor wholly and absolutely distinguished, this is, at least in part, because each term remains paradoxically both imprecise and embattled. For example, in *Life's Dominion* (1993), one of the most influential contemporary books making a case in favor of a right to die (to which I return at more length later), Ronald Dworkin claims that there is "a fundamental idea we almost all share in some form: that individual human life is sacred" (13). In other words, "we" believe that all life possesses "sanctity" in the sense of an "intrinsic" or "inviolable" value (70). This intrinsic value is analogous to the value we accord to works of art, to human cultures generally, and to "distinct animal species"—as opposed to "individual animals" (75). For Dworkin, both proponents and opponents of a right to die are actually acting out of a shared fundamental belief in this sanctity of life; they disagree only about how such sanctity should be defined and about how it should be fostered and preserved. Dworkin claims that if this underlying but invisible consensus can simply be brought to light, if we can begin to see that "what we share is more fundamental than our quarrels over its best interpretation" (71), then we will be better able resolve our "deep and painful" conflicts over who or what should have dominion over life and death. So far, however, the opponents of a right to die have obviously not been convinced. Robert P. George, for example, in his 2001 book *The Clash of Orthodoxies*, claims that, in making such an argument, Dworkin actually intends "to show that the lives of very young and very old or infirm human beings are not valuable," and that "the differences Dworkin describes as differences of *interpretation* of an allegedly shared fundamental value are, in truth, themselves fundamental" (41, emphasis original). Let me suspend any judgment as to the relative merits of these warring assertions in order to observe simply that, regardless of what I (or "we") think, the concepts of either "sanctity" itself or "the sanctity *of* life" cannot, at least in practice, even be defined in a manner that all parties are willing to accept.

Moreover, there is an evident problem with the idea of life's sanctity that *precedes*, so to speak, any analysis of the term's deployment or its practical implications. Let me illustrate this in a shorthand way with an incongruous juxtaposition of two brief passages. The first is from Samuel D. Williams' "Euthanasia" (1870), which begins by casting doubt on what he calls the "sacredness of life:"

> Nature certainly knows nothing of any such sacredness, for there is nothing of which she is so prodigal; and a man's life, in her eyes, is of no more value than a bird's. And hitherto, man has shown as little sense of the value of man's life as nature herself, whenever his passions or lusts or interests have been thwarted by his brother man, or have seemed likely to be forwarded by his brother man's destruction. . . . even to-day, and amid the most civilized countries of Europe, "the sacredness of man's life" is thrown to the winds, the moment national or political passion grows hot, or even when mere material interests are seriously threatened. (215)[2]

The second, from 2001, is from the same comic performance by the late George Carlin cited as the epigraph to the preface:

Even with what we preach about the sanctity of life, we don't practice it. Look at what we kill: Mosquitoes and flies, because they're pests. Lions and tigers, because it's fun. Chickens and pigs, because we're hungry. And people. We kill people. Because they're pests. And because it's fun! . . . So, at best, the sanctity of life is a selective thing. We choose which forms of life we feel are sacred, and we get to kill the rest. Pretty neat deal. You know how we got it? We made the whole thing up! Same way we made up the death penalty. The sanctity of life and the death penalty. We're such a versatile species. (Carlin 226–27)

Between them, these two passages are sufficient to indicate the two irreducible questions that attend any affirmation of the sanctity of life, questions whose absolute rigor and necessity remain inseparable from the laughter that is merely foregrounded in the second passage. As we will continue to see, all the obvious cases in which human beings have always reserved the right to take life—whether in war or judicial punishment on the one hand, or the daily exploitation of animals for human consumption on the other— manage to be cited as exemplary proofs of either the justice *or* the injustice of anything like an individual (human) right to die. In any serious discussion, one must surely begin by recognizing how the alleged sacredness of (human) life remains entirely at the command of the reasons of state; and how the concepts of dignity and sanctity, applied variously and inconsistently both to *life* in general and to *human* life in particular, manage to serve as the ground for that very distinction between the human and the animal that licenses the former to kill the latter, and also for arguments either for *or* against a human right to die.

Correspondingly, in the prolific contemporary discourse about this issue, one sees again and again a precarious balancing act in which dignity and sanctity are repeatedly affirmed *and* critiqued, questioned *and* reinterpreted, rejected *and* reclaimed, by thinkers and commentators on both sides of the debate. For example, Leon R. Kass begins his discussion of right-to-die issues by conceding that dignity and sanctity seem to "pull in opposite directions" and that "many of us" are disquieted by the possibility that "we may be forced to choose between them" (233). Then, in a patient and learned exposition drawing both on enlightenment philosophy and scriptural interpretation, Kass finally affirms that "human dignity and the sanctity of life are not only compatible, but, if rightly understood, go hand in hand" (234) because "the *sanctity* of human life rests absolutely on the *dignity*—the godlikeness—of human beings" (243). Acknowledging as a possible difficulty the paradox we have just observed, Kass nevertheless affirms, as strongly as possible, that human dignity licenses humanity to destroy animal life, because animals "can make nothing of their misery or mortality" (252) and, correspondingly, that "humanity, to uphold the dignity of the human, must sometimes shed human blood" (243).

In the present context, I highlight merely how Kass understands dignity and sanctity neither as simply synonymous nor as rigorously distinct. Those on the other side of the issue are similarly often compelled to reduce the two terms into a certain quasi-identity. For example, Raphael Cohen-Almagor's *The Right to Die with Dignity* (2001) begins, just as Kass does, by acknowledging the possibility that dignity and sanctity may seem to be opposed. He contrasts two "principled opinions" on the subject: one that "emphasizes the sanctity of life and sees its maintenance as a substantive intrinsic value," and another that "emphasizes the autonomy of the patient and his or her right to formulate a decision whether to continue living." The latter view, he suggests, is espoused by "liberals" "who "use the term *death with dignity*" to refer to this autonomy as it might be exercised in end-of-life decisions (1, italics original). Acknowledging that his own book "is written from a liberal perspective," Cohen-Almagor concludes, however, that "*both* viewpoints are motivated by the desire to maintain and protect human dignity" (2, emphasis added). Thus he suggests that "the sanctity of life model [is] justified in moral terms" provided only that it does not impose itself in a "paternalistic" way on patients for whom "the preservation of dignity may be valued more than the preservation of life" (2–3). Here again, dignity and sanctity seem to be at once distinguished and forced into alliance. For Cohen-Almagor, dignity ought to prevail over sanctity in practice, but only insofar as it reveals itself as so incalculable a value that it can sometimes be "valued more" than life itself—which would mean that such dignity must itself also be, in some inescapable sense, a kind of "sacred" value, a value beyond all price.

This kind of terminological and economic balancing act, so characteristic of this debate, is not the result of any carelessness on the part of these and other writers. Rather, it stems from the way the idea of *dignity* splits along the axis of calculation and incalculability, a splitting that then draws it into an ineluctable relation with the concept of *sanctity*. If dignity and sanctity seem sometimes to oppose one another with regard to a right to die, they do so along this very axis. Sanctity, a word which is by no means easy to define in itself, may be said to refer in general to that which is incalculably valuable, to incalculability itself. Dignity, at least in the specific sense of a death *with* dignity, must refer, by contrast, to the *conditions* in which a death occurs, conditions that must be calculated, calibrated, and managed so as to ensure that they are dignified. Yet the concept of "human dignity" that generally prevails today, not only in the debate about a right to die, but in the whole modern tradition of human rights, is at the same time grounded in Kant's vision of dignity as an incalculable value, an unconditional and incomparable worth. The idea of dignity, across a long and complex genealogy in Western discourse, seems always to divide itself in precisely this way, and thus to be characterized by a kind of internal gap or fissure that allows it to refer simultaneously to calculable conditions or practices (social status, bearing, deportment, manner, or style), and to a kind of metaphysical or ontotheological value—above all, to the incalculable value and worth that "humanity" ascribes to itself in order to define itself as such. It would appear to be this strange economy that makes it possible, as in our last example, for one thinker to declare human dignity and the sanctity of (human) life to be absolutely interdependent, while another envisions a human dignity that transcends mere life.

## CHAPTER THREE

# Dignity and Sovereignty

On September 15, 2006, just following the US Supreme Court's decision in *Hamdan v. Rumsfeld* (which considered the right of the executive branch to detain terrorist suspects outside the criminal justice system), and as Congress was beginning to debate in response the "Military Commissions Act of 2006," President George W. Bush spoke to the nation in a press conference. Asked whether the proposed legislation, that would strip federal courts of any jurisdiction over the detainees held at the US military prison at Guantánamo, Cuba, was "basically seeking support for torture, coerced evidence and secret hearings," Bush responded:

> This debate is occurring because of the Supreme Court's ruling that said that we must conduct ourselves under the Common Article III of the Geneva Convention. And that Common Article III says that there will be no outrages upon human dignity. It's . . . it's like . . . it's very vague. What does that mean, "outrages upon human dignity"? That's a statement that is wide open to interpretation. And what I'm proposing is that there be clarity in the law so that our professionals will have no doubt that that which they are doing is legal.[1]

In this striking moment—in which the sovereign suspends himself, ever so briefly, before the letter of the law, hesitating impatiently until he finds the very word on which his derision can settle—one seems to witness, in its own form and likeness, a certain confrontation between human dignity and state sovereignty that, it might be said, sums up a whole history of human emancipation.

At the time, Bush's derisive assessment of Common Article III of the Geneva Conventions (called "common" because it appears in all four of the

Geneva agreements going back to 1864) provoked an indignant response in some commentators. For example, Rosa Brooks, writing in the *Los Angeles Times* on September 22, declared that "the alternative interrogation methods championed by our president are torture, plain and simple. And there is no doubt at all that they're cruel, inhuman and degrading." A video clip of President Bush's words intercut with the notorious images of US soldiers torturing prisoners at Abu-Ghraib prison in Iraq was widely circulated on the Internet, as though to demonstrate that it should be easy to know exactly what Common Article III is supposed to prohibit. But is it? When one watches the sovereign set his sights (and his "professionals") on everything the law entrusts to this little phrase, "human dignity," can one really be certain of what is at stake? Or must one, on the contrary, and precisely in the name of "taming the sovereign" and the urgent responsibilities with which this concept of dignity has been invested, entertain Bush's doubts about its precision and its force? Indeed, in the video recording of this appearance one can perceive, when Bush articulates the word "dignity," the slightest hint of that nervous chuckle that was so often satirized by impersonators of the President. Even so attenuated a laughter might be said to emerge not incidentally but as a structural necessity of the whole problem here entertained; and one might, however reluctantly, feel almost moved to join in, despite the gravity and danger of the decision Bush is making and the unreserved sympathy owed to all those who would suffer in consequence.

To consider briefly just the most immediate example, Common Article III of the Third Geneva Convention, just after the reference to dignity that worries President Bush, also prohibits

> The passing of sentences and the carrying out of executions without previous judgment pronounced by a regularly constituted court, affording all the judicial guarantees which are recognized as indispensable by civilized peoples. (Roberts and Guelff 245).

It was actually to this clause that the majority decision in *Hamdan v. Rumsfeld* primarily referred in ruling against the administration's plan to try accused terrorists in military tribunals. They did so notwithstanding the Court's own previous acknowledgement, in *Hamdi v. Rumsfeld* from 2004, that "enemy combatant proceedings may be tailored to alleviate their uncommon potential to burden the Executive at a time of ongoing military conflict"— for example, by allowing the use of hearsay evidence and a presumption of guilt against the defendant (533-34). According to the court, therefore, Common Article III of Geneva *permits* practices such as detention, penal imprisonment, and even capital punishment, provided only that they follow *some* judicial process, even one well below the standard that prevails in American criminal courts.

To be sure, both American jurisprudence and international law *claim* to distinguish absolutely between the permissible violence of incarceration and execution and all "degrading" punitive practices. For example, Chief Justice Earl Warren declared famously in 1958 that "the basic concept underlying the Eighth Amendment" (which prohibits "cruel and unusual punishment") "is nothing less than the dignity of man" (*Trop v. Dulles* 100). The grandeur of such an assertion today necessarily encounters, among many other possible things that could be named, so-called super-max prisons in the United States where, as summarized by the Western District Court of Wisconsin in 2001, inmates "spend all but four hours per week confined to a cell" that is "illuminated 24 hours a day," and where they are permitted "no clocks, radios, watches, cassette players or televisions" (Pettigrew 208–9). Numerous recent studies of the effect of such conditions on prisoners have found them to be, as one recent article states dryly, "detrimental to the mental health of the inmates," producing a range of deleterious physical and psychological effects including "sleep disturbance, anxiety, paranoia, hallucinations and self-mutilation" (Groscup 78). Such examples of "lawful sanctions" in *domestic* American prisons (which will remain the status quo even if and when, for example, the infamous prison at Guantánamo is finally closed) can, of course, be safely assumed to be well within the limits of the Eighth Amendment as currently interpreted in American law.[2]

One must therefore conclude that neither the Eighth Amendment nor the clause of Geneva Common Article III that bothers President Bush prohibit *any* and *all* practices that threaten, attack, or assault human dignity, but rather, only "outrages" upon it: for example, what an Executive Order of July 20, 2007, now specifies and qualifies in meticulous detail as "willful and outrageous acts of personal abuse done for the purpose of humiliating or degrading the individual in a manner so serious that any reasonable person, considering the circumstances, would deem the acts to be beyond the bounds of human decency" (Bush, Executive Order 13440). Thus, even at the very heart of national and international law, human dignity is not so much protected or preserved, as suspended precariously just this side of a certain limit that is itself specifiable only as that which out-lies or out-rages all limit. So tenuous a standard, grounded only in what a hypothetical reason might judge to be excessive (but compared to what?) would appear quite unmistakably to remain, at the very least, "wide open to interpretation."

This fragility or interpretive fluidity of dignity seems all the more problematic in that this fundamental determination of the value of humanity
is one that is today accepted (at least nominally) by thinkers from all sides
of the political spectrum and nearly all state governments on earth. As is
very well known, the contemporary project of "human rights" begins by
affirming and declaring what the "Universal Declaration of Human Rights"
(1948) calls "the inherent dignity . . . of all members of the human family" (Brownlie and Goodwin-Gill, 24). Many modern state constitutions also
prominently and explicitly declare an allegiance to human dignity, including those of Germany, Portugal, Greece, and Spain (Eckert 41–42); and in
recent decades, the concept of dignity has been increasingly invoked in judicial decisions on a range of issues both in the United States and throughout the world (see McCrudden). How is one to think this conjunction: that
is, the widespread reliance of national and international law on a concept
of human dignity, and the equally central deployment of the term in debates about the end of life? One might venture to suggest that an alleged
individual *right to die* could not in principle be affirmed or denied except by
reference to a sovereign *right to death*. Why else has the word and concept
of *right* imposed itself in the first place on this debate, at least from Adolf
Jost's notorious pamphlet *Das Recht auf den Tod* from 1895? Jost's title might
be translated as either "the right to die" or "the right to death." Just so, the
whole debate about euthanasia and assisted suicide in general always seems
to necessitate the drawing of a line between a possible individual right to
control the conditions of his or her own dying, and what Foucault and
many others describe as the definitive sovereign right "to decide life and
death" (*History of Sexuality* 1:135; cf. Lifton 46). Both Jost's book and the
more famous or infamous *Die Freigabe der Vernichtung Lebensunwerten
Lebens* (*Permitting the Destruction of Life Unworthy of Life*[3]) by Karl Binding
and Alfred Hoche were, of course, later declared to have inspired the Nazi
euthanasia program of subsequent decades, and today are often cited in arguments against any relaxation of the laws against assisted suicide. These
texts are concerned above all to affirm the rights of sovereign state power
over the individual citizen or subject. They also, as Foucault and others
have argued, indicate a certain transition, perhaps still in process, between
a sovereign right to death preeminently exercised in punishment and war,
and a modern biopolitics proceeding via the management, preservation,
and normalization of a citizenry now conceived of in demographic terms as
a *population*. Either of these, however, must still be further distinguished, as
Robert Jay Lifton stipulates, from any affirmation of "the *individual's* 'right

to die' or 'right to death' or 'right to his or her own death,' as the ultimate human claim" (46).

There are therefore at least two actual or hypothetical "rights" that might be at issue here: the state's sovereign right to command the life *and* death of its citizens, and the individual's hypothetical right to *die* (or, that is, to *decide* on the conditions of his or her own death). Here again, these two rights are at once opposed and indissociable. At one time, the death of the individual on the scaffold or the battlefield would be the sign of his subjection to sovereign power; but today, as Foucault and Agamben famously argue, "it is over life, throughout its unfolding, that power establishes its dominion; death is power's limit, the moment that escapes it; death becomes the most secret aspect of existence, the most 'private'" (*History of Sexuality* 1:138). But if it is indeed a definitive characteristic of modern biopolitics that power should now establish itself not merely over death, but rather, over *life*, then one might have to question whether the establishment of a legal and political *right* to die might paradoxically extend the sway of biopower even beyond the limits Foucault envisions above. Wouldn't a formal, legal "right to die" have to be instituted, guaranteed, regulated, and enforced by the state? Would such a right, called for and celebrated as the expression of individual freedom and autonomy, in fact make it possible for power to colonize, if not *death* itself, then at least the entire process and experience of *dying*: that is, to assume a biopolitical control, masked in the form of the individual choice that will be claimed to be operative, over all the most intimate conditions by which (human) life ends, even (as we shall see) by calculating with obsessive precision the duration of its coming-to-pass? To raise such questions, however, is by no means to concede the argument already briefly referenced: that the establishment of a right to die, in however limited a form, necessarily places society on a "slippery slope" towards something like the Nazi program of involuntary euthanasia for all individuals declared for any reason to be unworthy of life. But it would nevertheless remain to be asked, at least: would the establishment of a right to die involve, in any sense, a *withdrawal* of sovereign power over the life and death of individuals, or, on the contrary, an abandonment of all limits to power's dominion?

Along the same lines, consider, for example, how at the time of this writing, a political debate in the United States about reforming health insurance has been marked by allegations that any such program would establish "death panels" to decide whether disabled or elderly individuals would receive medical treatment or not. The original source of such allegations seems to have been former New York Lieutenant Governor Betsy

McCaughey (a frequent critic of health insurance reform since the Clinton administration), who claimed in a radio interview that, under the proposals being considered, "Congress would make it mandatory, absolutely require, that every five years, people in Medicare have a required counseling session that will tell them how to end their life sooner" (Politifact). Then Governor Sarah Palin of Alaska gave such allegations their name by writing online that "The America I know and love is not one in which my parents or my baby with Down Syndrome will have to stand in front of Obama's 'death panel' so his bureaucrats can decide, based on a subjective judgment of their 'level of productivity in society,' whether they are worthy of health care." In any serious discussion of the right to die, it must first be stipulated that such allegations were baseless, and the phrase "death panel" no more than a polemical misnomer. As Clarence Page clarifies in the *Chicago Tribune* of November 1, 2009, the provisions in question, which "have been a part of federal health care law with support from both parties" for many years, "only offer to make funds available at least every five years for seniors and their families to receive end-of-life counseling from their doctors or other health care providers if they want it." Thus a proposal clearly intended to maximize *individual* choice about the conditions of death was construed as a proposal to maximize the state's power to decide on the life and death of individuals. But has so potent a misprision been implicitly licensed and facilitated in advance by the hidden link between the (individual) right to die and the (sovereign) right to death (and life)?

Even more broadly, to envision the history and continuing project of human emancipation as a clash between (individual) dignity and (state) sovereignty is also to confront a certain unsettling irony: for these two terms and concepts are ineluctably connected both semantically and discursively. A few brief opening examples will begin to suggest both the fatal interconnection of the two concepts and a kind of groundlessness or incompletion that, as a paradoxical consequence, seems always to attend the evolving concept of human dignity. Jacques Derrida has drawn attention to a crucial passage from the *Republic* where Plato compares the Form of the Good to the sun. As the sun provides for both the visibility and the generation of all things, so, Plato says,

> In like manner, then, you are to say that the objects of knowledge not only receive from the presence of the good their being known, but their very existence and essence is derived to them from it, though the good itself is not essence but still transcends essence in dignity [or majesty] and surpassing power [*presbeia kai dunamei*]. (509b; cited Derrida, *Rogues* 138–39)

Because not just the existence but even the very essence of all other objects of knowledge are derived from the form of the Good, the latter transcends essence, says Plato, in two ways: in its power and in what Paul Shorey's well-known English translation calls its "dignity" (*presbeia*). Derrida argues, however, for the greater precision of Chambrey's French translation as "*majesté*." As he explains:

> For *presbeia* is the honor and dignity attached to age, to what precedes and comes first, to seniority and primogeniture, but also to the principate, to the precedence of *what* or *who* has the privilege of the predecessor or forebear, of the ancestor, the father or grandfather—and thus of that which begins and commands. . . . Again in Roman political law, *majestas*, the grandeur of what is absolutely grand, superior to comparative grandeur itself, a grandeur most high, higher than height itself, more elevated than magnitude itself, is the word most often translated as *sovereignty*. (*Rogues* 139)

Derrida's observations raise a question, though this is not his own point at the moment, about the apparent semantic link between a concept of *dignity* that, especially in its developed and collective form, aspires to a kind of democratic universality, and a concept of *sovereignty* that designates the summit, the most-high, the one and indivisible. But given that *presbeia*, whether understood as majesty, sovereignty, or dignity, already means quite precisely the supreme honor of having (the) power (to decide), why does Plato feel it necessary to say that the Good is characterized both by a "dignity" or "majesty" on the one hand, and by a "surpassing power" on the other? Why does the particular *value* (the fitness, power, honor) of the One need to be doubly named? If on the one hand the dignity of the Good is singular and sovereign, on the other hand, it can only be designated in terms of a certain duplicity by which it must be understood as both powerful *and* valuable: or, that is, as both the source from which all power and value emanate and as a kind of self-sufficient site to which, as Socrates puts it, "honor belongs."

The contemporary deployment of human dignity, similarly, is obviously at times still shaped both by a Platonic and Stoic tradition of classical philosophy and by Judeo-Christian theology. It remains open to question, however, whether there is even a distinctively Judeo-Christian vision of human dignity per se. To be sure, a basic assumption that humanity has a special worth, value, and status in the realm of the created might be deemed a fundamental principle across the three interrelated religious traditions that Derrida calls Abrahamic. In the discourse of contemporary Judaism and Christianity, this special worth and status of humanity is indeed commonly referred to as its "dignity." The Vulgate text of the Bible, however, never uses the phrase *dignitas hominis* (Cancik 21), and the case for a scriptural source of the modern concept of human dignity rests primarily on a single famous passage from Psalm 8:

> What is man that thou are mindful of him? And the son of man, that thou visitest him? For Thou has made him a little lower than the Angels and hast crowned him with glory [*kavod*] and honour [*hadar*].

The Hebrew word *kavod* (or *kabôd*: Strong 3519) is translated in almost all major English versions of the Bible, including relatively more literal or modern ones, as either "honor" or "glory."[4] In other contexts, however, the word can be and has been translated as "dignity." The Talmud uses the phrase *kavod ha-beriyot*, "the dignity of the created," and, correspondingly, *kavod ha-adam* would be the modern Hebrew phrase for "the dignity of man." Some modern Biblical translations accordingly translate *kavod* this way in other scriptural passages. For example, in Exodus, the Israelites are enjoined, as the King James translation has it, to

> Make holy garments for Aaron thy brother for glory [*kavod*] and for beauty. (Exodus 28:2)

In this case the two final terms have been translated as "dignity and honor" (New International Bible), "dignity and grandeur" (New English Bible), or "dignity and adornment" (Jewish Study Bible).

Although many other passages from the Bible might be said to affirm the value or status of humanity (above all the reference in Genesis to humanity being created in the image of God), the passage from Psalm 8 seems to me the only reference in the Hebrew scriptures to something that could be considered an intrinsic and universal "human dignity" as such. The psalmist actually writes, however, that humanity has been crowned (or possibly "encompassed") by God with both *kavod* (glory) and *hadar* (honor). These two terms, while not simply synonymous, would be nearly impossible to distinguish precisely. The word *kavod* in this passage is itself translated as "honor" in *Young's Literal Translation* (1862), and as "honneur" in the French *Bible du Semeur* (2000), which also gives *hadar* as "gloire." Correspondingly, the word *hadar* is occasionally translated as "dignity." In *Proverbs*, it is said of a virtuous woman, as the King James version has it, that "strength [*oze*] and honor [*hadar*] are her clothing" (31:25), a line which the New English Bible gives as "she is clothed in dignity and power." In Francis Rous' well-known

English metrical translation of the psalms, the line from Psalm 8 was originally translated as "with glory, and with honour great" (1641 edition); but
in editions published after his death, the line has become "with glory and
with dignitie" (1673 edition). Such examples are perhaps sufficient to indicate what seems to be a terminal semantic undecidability about the precise relations among this constellation of three modes of excellence: dignity,
glory, and honor. How, then, is the distinction, if any, between the psalm's
two nearly interchangeable words to be understood? Has God given humanity *two* essential and definitive characteristics, or has the psalmist used two
similar but slightly different names to designate humanity's singular status
or stature in the divine creation?

*Kavod*, in its most basic semantic sense, refers to a kind of weightiness or
heaviness (Lorberbaum 56), or, as Vine puts it, "a heavy or imposing quantity of things" (Vine 114). Isaiah says of Eliakim, for example,

> I will fasten him as a nail in a sure place; and he shall be for a glorious throne
> to his father's house. And they shall hang upon him all the glory [*kavod*] of his
> father's house, the offspring and the issue. (22:23-24)

*Kavod* is also frequently used in the Hebrew scriptures to refer to a quality of God himself, as when Moses beseeches God to "shew me thy glory"
(Exodus 33:18), or when he tells the children of Israel that if they obey
God's commands "the glory of the Lord shall appear unto you" (Leviticus
10:6). The word sometimes also has, as Vine observes, "the more concrete
idea of a fullness of things including fortified cities, sovereignty (self-
rule) and people"—for example, when Isaiah speaks of a day when, just
as Damascus and other great cities and kingdoms have been destroyed, so
"the glory [*kavod*] of Jacob shall be made thin" (17:4). *Hadar*, on the other
hand, as Vine puts it, "is a counterpart to Hebrew words for 'glory' and
'dignity,'" and denotes "a combination of physical attractiveness and social
position" (115). The Vulgate gives the famous line of Psalm 8 as *gloria vel
decore coronabis eum*, so that God has crowned humanity with glory and
with *decus*, which in classical Latin yet again sometimes denotes honor or
glory, or, more broadly, such things as dignity, decorum, beauty, grace, or
splendor (OLD, *decus, decoris*). At most, therefore, one might understand
the double gift of God as being, on the one hand, a kind of fullness, power,
and sovereignty, a weightiness and plenitude, and on the one hand, a kind
of gracefulness or beauty. (Such a pair of qualities, I note in passing, would
distantly anticipate a Romantic literary criticism in which *dignity* and *grace*
are taken as two opposed forms of aesthetic experience: the one a kind

of grandeur or gravity, the other a kind of fluidity and flexibility.⁵) Since, however, both *hadar* and *kavod* can be plausibly translated as dignity, the latter continues to be a kind of absent presence or floating signifier in a text that seems to understand the transcendent value of humanity as a duplicity within unity.

To return to the contemporary deployment of the term in human rights discourse, one finds that the word "dignity" still seems to require a supplement. The Charter of the United Nations opens by stating the intention of the signing states "to reaffirm faith . . . in *the dignity and worth* of the human person" (Brownlie and Goodwin-Gill 3, emphases added), a formulation later repeated exactly in the Universal Declaration of Human Rights. This double formula, dignity and worth, has become a standard locution today, perhaps through emulation of these widely read and widely translated texts. For example, Martin Luther King Jr., in a speech to the Southern Christian Leadership Conference in 1967, declared that "we must massively assert our dignity and worth." Similarly, the first of the "Seven Principles" of the Unitarian Universalist church is "The inherent *worth and dignity* of every person." Wesley J. Smith, in one of his several books opposing euthanasia and assisted suicide, accuses advocates for a right to die of equating "dependency and disability" with "a lack of human dignity and human worth" (*Forced Exit* 207); in another book, similarly, Smith asserts that to calculate the relative value of human lives in the utilitarian manner "strips *worth and dignity* from people" (*Culture of Death* 28, emphases added). This conventional double formulation seems, as it were, to efface precisely the question that must be asked: what is the relation between humanity's *dignity* and its *worth*? It is as though the word dignity either is not sufficient to state the worth of humanity, or states a quality somehow more than or different than mere general worth. Moreover, the Universal Declaration begins by affirming, in its preamble, "the *dignity and worth* of the human person," then goes on to say that "everyone, as a member of society . . . is entitled to realization . . . of the economic, social and cultural rights *indispensable for his dignity*" (Article 22); and then, still later, declares that "Everyone who works has the right to just and favourable remuneration ensuring for himself and his family an existence *worthy of human dignity*" (Article 23; Brownlie and Goodwin-Gill 24–27, emphases added). Since, again, dignity already refers to the worth or value of humanity, this article in effect guarantees human beings an existence worthy of their worth. But how can dignity be at once immanent to a human being and yet entirely independent of that being's conditions of existence? How can dignity be both the theoretical ground and source of human rights, and the concrete product of their realization? Dignity must be a form of worth that is somehow distinct from a being's own worth, something that belongs to or is proper to a being, but that is distinct from the being's being.

These examples from ancient and contemporary discourse reveal something that remains the case at a more fundamental theoretical level as well: the way in which *human dignity* seems always in need of supplementation, and threatened by a certain groundlessness or incompletion. In his Nobel Prize lecture (November 10, 2001), Kofi Annan, at that time Secretary General of the United Nations, spoke eloquently of a profound class divide between the haves and have-nots of a global economy, and declared that

> No one today can claim ignorance of the cost that this divide imposes on the poor and dispossessed who are no less deserving of human dignity, fundamental freedoms, security, food and education than any of us.

In the face of such an assertion, whose substance compels our assent, one must still ask about the gap opening in Annan's sentence between "dignity" and all those other things. Is it really possible to imagine a human being who was truly guaranteed freedom, security, food, and education who would *not*, precisely as such, also have dignity? What strange economy elevates dignity over all of its absolute conditions of possibility, and how exactly are we to grasp or define this odd surplus value and worth that we insistently accord to ourselves?

## CHAPTER FOUR

# Human Dignity from Cicero to Kant

So far, we have begun to observe a certain fatal irony by which a concept today commonly understood as a site of resistance to sovereignty should prove to be semantically and conceptually inseparable from it. We have also noted a strange economy by which dignity seeks to name an absolute human essence or value that always seems to require a supplement. Such problems, which we have noted so far by considering various semantic and etymological questions, seem also to attend the developing concept of "human dignity" itself from its earliest appearances in Western philosophy and thought. The main lines of a basic genealogy of the concept of dignity are by now well known. Here, without claiming to provide anything like a comprehensive account of this long history, I will consider closely a handful of texts in which "human dignity" seems to name a value that is, by turns or at once, both conditional and unconditional, a value accordingly always hollowed out by exceptions and thus characterized by a kind of groundlessness or incompletion.

In a study of the etymological and intellectual origins of the word and concept of dignity, Hubert Cancik confirms what has long been suggested: that the term itself originates with Panaetius of Rhodes in the second century BCE, and enters the mainstream of Western discourse via Cicero's *De Officiis* ("On Duties"), a text based at least in part on a now-lost work of the same title by Panaetius (Cancik 19). Cicero himself employs the word *dignitas* frequently throughout his considerable canon of texts, usually in the sense of office, authority, social status, or personal worthiness. In *De Inventione*, Cicero defines *dignitas* as "someone's virtuous authority which makes him worthy to be honoured with regard and respect [*Dignitas est ali-cuius honesta et cultu et honore et verecundia digna auctoritas*]" (cited Cancik 23). Even so relatively simple a definition, however, has the kind of circular or tautological semantic logic that we have already occasionally observed in the contemporary deployment of the word. Dignity is an honor that makes someone honorable, an authority that makes someone worthy to be honored as such. To be *dignified* is to have, to comport one's self with, to be seen as having, *dignity*. The special sense of a "human dignity" as such appears in only a single passage in *De Officiis*. In this text as a whole, however, Cicero also uses the word *dignitas* with so broad a range of meaning, and in conjunction with so many similar or overlapping words, as to strain the resources of translation almost past their breaking point. What will accordingly interest us here is not so much Cicero's text in itself—which has been studied for centuries and elucidated almost line by line in Andrew R. Dyck's magisterial *Commentary* as recently as 1996—but rather, what that text and its translations indicate about the myriad meanings that persist in the concept of human dignity.

Early in Book 1 of *De Officiis*, according to Walter Miller's well-known Loeb Library translation (1917), Cicero identifies four sources of "moral goodness," defining the last of these four as "orderliness and moderation of everything that is said and done, wherein consist temperance and self-control" (1.15).[1] He then concludes, "if we bring a certain amount of propriety and order into the transactions of daily life, we shall be conserving moral rectitude and moral dignity [*honestatem et decus conservabimus*]" (1:17). While it is certainly plausible to translate the word *decus* in this passage as "moral dignity," the choice is not inevitable, for *decus* can also denote a wide variety of social and moral qualities or attributes, such as what the Oxford Latin Dictionary (OLD) gives as "high esteem, honour, glory, honourable or seemly behavior, dignity, decorum" (*decus, decoris*). Miller's translation perhaps betrays a certain anxiety about the concept at issue by stipulating that it is a specifically *moral* dignity. For *decus* is also, of course, the cousin of modern English words such as "decorate" and "decorum," and could in classical Latin itself also have the sense of "a pleasing appearance, beauty, grace" (OLD). John Higginbotham, in his 1967 edition of *De Officiis*, gives the final words of the sentence cited above as "we shall preserve our honour and respect"; M. T. Griffin and E. M. Atkins, in their 1991 edition, give them as "we shall conserve honourableness and seemliness"; and P. G. Walsh, in his 2000 edition, gives them as "we shall maintain decency and decorum." Whatever the strengths of each of these rather different readings, the variety itself indicates an irresolvable uncertainty about the particular qualities Cicero seeks to conserve. Such uncertainty is merely intensified when one considers that *honestas*, which Miller gives as "moral rectitude" (a phrase already difficult to distinguish precisely from "moral dignity"), might also be translated as "title to respect, honourableness, honour" and "integrity" (OLD, *honestas, honestatis*).

We are already beginning to see how the modern English word "dignity" hovers in between its most literal Latin analogue (*dignitas*) and other similar but distinct words. Similarly, the concept of "dignity" that seems to be operative in Cicero's text seems always to slip between the two rather different senses that might be indicated by the English words *dignity* and *decorum*—that is, between dignity as an immanent essence or intrinsic worth, and dignity as a decorous comportment or bearing. These two senses seem to be positioned in terms of the classical metaphysical opposition of essence and manifestation, so that "dignity" refers to an inner worthiness, and "decorum" to its outward expression. Yet, at least in classical Latin, each of these two words or concepts seems to bear in itself the same metaphysical ambiguity, the same possible division between an inside and an outside, an essence and a manifestation. For example, when Cicero discusses the concept of *decorum* itself, he identifies it as a key form of *honestas*, which, as we have just seen, Miller translates as "moral rectitude" (1:93). The Latin word *decorum* has passed directly into modern English; yet Cicero's translators do not use this word in translating *decorum* in Cicero's text, but give it, rather, as "propriety" (Miller), "seemliness" (Griffin and Atkins), or "the fitting" (Walsh). This *decorum*, Cicero argues, is a

> considerateness and self-control, which give, as it were, a sort of polish to life; it embraces also temperance, complete subjection of all the passions, and moderation in all things. . . . Such is its essential nature, that it is inseparable from moral goodness; for what is proper is morally right, and what is morally right is proper [*quod decet, honestum est et, quod honestum est, decet*]. (1:93–94)

With *decorum* as with *dignity*, the process of definition comes to rest in tautology. Moral goodness or rectitude is inseparable, both in principle and in practice, from the decorum with which it presents itself, from its polish or seemliness.

Therefore, as Cicero concedes in the next sentence, "the nature of the difference between morality and propriety can be more easily felt than expressed" (1:94). In his detailed commentary on *De Officiis*, Andrew R. Dyck suggests that this "is perhaps the most difficult section in the entire essay," in part for reasons having to do with the relation between Cicero's text and its Greek model, but also because Cicero has taken "a term from the aesthetic sphere" and adapted it to "ethical uses" (Dyck 241). This conjunction of aesthetics and ethics does seem to produce certain difficulties. The verb *decet* ("to add grace to, to adorn, to become"), which is deployed impersonally in this passage to mean what is proper or fitting, is itself the source of the noun *decus*. In the passage above, Cicero was distinguishing between (and yet linking together as an intimate causational and expressive duo), propriety or appropriateness (*decus*) and moral rectitude (*honestas*). Thus, an essence, a definitive and intrinsic quality (moral rectitude), is said to manifest or express itself as a grace, beauty, or decorum of body and action. But because *decus* can already be plausibly translated as "moral dignity"—that is, not merely as grace or decorum but *as* moral essence—it cannot exactly be opposed to such moral rectitude in the familiar metaphysical way, as denoting its mere appearance or manifestation. One might suggest that a certain concept of "dignity" is being asked to bridge or mediate between the two sides of precisely such an opposition.

Just before the lines already cited, Cicero also claims that nobility of soul [*animi excellentia*] may be revealed not only in increasing one's resources and acquiring advantages for one's self and one's family but, far more, in rising superior to these very things. *Excellentia*, meaning "superiority, preeminence, excellence" (OLD), thus joins a chain of similar and overlapping superlatives that all involve a process of *exceeding*, a rising or raising above. Cicero's point is that such excellence or superiority manifests itself not just in acquiring or having the advantages of wealth, but also in being "above" such things, as one might put it in modern English. An all-important social and moral quality with many possible names (grace, honor, dignity, decorum, and so forth) must be, as Cicero puts it in the line cited above, conserved or preserved by the right kind of behavior. Here again, *dignitas* and its various semantic cousins are the names both of an inward quality (so that orderly actions merely express or make manifest a quality already present in the being who acts), *and* the expression or manifestation of that quality, the bearing or behavior or comportment that draws and deserves social esteem. Thus excellence requires both calculation ("increasing one's resources and acquiring advantages"), and an incalculable process of rising above all that.

Slightly later, similarly, when Cicero discusses the duties of public life and the responsibilities that come with wealth, he again sets down certain rules for behavior; and concludes that "By observing these rules, one may live in magnificence, dignity, and independence and yet in honour, truth and charity toward all [*licet magnifice, graviter animoseque vivere atque etiam simpliciter, fideliter, vere hominum amice*]" (1:92). This time, Miller is translating the adverb *graviter*, from the adjective *gravis*, as dignity. This extraordinarily complex word conveys in Latin a whole constellation of literal and figural meanings emerging from a basic sense of heaviness or weightiness. It can mean, for example (to sample only a few of the myriad senses listed by the OLD) severely, solemnly, gravely, seriously, and, of course, with dignity. So in this passage the translator again has considerable interpretive latitude. Higginbotham gives it as:

> The man who observes these rules can combine fine, dignified and vigorous with honest, faithful and generous living.

Griffin and Atkins give it as:

> A man who observes these rules may live not only in a grand, impressive and spirited manner, but also with simplicity and trustworthiness, a true friend of other men.

And Walsh, finally, gives it as:

> The man who observes these injunctions can live a splendid, dignified, and vigorous life while simultaneously exhibiting simplicity, loyalty and truth.

The interpretive variety that, a moment ago, indicated the proximity of dignity to qualities of grace or decorum, here indicates its proximity to qualities of grandeur or impressiveness (the quality that in modern English might be called "gravitas": a twentieth-century coinage [whose first citation in the Oxford English Dictionary is from 1924] that in effect re-Latinizes the earlier "gravity" to denote "the quality of being grave"). This would be in keeping with the normative ideal of a life that combines two sets of distinct yet complementary qualities. Thus Cicero speaks of living both wealthily *and* virtuously, both grandly *and* charitably, both with dignity (as high status and as gravity), *and* with a certain openness or unaffectedness that tempers it.

In the passages considered so far, Cicero's text (like the scriptural passage considered earlier) might even seem to anticipate a Romantic literary criticism in which dignity and grace are taken as two opposed forms of aesthetic experience (the one a kind of grandeur or gravity, the other a kind of fluidity and flexibility). But Cicero elsewhere insists that these two sets of qualities, these two forms or manifestations of dignity, are radically distinct, and he associates the word *dignitas* exclusively with the first of them. Late in Book I, for example, he claims that "there are two orders of beauty: in the one, loveliness predominates; in the other, dignity [*altero venustas sit, in altero dignitas*]; of these, we ought to regard loveliness as the attribute of woman and dignity [*dignitatem*] as the attribute of man" (1:130). Here a feminine *venustas*, loveliness, charm, or grace, is now opposed to *dignitas* as a specifically masculine beauty, a simplicity, uprightness, straightforwardness, or wholesomeness. Therefore, Cicero advises worthy men to avoid "all finery not suitable to a man's dignity," as well as affected behavior, such as that of actors on the stage, or that taught in the Palestria, the Greek-style gymnasium which some Romans considered to be a "nursery of foppish manners" (1:130; Holden 245). The semantic and social logic again approaches tautology: worthy men must avoid behavior that is not worthy of a man, or not worthy of their own worthiness. Moreover, the problematic of gender, doubly evoked here both by the contrast between men and women, and between worthy men and actors or fops, exacerbates the problem that is beginning to emerge. For dignity is now a doubly exclusionary quality: a worthiness that is proper to a man but which many men's behavior contradicts, and that women neither have nor ought to have.

All of this must obviously be kept in mind when considering the famous passage where Cicero refers, for the first and only time, to dignity as an innate or intrinsic characteristic of human nature in general:

> From this we see that sensual pleasure is quite unworthy of the dignity of man [*non satis esse dignam hominis praestantia*] and that we ought to despise it and cast it from us . . . And if we will only bear in mind the superiority and dignity of our nature [*quae sit in natura excellentia et dignitas*], we shall realize how wrong it is to abandon ourselves to excess and to live in luxury and voluptuousness. (1:106)

As Cancik suggests, this passage is probably the ultimate source in Western thought for the idea of "human dignity." Yet Cicero himself names such an idea only in passing, and he allows it to stand only with essential qualifications. In the first sentence cited here, Cicero actually affirms the *praestantia*, the excellence or preeminence of man (OLD), and suggests, to put it slightly more literally than Miller does, that sensual pleasure is "insufficiently worthy of man's superior status" (Walsh), or "not sufficiently worthy of the superiority of man" (Griffin and Atkins). But of course, when Cicero names this excellence, this superiority or worth of man, in the second sentence above, he now specifically does call it *dignitas*. So it is almost irresistibly tempting to read this second line as referring to human dignity in a manner that is at least close to the modern sense of the phrase. Here, Walsh hews close to Miller in translating the line as "the high worth and dignity of our nature," and Higginbotham as "the quality of human dignity." But Griffin and Atkins resist even this temptation by giving the phrase as "the excellence and worthiness of our nature." Nevertheless, Cicero is clearly naming and affirming a kind of innate worthiness, excellence, or superiority of humanity in general that, in modern English, can or must be called human dignity. Yet Cicero's point remains a prescriptive one, for he affirms the dignity of humanity only in the process of suggesting that human beings often do not act in accordance with it.

Therefore, in the following paragraph, Cicero will make an essential qualification. Human beings, he writes,

> are invested by Nature with two characters, as it were: one of these is universal, arising from the fact of our being all alike endowed with reason and with that superiority which lifts us above the brute. From this all morality and propriety are derived, and upon it depends the rational method of ascertaining our duty. The other character is the one that is assigned to individuals in particular. (1:107)

The universal character of humanity appears to lie in precisely those qualities that constitute its dignity. Although "there are great differences" among individuals, human beings are "*all alike* endowed" with a certain dignity consisting in particular of their capacity for reason, a "superiority that lifts us above the brute." Even if dignity is at most a kind of potential to which human beings' actual behavior often does not measure up, it can still be sought for and esteemed as such. As Cicero writes, just before the passage we have been reading:

> it is essential to every inquiry about duty that we keep before our eyes how far superior man is by nature to cattle and other beasts: they have no thought except for sensual pleasure and this they are impelled by every instinct to seek; but man's mind is nurtured by study and meditation; he is always either investigating or doing, and he is captivated by the pleasure of seeing and hearing. (1:105)

It is "from this," Cicero goes on to say in the passage we were reading above—that is, from the superiority of (rational and sensible) human beings to (merely instinctive and sensual) animals—that we should see that bodily pleasure is unworthy of human dignity. The dignity with which human

beings are all alike endowed is precisely their superiority to all other creatures, and their general ability to distinguish themselves, and to be distinguished from, an animality that is correspondingly understood as an
absolutely universal or general quality of every other earthly being. Thus
dignity in this developed usage unmistakably retains at least some trace
of the word's originary sense of status or rank; for "human dignity" still
necessarily refers in some sense to humanity's high status on an assumed
ontological hierarchy.

This double vision of dignity as both an individual and a universal quality
also involves, as we began to see above, a particular relation of calculation
and incalculability. Dignity is a kind of ideal against which men's actual or
individual beings are often found wanting (and to which it is the essential
role of philosophy to recall them); and it is a definitive characteristic of humanity transcending all such calculations because it is universally shared.
One might even say that this universality is practically the only really distinctive thing about the "concept" of human dignity in itself, the only way
of defining it that can be wrenched entirely free from all the merely corporeal and social forms of value that it also often names, from honor, gravity,
grace, and so forth. On the one hand, dignity as a generic concept always
seems to remain vulnerable to a kind of reduction by which it becomes
no more than a mode of social self-presentation. On the other hand, even
human dignity in its elusive transcendent or universal sense is always, for
Cicero, hollowed out with exceptions. Cicero suggests, for example, that

> even if a man is more than ordinarily inclined to sensual pleasures, provided,
> of course, that he be not quite on a level with the beasts of the field (for some
> people are men only in name, not in fact) [(*sunt enim quidam homines non re, sed
> nomine*)],—if, I say, he is a little too susceptible to the attractions of pleasure, he
> hides the fact, however much he may be caught in its toils, and for very shame
> conceals his appetite. (1:105)

Even those "more than ordinarily inclined" to the sensual pleasure that
has just been definitively associated with animality, still retain a sense of
shame, an impulse of concealment, that indicates and preserves their superiority to the animals. The excessive expenditure of sense keeps something
in reserve, so that dignity and humanity are never entirely lost. But not *all*
prove to be capable even of the shame that thus preserves human dignity
when reason and temperance are lacking. Some human beings are always-
already "on a level with the beasts of the field," being "men only in name,
not in fact." Here, as a kind of parenthetical digression, an interruption of

a digression, a small rhetorical stutter that fatally qualifies the very thing otherwise affirmed, is the gap or fissure on which Cicero's whole vision of human dignity seems to rest. This gap opens precisely *in* and *as* the fatal duplicity of the name (*non re, sed nomine*). Dignity, it appears, is at once universal *and* exclusive. Its value transcends individual difference and yet requires precise and particular acts of calculation (in dress, manner, behavior, and so forth) in order to preserve it in any given individual. It has to do at once with modes of behavior and self-presentation that can be cultivated and calculated, and with an essence that precedes and transcends behavior. And therefore, finally, dignity is the definitive characteristic of all human beings except for those judged not to *be* human.

This strangely self-cancelling argument seems to awaken a note of comic skepticism; and, as it happens, Cicero had been discussing comedy just before this famous passage about human dignity. Following a long exposition of the various forms and instances of honor, duty, propriety, and the like, Cicero adds, as if in passing, what would become another often-cited observation:

> Nature has not brought us into the world to act as if we were created for play or jest, but rather for earnestness and for some more serious and important pursuits. We may, of course, indulge in sport and jest, but in the same way as we enjoy sleep or other relaxations, and only when we have satisfied the claims of our earnest, serious tasks. Further than that, the manner of jesting itself ought not to be extravagant or immoderate, but refined and witty (1.103)

In the broad tradition of humanist thought in which Cicero's text figures so prominently, both the capacity for reason and the ability to laugh have been commonly cited as distinctive features of human nature. But only the first of these, as Cicero indicates here, can be directly linked to human dignity. This is in keeping with Cicero's account as a whole, in which human beings must be enjoined, above all, to discern, recognize, understand, or bear in mind their dignity, precisely so that they may always be brought back to it from all the many things that adulterate its purity: appetite, ambition, bodily pleasure, jesting, and so forth. Thus the definitive characteristic *of* human dignity (reason) must always be employed to maintain and preserve it; and thus, as we have seen, the incalculable value of such dignity remains in service of a certain economy, of the production and conservation of itself. Laughter and comedy, by contrast, are opponents of dignity, and prime instances of the kind of thing that reason must keep in check. In this passage, therefore, adding one more to the catalog of binary oppositions on which his argument turns (*venustas* versus *dignitas*, sensual pleasure versus reason, animal versus human, and so forth), Cicero contrasts two different kinds of comedy: "the one, coarse, rude, vicious, indecent; the other, refined, polite, clever, witty." Although the first kind is unfit for gentlemen, the second one is "becoming to the most dignified person [*gravissimo homine dignus*]" (1: 104). Cicero's distinction is clear enough, even if different people might disagree about which specific instances of the comic should be considered coarse or polite, indecent or witty, dignified or undignified.

This apparently simple point, however, is another textual crux, for the manuscripts of *De Officiis* actually say that the second kind of comedy, the dignified kind, is simply *homine dignus*, becoming to or worthy of a man, which is clearly insufficient, since Cicero's whole point has to do with distinguishing between different kinds of comedy and different kinds of men. Therefore, "to fill an obvious gap" (Griffin and Atkins, 1:104n; cf. Dyck 266), subsequent editors have added various adjectives to allow Cicero to say that refined comedy is worthy of a "great" man, a "free" man, or (as Miller gives it above) a "most dignified" man. One might venture to draw a rather broad conclusion from this small textual problem—at least, to adapt Cicero's words, *si tempore fit, ut si remisso animo*, if the time be right and if one is in a suitably relaxed frame of mind (1:104). It would be this: the concept of human dignity, in Cicero's text and beyond, seems itself to be a kind of emendation, a supplement, a conjecture, something deployed not *despite* but *because of* its inescapable conceptual groundlessness, and called on, here and elsewhere, to fill an obvious gap.

With regard to such dignity, one might venture to suggest that it was Cicero's shaky logic of exclusion and exception, as much as or more than any substantive precision of meaning, that would be transmitted to medieval theologians and Renaissance humanists, for whom *De Officiis* was among the most widely read and cited of classical texts (MacKendrick 259-61). In both medieval and early-modern discourse, the various linguistic cousins of *dignus* and *dignitas* continue to be primarily deployed in a manner that flickers between the three distinct but interrelated senses of worth, bearing, and status. Nevertheless, the concept of "human dignity" in the rest of the tradition would be profoundly conditioned by a few themes of late medieval theology. The Oxford English Dictionary gives the first or primary meaning of the word "dignity" in English as "The quality of being worthy or honourable; worthiness, worth, nobleness, excellence," and cites the earliest example of this sense from the *Ancren Riwle* (1225, just five years before the OED's earliest instance of "dignity" in its second sense, aristocratic status):

Nor is it easily seen of what dignity [*dignite*] she [the soul] is, nor how noble [*heih*] is her nature. (Morton 140-41)

But are the two clauses that constitute this sentence in apposition, or does the author intend to ascribe two distinct qualities to the soul? The answer to this question is itself not very easily seen. If, with the word dignity, the text ascribes to the soul simply an essential worthiness, value, or excellence, then how exactly is this to be distinguished from a high or noble nature? Even more broadly (to return to the question broached earlier), why does the soul's worthiness need to be named twice? Why does the designation of the soul's dignity (its worthiness) require further definition as a highness or nobility of nature? Given that the *Ancren Riwle* as a whole, including the very section where these lines appear, is largely concerned with enumerating devotional practices to ensure that anchorites "fall not into the filth of sin" (141), the dignity and worth of the soul appears here again as a quality always in need of maintenance via the same forms of practice that manifest it.

The implicit metaphysical structure, by which the concept of dignity aspires to unite intrinsic and extrinsic senses, is particularly obvious in the early-modern commonplace about how aristocratic status should manifest itself in true nobility of character. One obvious source for this commonplace is *The Consolation of Philosophy*, in which Boethius writes:

> But high offices [*dignitates*] bring to him who acquire them honour and respect. Yet is there really this power in offices [*magistratibus*], that they instill virtues into the minds of those who fill them, and drive away vices? Surely they do not usually drive off wickedness but rather make it notorious? That is why we are indignant [*indignemur*] that they are often bestowed on wicked men. . . . Do you see how much dishonour high offices [*dignitates*] bring on bad men? Their baseness [*indignitas*] would surely be less obvious if they were not well known for many honours. For we cannot judge those worthy of respect [*dignos*] because of their offices whom we judge unworthy [*indignos*] of the offices themselves. But if you saw someone endowed with wisdom, could you think him unworthy [*non dignum*] of respect or of that wisdom with which he is endowed? Of course not. So there is some worth [*dignitas*] proper to virtue which is immediately transferred to those in whom virtue is joined. Now since honours acclaimed by the mob cannot do this, it is clear that they do not possess the beauty proper to real worth [*dignitatis*]. (Boethius 246-47)

In such a passage, the various permutations of *dignus and dignitas* float between the meanings of worth and status in a manner the translation partially obscures, for example, by translating both *dignitas* and *magistratus* as "office," and by translating *dignitas* simply as "worth" in the last two sentences.

Both *dignus and dignitas* also refer, by turns, either to a value that is immanent in a being (dignity as "real worth") or to a kind of extrinsic regard or
valuation (dignity as "respect," the esteem owed or given to worth). When
Boethius writes of the *indignitas*, the "baseness," that is made even more obvious by misplaced honors, an English speaker might be tempted to give
the word as "indignity" were it not that this modern word must be reserved
for the sense Boethius also expresses in the passage with the verb *indignor*,
"to regard with indignation, take offence at, resent, disdain, etc." (OLD). *Indignation*, here, denotes a kind of affective response to the perceived dis-
juncture between dignity as inherent worth and dignity as status, office, or
condition. Such semantic or translational issues indicate how the word dignity always highlights or brings into focus that very gap between worth and
status that it also seeks above all to bridge. Notice, too, that the real worth or
dignity that Boethius affirms is declared to be always potentially or actually
*absent*, given the evident fact that honors are often misplaced and the "mob"
always swayed by the mere appearance of virtue and value.

Thomas Aquinas' *Summa Theologica*, similarly, builds on such themes to
develop what is still widely regarded as providing a coherent and distinctively Christian vision of human dignity. In Aquinas' text, however, *dignitas*
serves at once as a term invested with complex philosophic and theological
meanings and as a relatively simple word denoting status or worth. At a famous moment in the first part of the *Summa*, Aquinas discusses the concept
of "person":

> Although this name "person" may not belong to God as regards the origin of
> the term, nevertheless it excellently belongs to God in its objective meaning.
> For as famous men were represented in comedies and tragedies, the name "per-
> son" was given to signify those who held high dignity. Hence, those who held
> high rank in the Church came to be called "persons." Thence by some the
> definition of person is given as "hypostasis distinct by reason of dignity" [*hy-
> postasis proprietate distincta ad dignitatem pertinente*]. And because subsistence
> in a rational nature is of high dignity, therefore every individual of the rational
> nature is called a "person." Now the dignity [*dignitas*] of the divine nature ex-
> cels every other dignity; and thus the name "person" pre-eminently belongs to
> God. (1: Q 29, A 3)[2]

This passage remains of great interest even if one largely suspends the difficult theological and philosophic questions that surround the terms and
concepts of *hypostasis* and *substance* and their respective relation to the Ar-
istotelian concept of essence or being *(ousia)*. Aquinas makes clear he is

intervening in what was already an extensive debate, and the schematic definition of human dignity that he both transmits and shapes does appear to condition the concept that prevails today.

Via the concept of the *person*, Aquinas inextricably links the *high dignity* [*magnae dignitatis*] of the (individual) being with the sovereignty of the summit, the higher than high, the being whose dignity *excels* and whose worth is especially worthy. Aquinas also acknowledges that to call God a "person," and indeed to employ this term as the name of a privileged ontological and theological category, is somewhat unexpected. As Boethius had also observed, the term originates in the theater and has, among its meanings, "mask." It is also strange that the term denoting the very category of the origin should not originally be the (semantic) property of the origin. As Boethius and others had also already observed, the Latin *persona* derives from the Greek *prosopon* that, either in Aristotle or in the Septuagint, designates, as Giles Emery summarizes, "the part of the human body between the cranium and the neck, that is, the face, the countenance, that which appears in front" (Emery 109n3). Dignity is, here again, a kind of highness or elevation that is at once literal and figural: it denotes a status *and* an essential worthiness, and both are at once indicated *and* embodied by the erect carriage of the human being that lifts the face above the feet and the soul above the soil (cf. Nancy, *The Creation of the World* 96).

According to the tradition Aquinas is following and elaborating, this dignity of the human is at once a *specific* form of worth and value (a "rational nature" that is itself of "high dignity") and, so to speak, simply *value* or *valuation* itself. This is precisely the progress of the argument as Aquinas unfolds it: he says that (1) the word *person* originally referred to (a representation of) someone of high dignity in the sense of status or office; (2) rational nature also has dignity in the sense of an absolute worth or value; (3) accordingly, all who possess or subsist in this rational nature also have dignity; and, finally, (4) God, whose dignity (in the sense of both status *and* worth) is supreme, is therefore supremely deserving of being called, being *valued as*, a person. The formula that Aquinas cites, *persona est hypostasis proprietate distincta ad dignitatem pertinente*, can be translated, more literally, as "the person is a hypostasis distinguished by a property pertaining to dignity" (Emery, *Trinitarian Theology* 109); or, as the translators I have been citing themselves translate the same phrase elsewhere: "a hypostasis distinguished by a property of dignity" (1: Q 40, A 3). Boethius had written, somewhat more simply, that a person is an "individual substance of a rational nature"; and the later version of this definition seems to emphasize above all that humanity is essentially *defined by* the same characteristic (reason) that gives it its dignity or value.

In the passage above, however, the crucial definition of the person that Aquinas cites does not even name the *specific* property or quality, a rational nature, that pertains to dignity or nobility, which Aquinas himself accordingly names in the next sentence of his text. The formula itself thus has a kind of tautological or circular logic that emphasizes the general self-identity of the definitive quality and the consequent value that attaches to its bearer. To give the phrase "by reason of dignity" (as the Fathers of the English Dominican Province do in the cited passage above) is to highlight, as the Latin does not, how reason plays the part at once of the definitive characteristic of the person *and* the faculty by which such a characteristic can and must be recognized, judged, and valued. Or, to put it another way, the English phrase calls for an exercise of rational judgment by the being whose capacity for rational judgment is the very thing intended to be conclusive *in* the judgment. The whole argument thus starts to resemble a sort of riddle or pun. Why is a human being a person? By reason of dignity and by the dignity of reason.

In one other well-known section of the *Summa* (also a classic source, as it happens, for the Christian prohibition of suicide, a topic to which I return in chapter 7), Aquinas is addressing the question of whether it is lawful to kill a sinner. He argues, first:

> As stated above (Article 1), it is lawful to kill dumb animals, in so far as they are naturally directed to man's use, as the imperfect is directed to the perfect. Now every part is directed to the whole, as imperfect to perfect, wherefore every part is naturally for the sake of the whole. For this reason we observe that if the health of the whole body demands the excision of a member, through its being decayed or infectious to the other members, it will be both praiseworthy and advantageous to have it cut away. Now every individual person is compared to the whole community, as part to whole. Therefore if a man be dangerous and infectious to the community, on account of some sin, it is praiseworthy and advantageous that he be killed in order to safeguard the common good. (2: 2, Q 64, A2)

According to what remains this extremely familiar argument, the right to kill animals is the precise analogue of the right to kill "dangerous and infectious" human beings. Indeed, the latter is linked to the former as its logical corollary, and both are accordingly the paradigmatic examples of a general sovereign right to death. As we will see later, Aquinas' surgical metaphor, in which the cutting away of an infected member to save the whole body figures a legitimate, proportionate, and permissible violence, emerges recurrently within a general philosophic discourse about suicide. In the third of Aquinas' possible objections, it is claimed that

> it is not lawful, for any good end whatever, to do that which is evil in itself. . . . Now to kill a man is evil in itself, since we are bound to have charity towards all men, and "we wish our friends to live and to exist."

To this Aquinas responds,

> By sinning man departs from the order of reason, and consequently falls away from the dignity of his manhood [*dignitate humana*], in so far as he is naturally free, and exists for himself, and he falls into the slavish state of the beasts, by being disposed of according as he is useful to others. . . . Hence, although it be evil in itself to kill a man so long as he preserve his dignity, yet it may be good to kill a man who has sinned, even as it is to kill a beast.

If the Fathers of the English Dominican Province, in their standard English translation of the *Summa*, show a certain rhetorical flourish above in rendering the definition of the person, here they seem to show a certain reticence. Isn't it nearly irresistible to translate the highlighted phrase in the first sentence (as, for example, Timothy McDermott does in his more recent, "concise" translation of the *Summa*), as "falling away from their human dignity" (McDermott 389)? In any case, this is also obviously one more place where a kind of human dignity is affirmed in its always-potential absence. For Aquinas, to kill a man who has sinned is no more than to kill an animal; and to kill a man is not to *take* his dignity but simply to respond, rationally, to the man's own failure to *preserve* it.

Such formulations, as we will see later in the book, remain potent in the contemporary discourse about human dignity, including the debate about a right to die. In these foundational discourses, human dignity proves to be a fugitive concept, not only because it continues to convey a constellation of related but potentially distinct senses, but also because it names a kind of essence always in peril of becoming disjoined from its appearance or manifestation. Chaucer famously writes, in his poem "Gentilessse":

> For unto vertu longeth dignitee,
> And noght the revers, saufly dar I deme,
> Al were he mytre, croune, or diademe.   (654)

Although the OED cites this passage as another instance of the English word dignity being used to refer to the quality of worthiness, nobility, or excellence, it would be difficult to make sense of the lines unless dignity is also understood in the OED's second sense, as an honorable or high estate. It is of course the latter that Chaucer is distinguishing from "virtue" in the sense of "conformity of life and conduct with the principles of morality" (OED). The whole point of Chaucer's play on words is that virtue always or intrinsically has "dignity" in the sense of worthiness and value, even though dignity, in the extrinsic sense of status or rank, does not always or necessarily have virtue. As Chaucer writes in the poem's final stanza:

> Vyce may well be heir to old richesse,
> But ther may no man, as men may wel see,
> Bequethe his heir his vertuous noblesse
> (That is appropred unto no degree,
> But to the firste fader in magestee.   (654)

"Vertuous noblesse," the dignity or worthiness of virtue itself, transcends the necessary calculations of social life: it cannot be bequeathed to an heir (as wealth, status, or title can), and it cannot be "appropred" (that is, reserved or exclusively assigned) to any particular social "degree." This incalculable value could only be attached as a property or possession to the degree of the summit, to absolute sovereignty, to the "majesty" that here displaces the word dignity in the poem's final stanza. Here again, therefore, dignity in its very concept seems on the one hand to be always striving to universalize itself (at least via the Christian notion of the dignity of the soul's nature and of humanity as the bearer of the divine image), and, on the other hand, to be inevitably associated with a sovereignty whose definitive characteristic is to be one and indivisible.

Dignity as an always-potential, or almost literal absence: surely the crowning instance of such a meaning would have to be Pico de Mirandola's *Oration* of 1496. This text is always referred to today as *On the Dignity of Man*, but in its original publication and most of its subsequent reprintings over the next few decades, it was titled simply *Oratio Quaedam Elegantissima*, "a most elegant oration." Only in 1557 did it become *On the Dignity of Man* in a collection published in Basel and *A Very Elegant Oration on the High Nobility and Dignity of Man* in a Venice edition (Kristeller 173; Copenhaver). One might again ask in passing why the editors of the Venice edition thought it necessary to give a double name to Pico's titular concept. As I suggested earlier, it is as though the word dignity, which among its varied senses already denotes aristocratic estate, often invites a supplement to guarantee its full consignment of intended meaning. Still, to call what Pico is affirming in the essay "human dignity" must have seemed inevitable. The essay explicitly positions itself as following what Pico calls "the numerous considerations advanced by many men to explain the excellence of human nature" (2:3)—books such as Giannozzo Manetti's *De Dignitate et Excellentia Homines* (1452), which was itself an emulation of an earlier treatise by Bartolomeo Fazio (Manetti 66).[3] Indeed, early-modern humanism in any of its varieties has often been understood as essentially affirming what Herschel Baker calls, in his survey of Renaissance philosophy from 1947, *The Dignity of Man*. Baker's book, published just in between the signing of the charter of the United Nations and the ratification of the Universal Declaration of Human Rights, seems in its choice of title to participate in an explosive resurgence of interest in the concept of human dignity in the aftermath of the Second World War. Brian P. Copenhaver suggests, similarly, that the textbook *The Renaissance Philosophy of Man*, published by Ernst Cassirer, Paul Oskar Kristeller and John Herman Randall in 1948 and still in print today after more than half a century, was intended by its authors to reclaim texts such as Pico de Mirandola's *On the Dignity of Man* not only for a post-Kantian ethical philosophy but, more generally, as founding documents of a new "humanist charter of human freedom and dignity".

In his own historical context, Pico's vision was no doubt a radical one, for he envisions a humanity who is not simply the *imago dei* but, rather, a "creature of indeterminate image" (5:18). Or, as Ernst Cassirer articulates this now-familiar point, for Pico, humanity's "likeness and resemblance to God is not a gift bestowed on man to begin with, but an achievement for him to work out"; and "the 'dignity of man' . . . consists in the fact that the work of man is the expression of his own will" (321; 344). It is this potential that makes humanity, as Pico repeats four times in the oration's opening sections, "admirable." But even assuming that "dignity" is indeed the right word for the groundlessness wherein consists the ontological preeminence of humanity, the argument necessarily marks dignity with a certain inner tension. For human dignity seems to reside both in humanity's general potential for self-fashioning and in the particular self that is fashioned and achieved by *some* though not *all* humans.

In any case, Pico himself never exactly names as "human dignity" the definitive quality or characteristic of humanity that he celebrates. In the famous opening sections, Pico declares that he is not satisfied with the reasons advanced to explain the "excellence" of human nature [*praestantia*; the same word we saw above being translated as "dignity" in the famous passage from Cicero]. But now, he says, he has "come to understand why man is the most fortunate of beings and consequently worthy of all admiration [*dignum omni admiratione*] (3.6). At the end of the first movement of the oration, Pico observes that in the court of heaven, angels occupy the first places; and he accordingly demands that humanity "emulate their dignity and glory," because we are "unable to endure second place" (10:52). But what precisely are the two qualities of the angels which humanity is to emulate? If we are to emulate both the angels' status in the cosmic hierarchy (the whole passage might be said to figure our relation to the angels as a sporting match) and their essential worth, excellence, or superiority, then which Latin or English word matches each of these two senses?

If dignity thus seems to be a kind of absent presence in this text, one might suggest that this is precisely because the "dignity" of humanity finally resides not in any one particular characteristic but, rather, in its fundamental capacity to make and remake itself. But the word and concept of dignity in this text is thus forced, as it were, to do double duty: it denotes the value and worth of a humanity essentially defined by its power "to degenerate into the lower forms of life, which are brutish; [or] to be reborn into the higher orders, which are divine" (5:23); and also, as we have just seen, it denotes the value and worth *of* those higher orders. Pico's very affirmation of the limitless range of human freedom—humanity's power both to *de*generate and to be *re*generated [*Poteris . . . degenerare; poteris . . . regenerari*]—necessarily means that the crucial border between humanity and animality is a dynamic one that must in principle be capable of transversal. Humanity's freedom as such (that is, the freedom that is proper to it, the freedom that *is* its dignity) actually *compels* humanity to move only towards those higher orders, because otherwise they sink to the level of "brutes" who are correspondingly *defined* by their lack of such freedom. "As soon as they are born," he writes, "brutes bring with them . . . all that they are going to possess," whereas humanity has been given "every sort of seed and sprouts of every kind of life" (6: 26–28). Indeed, the word "brute" insistently punctuates the first few pages of the oration, indicating as clearly as possible how animality marks the downward limit of the human. But the *excellence* of the human remains, here again, at once the *capacity* and the *obligation* to excel. As Pico observes,

> If you see someone, a slave to his belly, crawling on the ground, it is not a man you see but a plant; if you see someone who, as though blinded by Calipso with empty imaginations, under a seductive spell, is enslaved by his senses, it a brute you see, not a man. (8:40)

Here again, therefore, human dignity remains suspended within the duplicity of the word that might not signify, the name that might not name. If you see a man given to animalistic behavior, then what you are seeing is a brute and not a man (*brutum est, non homo*). By contrast, to his fellow men in the proper sense, Pico enjoins that we should "spurn earthly things" (*dedignemur terrestria*)—or, in other words (given that Pico's verb here is another linguistic cousin of *dignus* and *dignitas*), let us accord no dignity to them (10:41).

In the famous passage from the beginning of the oration, God is imagined declaring to humanity: "you may, as the free and extraordinary shaper of yourself, fashion yourself in the form you will prefer [*ut tui ipsius quasi arbitrarius honorariusque plastes*]" (5). But if such a point is the very crux of Pico's definition of human dignity, then that definition seems to be marked by a sort of impossible tension between actuality and potentiality. As another translation gives the line, perhaps a little more precisely, Pico's God says to humanity that "*as though* the maker and molder of yourself, you may fashion yourself into whatever form you prefer" (Bondanella and Musa 181, emphases added). That is, Pico seems to say both that humanity shapes itself freely and that humanity shapes itself *as though it were* or *as if it could be* (*quasi*) the free maker, molder, and shaper of itself. A certain fatal question thus remains unanswered in this text, despite the rhetorical and figural beauties that have inspired so many readers from the Renaissance to our own times. Dignity as freedom and dignity as the definitive and universal characteristic of humanity: how are these to be reconciled? If dignity names both humanity's potential for self-fashioning and the achieved potential, the particular kind of self that may (or may not) be fashioned, then humanity is "free" only insofar as it chooses correctly to reject animality and manifest itself through reason. Thus both the freedom and the universality of dignity evaporate the very moment that it begins to exercise itself in its own most proper form.

Although, in our own times, an impulse of "self-fashioning" has been identified as a definitive characteristic of early-modern culture in general, the deployment of the word dignity in the period seems to remain largely untouched by the special sense that Pico may (or may not) have been trying to give. Shakespeare, for example, uses the word neither with any precision nor with any particular valence. In Shakespeare's text, the word usually floats between a general sense of excellence or high worth and the specific sense of rank or aristocratic status. He writes, for example, of "two houses, both alike in dignity," in *Romeo and Juliet*, and of knights who are to be given "dignities becoming your estates" (*Cymbeline* 5.5.3390). In *Henry IV, Part 1*, Westmoreland says, of Hotspur and Prince Henry,

> This is his uncle's teaching; this is Worcester,
> Malevolent to you in all aspects;
> Which makes him prune himself, and bristle up
> The crest of youth against your *dignity*.
>
> (1.1.96-100, emphasis added)

Here, the word obviously encompasses both a general sense of personal worth and a more specific sense of aristocratic rank. At most, Shakespeare's usage might suggest that the word had for him a kind of vaguely metaphysical or theological connotation. When the Ghost of Hamlet's father claims that his love for Gertrude

> was of that *dignity*
> That it went hand in hand even with the vow
> I made to her in marriage (*Hamlet* 1.5.48-50)

or when Helena, in *Midsummer Night's Dream*, asserts that

> Things base and vile, holding no quantity,
> Love can transpose to form and *dignity* (1.1.237),

the word is usually glossed as meaning simply "worth"; but given the sacramental reference in the first passage, and the faintly neo-Platonic associations of the second, it might be suggested that the word conveys something somehow grander than this general sense. Although it would be easy enough to cite other passages—Hamlet on Man as "the paragon of animals" will obviously come to mind—that can be taken as evidence for a Shakespearean humanism in general, he never uses the word dignity in any such context.

If anything, in this period the word dignity seems primarily to name something that is, so to speak, always imperiled by the thousand natural shocks that flesh is heir to, and honored as much in the breach as the observance. Spenser writes, for example,

> Of all Gods workes, which do this world adorne,
> There is no one more faire and excellent,
> Then is mans body both for powre and forme,
> Whiles it is kept in sober gouernment;
> But none then it, more fowle and indecent,
> Distempred through misrule and passions bace:
> It growes a Monster, and incontinent
> Doth loose his *dignitie and natiue grace*.
>
> (*Faerie Queene* II:9:1; emphases added)

Dignity here refers to a specifically corporeal quality: the "native grace" of the body's "power and form" when it is soberly governed and kept in temper. Similarly, in Anthony Nixon's book *The Dignitie of Man* from 1612, the titular term refers to what is called in the subtitle *The Perfections of His Soule and Bodie*, perfections which are presented as always precarious, always subject, to cite just a few examples, to an *"Intemperance"* that "inflameth, provoketh, and troubleth the tranquilitie of the soule" (79) or to a *"Voluptuousnes"* that "mortifieth the Spirits," "weakeneth the body," and "breedeth diseases" (83–84). Only a little more broadly, Thomas Stoughton in 1610 provides a book-length treatment of a subject that he describes on the title page as "The dignity of Gods children" and the "base . . . condition of all other." It would be hard to imagine a more succinct summary of human dignity as essentially a category of exclusion.

Still, such examples do make clear that a general concept of what might be called human dignity, however inconsistent or imprecise, was probably familiar to any learned individual by the early decades of the seventeenth century. In *The Advancement of Learning*, Francis Bacon refers in passing to "those delightfull and elegant discourses, which haue bin made of the dignitie of Man" (94), indicating clearly that this point was already an entirely conventional one. Although he seems to suggest in the same passage that his own book is not merely a recapitulation of such themes, in his text Bacon also affirms above all what he repeatedly calls the "dignity" of knowledge.[4] His book, titled in its 1605 publication *Of the proficience and advancement of Learning, divine and humane*, became in its 1623 Latin version *De dignitate & augmentis scientiarum*, as though to affirm even more strongly this defense of learning's dignity. Bacon seems to use the word primarily to denote "high worth." Since he also suggests repeatedly that those who profess the sciences and liberal arts are worthy of an esteem and respect that they do not always receive, it is obvious that what is being defended about learning includes its social status. More generally, in Bacon's account dignity is a kind of incalculable value that, however, must be subjected to a certain process of calculation: men seldom "give a true account of their guift [*sic*] of reason" (31), and his own intent is "to weigh the dignitie of knowledge in the balance with other things, and to take the true value thereof" (33).

Moreover, for Bacon, the dignity of learning—if not its *value* in some ultimate or transcendent sense, then the *valuation* accorded to it as a practice—is always precarious. Learning must be delivered from "the discredites and disgraces which it hath receiued" (5) and from the distempers (23), errors and vanities (21), vices and disease (25) to which it is always itself subject. The true dignity of learning must therefore be rigorously distinguished from a kind of pseudo-dignity, or what he often describes as "affectation" (e.g., 4, 23, 59). For example, considering the accusation that learning softens men's minds, making them unapt for arms and "more readie to argue, than to obey" (9), Bacon says that such accusations "haue rather a countenance of gravitie, than any ground of Iustice" (10). Of Cato the Censor, he writes later, "his former censure of the Grecian learning was rather an *affected gravitie*, than according to the inward sence of his owne opinion," and he suggests, a few lines later, that his argument should "serve for answere to Politiques, which in their humorous severitie, or in their *fayned gravitie* have presumed to throwe imputations upon learning" (14–15, emphases added). By *gravity,* Bacon clearly refers to a quality of mind and expression unmistakably associated with what he otherwise calls "dignity": he writes elsewhere, for example, of "graue solemne wittes" who "haue more dignity than foelicity" (172). The project of the *Advancement* is thus to free learning in the proper sense from everything that commonly adulterates its purity or simulates its value and appearance.

We seem to be apprehending here an early deployment of the third pole of dignity's contemporary usage as we summarized it in chapter 2: a kind of style or manner, a self-presentation or mode of bodily comportment. In his essay "On Beauty," for example, Bacon writes that

> Virtue is like a rich stone, best plain set; and surely virtue is best, in a body that is comely, though not of delicate features; and that hath rather *dignity of presence,* than beauty of aspect. (*Major Works* 425; emphases added)

This "dignity of presence" appears to be the *positive* counterpart of the dignity that can be feigned or affected. Here, dignity denotes, as it were, a *quality* rather than a *quantity*: a set of highly particular characteristics, rather than value, worth, or status in general. The Oxford English Dictionary dates the first instance of this sense (dignity as "nobility or befitting elevation of aspect, manner, or style; becoming or fit stateliness, gravity") a few decades later, in Milton's *Paradise Lost,* from the lines in which Adam describes his first sight of Eve:

> Grace was in all her steps, Heav'n in her Eye,
> In every gesture dignitie and love.   (8:488–89)

Since Eve has both "naked beauty" (4:714) and this gestural or corporeal "dignity," the meaning of the latter as Milton uses it seems very close to Bacon's image of a "dignity of presence." Indeed, since dignity has always been associated with a literal and figural uprightness, the idea of a befitting manner or style of bodily comportment has always been at least implicitly operative in the concept. This moment in *Paradise Lost* echoes the earlier moment in which Satan, trespassing in the Garden of Eden, sees Adam and Eve walking side by side among

> all kind
> Of living Creatures, new to sight and strange:
> Two of far nobler shape, erect and tall,
> Godlike erect, with Native Honour clad
> In naked Majestie seemd Lords of all.    (4:287–90)

Here again is the common figure of a corporeal uprightness that indicates, embodies, and manifests an immanent worth and high ontological status and within which the senses of dignity and sovereignty commingle; and here again, as has often been observed, the reader encounters this vision of humanity's native grace and dignity through the eyes of Satan, and hence already as fatally imperiled.

Thus, as we have been seeing throughout, the semantic triangle of worth, status, and bearing seems to emerge as though inevitably, precisely because of a certain metaphysical and theological logic that informs the concept at every level of its meaning. The third pole of meaning, dignity as bearing or style, seems to have become today perhaps the most common usage of the word; indeed, one might speak today of both "living" *and* of "dying" with dignity. In either case, dignity appears unmistakably to be something *added on* either to life or to death as a kind of interpretive judgment as to the conditions of either. In this case, one must postulate a "dignity" that is a distinctive characteristic of human beings and yet that is not quite the same thing as "human dignity" in general; a dignity that that is not innate or intrinsic, but dependent on certain conditions of possibility; a dignity that combines qualities of independence, autonomy, rationality, and moral rectitude with a bodily soundness and upright bearing, a stateliness, gravity or seemliness of style, bearing and manner.

But precisely insofar as a certain concept of dignity seems in this way to unite an essence and an appearance, it seems to maintain its ineluctable association with a figure of sovereignty. This seems to be the case even in one of the definitional terms inevitably associated with dignity in its third pole of meaning: *state*liness. The sixteenth and seventeenth centuries were of course the very period in which the classical political theory of sovereignty began to emerge, in the form, as has often been argued, of secularized theological concepts. Correspondingly, insofar as there is a nascent concept of "human dignity" in the early-modern period at all, it seems to be understood paradoxically: at once as the self-sovereignty of an individual defined by his freedom, and as a kind of *being-for* sovereignty, a *being-towards* the summit. This is particularly clear in Bacon's *Advancement,* which acknowledges as a possible fault of learning the possibility that "learned men . . . haue esteemed the preseruation, good, and honor of their Countreys or Maisters before their own fortunes or safeties" (18). But this is necessarily the case, he suggests, because

> Learning endueth mens mindes with a true sence of the frailtie of their persons, the casualtie of their fortunes, and the dignitie of their soule and vocation; so that it is impossible for them to esteeme that any greatnesse of their owne fortune can bee, a true or worthy end of their being and ordainment; and therefore are desirous to give their account to God, and so likewise to their Maisters under God (as Kinges and the States that they serve). (18)

In this passage, the rhetorical sequence that unites, as analogous and fundamental truths of the human situation, the "frailty" of the body and the "casualty" (that is, the precariousness or uncertainty) of fortune, is both completed and interrupted by Bacon's invocation of the "dignity" of the soul. But what is the relation between a dignity of soul that essentially transcends its embodiment and what we earlier heard Bacon call a "dignity of presence" that is precisely a mode *of* embodiment? One might suggest that it is the divergence or contradiction between these two wherein lies the ineluctable link between dignity and sovereignty. To *recognize* how the dignity of the soul transcends the weaknesses and perils of mortal existence, Bacon argues, is to desire to serve states, kings, and God. Bacon even seems to say that to serve the one (to recognize the soul's dignity as the only "true and worthy end") is already to serve the other, because dignity and sovereignty are alike constituted *by* this very process of recognition, this presenting of a true "account" to God and to one's "maisters under God." Thus too, I observe in passing, both learning itself and the "true sence" it gives essentially involve a process of calculation, a taking and giving of account, and yet themselves have an incalculable value that transcends all "greatness" of personal fortune: a height that is, as Milton would put it, "above all highth" (*Paradise Lost* 3:57).

In one more passage from the *Advancement,* Bacon once again puts in play a certain concept of dignity and a certain concept of sovereignty in a manner that both opposes them and collapses them into near-identity. Bacon is discussing what he calls "matters of power and commandement," and he asks:

> whether in right reason, there be any comparable with that, wherewith knowl-
> edge investeth and crowneth mans nature. We see the dignitie of the com-
> maundement, is according to the dignitie of the commaunded: to have com-
> maundement over beasts, as Heard-men have, is a thing contemptible: to have
> commandement over children, as Schoole-Masters have, is a matter of small
> honor: to have commandement over Gally-slaves, is a disparagement, rather
> than an honour. Neither is the commaundement of Tyrants, much better over
> people, which have put off the Generositie of their mindes: And therefore it
> was ever holden, that honors in free Monarchies and Common-wealths, had
> a sweetnesse more, than in Tyrannies, because the commandement extendeth
> more over the wils of men, and not only over their deeds and services. . . . But
> yet the commandement of knowledge, is yet higher, than the commandement
> over the will: for it is a commandement over the reason, beleefe, and under-
> standing of man, which is the highest part of the minde, and giveth law to the
> will it selfe. (50–51)

In the first few lines, Bacon makes a series of negative observations intended to set up the positive observation that immediately follows. In this context, the word dignity is used in effect as a way to measure rank, honor, or status. A herdsman or a schoolmaster has "small honor," and thus small dignity as well, since their dignity accords with those they command. In this sense, therefore, dignity is conceptually opposed to sovereignty, as the mark, to-ken, or measure of the hierarchy of relative value and power over which sovereignty towers, indivisible and absolute. (Indeed, one might even say that sovereignty somehow breaks free from the economy and the hierarchy of relative dignity that it also crowns; for does not the sovereign ultimately command herdsmen and schoolmasters and all, with no diminution of his surpassing dignity?)

Yet Bacon's passage also seems to force the concepts of dignity and sov-ereignty into association. First, Bacon briefly imagines "free Monarchies and Common-wealths" where citizens willingly surrender to a "comman-dement" that is here figured as the command of knowledge itself, exert-ing its sway over "reason, beleefe, and understanding" (the very seat of dignity). In such free commonwealths, one might say that dignity simply is the ultimate sovereignty; or at least that would be the rhetorical point of the contrast with the tyrant, under whom men give their deeds and ser-vices to sovereign command, but not the final assent of reason, belief, and understanding (their dignity). Nevertheless, as with the learned men Bacon describes in the previous passage, these citizens are "desirous to give their account to . . . the States that they serve," so that here again, their dignity is constituted precisely by a *being-for* the summit. Then, a few lines later, Bacon finally articulates the full positive conclusion to which these mixed examples seem intended to lead, which is that "the just and lawfull *soveraignetie* over mens understanding, by force of truth rightly interpreted, is that which approacheth nearest to the similitude of the divine rule" (51, emphasis added). This sovereignty over the understanding is the unique characteristic or definitive quality of learning, the very ground of its dignity or value. So the dignity of learning *is* its sovereignty, its surpassing-power *over* all other powers.

The concept of dignity as we have followed it selectively here seems to reach its pinnacle (a peculiarly apt figure) with Kant's ethics, which is often understood as the single greatest source of the concept of dignity that prevails in contemporary usage, especially in human rights discourse. A myriad of small permutations in the concept of human dignity can no doubt be observed in the long history of regicide and revolution that stands between Bacon and Kant, but the conceptual problems that bedevil and conjoin them endure. The key points I've been trying to bring to light in this selective historical overview can best be further illustrated by Kant, whose concept of dignity obviously remains potent today. But Kant's use of dignity has already been discussed so often and so thoroughly as to command a certain reticence in holding it up to renewed consideration. Oliver Sensen, for example, has surveyed in detail all 111 instances of the term in Kant's published works as well as the interpretations of the concept in Kant's commentators. He confirms that Kant most often uses the word in its oldest and simplest senses, to mean either aristocratic rank ("the dignity of a monarch") or high status and worth, as when he speaks of the dignity of a teacher or a minister, or of the dignity of mathematics among the disciplines (Sensen 179; 164). The concept of "human dignity," the dignity of humanity, emerges prominently only in a few famous passages, primarily from the *Groundwork of the Metaphysic of Morals*. Yet, as Sensen also observes, Kant does not invoke dignity at all in some of the places one might expect him to, such as the third section of the *Groundwork*. Kant's concept of "human dignity" therefore "carries no justifactory weight," and remains largely in accordance with what Sensen calls a "traditionalist paradigm," by which dignity refers both to the freedom, autonomy, and capacity for reason that distinguishes humanity from all other natural beings *and* to a certain kind of self that it is the duty or obligation of such a being to achieve (e.g., Sensen 153 and passim). Above all, for Kant, dignity always "refers to an elevation rather than a value per se" (165). Thus the Kantian concept of "human dignity" is perhaps less innovative than it has often seemed; and Kant's own elaboration of the concept itself contributes to making it such "notoriously contested territory" (McCrudden 659).

To be sure, in the often-cited lines from the *Groundwork*, human dignity seems to name the incalculable value that transcends every other kind of value that might be found in a human being. What Kant calls "skill and diligence in work" (which satisfies our needs) has a merely "market price," and such things as "wit, lively imagination and humor" (things that satisfy a taste beyond need, and that give "delight in the mere purposeless play of our mental powers") have a "fancy price." But "that which constitutes the condition under which alone something can be an end in itself"—that is, the capacity for exercising reason in moral decisions by means of a categorical imperative, the capacity for willing that one's own moral choice be a universal law—"has not merely a relative worth, that is, a price, but an inner worth, that is *dignity*" (4:435). Kant thus seems to define or postulate dignity as an incalculable value inherent in each person; and thus it is commonly argued, as it is by Allen W. Wood, that "Kantian ethics rests on a single fundamental value—the dignity or absolute worth of rational nature, as giving moral law and as setting rational ends" (Wood 94). The idea that each human subject possesses this absolute, inalienable, and incalculable value called dignity, as Derrida puts it, "remains the indispensable axiomatic . . . of the discourses and international institutions concerning human rights and other modern juridical performatives" (*Rogues* 133). I have observed previously, however, the common locution by which one speaks of the "dignity and worth" of humanity, as though to indicate that the worth of dignity itself was not quite adequate to guarantee humanity its rights; and the duplicity with which dignity is said to be at once the *ground* of rights and something that *requires* certain rights for its own fulfillment.

Kant's own exposition of the term seems to condition at once whatever efficacy the term has had in the nascent field of "human rights," and the groundlessness that often threatens the word's discursive deployment today. For Kant, dignity is not an immanent characteristic, not even a specific faculty or capability, of a given human being: rather, it names something incalculably precious (morality, duty, rational choice, freedom) of which that human being as a person is (sometimes) capable, and that allows that person to be treated as *"absolutely precious* and worthy of respect" (Derrida, *Negotiations* 324). Therefore, Kant does not really understand humanity as "having" dignity; rather, as he writes, "Morality and humanity *insofar as it is capable of morality* is that which alone has dignity" (4:435, p. 42; emphases added). Such a formulation, which by yoking human dignity to specific forms of behavior as opposed to others makes such dignity at once universal *and* exclusive, seems not only to recapitulate all the many earlier formulations surveyed in this chapter, but also to survive more or less unchanged beyond the limits of the Kantian system in general. Hegel, for example, would later argue in *The Philosophy of Right* that "the subjective will has worth and dignity *only in so far* as its insight and intention are in conformity with the good" (Hegel 158 [par. 131], emphases added).

Kant himself also repeatedly associates this dignity with a sublimity which, of course, he himself would elsewhere define as a height beyond all height, as that which is "surpassingly large" (Sensen 178; cf. Rosen 28-30). In the *Groundwork*, Kant writes of "the sublimity and inner dignity of the command in a duty," both of which are greater or more manifest if they are obeyed without interest or what he calls here "subjective causes" (4:425). Later, just following his postulation of this ideal kingdom of ends in which each member is a lawmaker as well as a subject, Kant observes

> From what has just been said it is now easy to explain how it happens that, although in thinking the concept of duty we think of subjection to the law, yet at the same time we represent a certain sublimity and *dignity* in the person who fulfills all his duties. For there is indeed no sublimity in him insofar as he is *subject* to the moral law, but there certainly is insofar as he is at the same time *lawgiving* with respect to it and only for that reason subordinated to it. (4:439-40; emphases original)

A dutiful person who obeys the moral law seems to have (or can be "represented" as having) dignity. But this is only as one might say that a given landscape is "sublime," even though the sublimity is not really an objective characteristic of the landscape but only a name for the subjective (though subjectively-universal) response that one has in seeing it. In fact, dignity pertains only to the lawgiving aspect of humanity. Dignity is a self-sovereignty or sovereignty *of* self, in that the very thing that makes a human being worthy of respect is the capacity to act morally while "being free from all influences of contingent grounds" (4:427). Or, as Kant puts it slightly later, "it is just in this independence of maxims from all such incentives that their sublimity consists, and the worthiness of every rational subject to be a lawgiving member in the kingdom of ends; for otherwise he would have to be represented only as subject of the natural law of his needs" (4:439). Members of the kingdom of ends are *subject* both to the natural law of their bodily needs and to the universal moral law that they have themselves willed and legislated; they are also "sovereign"—though in this case only with regard to the latter. It is only insofar as one can act *as if* one were free from needs (following maxims independent of all incentives to interest) that one can be represented as sublime, dignified.

In all this, Kantian dignity seems to involve two obligations that divide along the lines of calculation and incalculability but whose relation is neither one of simple opposition nor a conceptual subordination by which one would be a subcategory of the other. On the one hand, "dignity" names the respect that one is obligated to give to all other persons regardless of any calculation one might make about them (regarding, for example, their talents and abilities, and whether or not they actually seem to us to act rationally). On the other hand, "dignity" designates or determines, as it were, a certain downward *limit* of human behavior beyond which the being in question would no longer seem, in the familiar implicitly tautological formulation, worthy of his own worth. In the *Groundwork,* the opposition of price and value—or, perhaps more precisely, of value and dignity, the latter being precisely that which is *priceless*—is actually only said to be operative in what Kant famously, if somewhat obscurely, calls the "kingdom of ends": an imagined, ideal community of rational beings each of whom at once wills and obeys the same absolute moral law. It is "in the kingdom of ends," Kant writes, that "everything has either a price or a dignity" (4:434). In *The Metaphysics of Morals,* Kant suggests that "the dignity of humanity" can be recognized in certain examples—which he gives, however, in negative form, and in the form of a specific set of injunctions or prescriptions:

> Be no man's lackey. Do not let others tread with impunity on your rights.— Contract no debt for which you cannot give full security.—Do not accept favors you could do without, and do not be a parasite or a flatterer or (what really differs from these only in degree) a beggar. Be thrifty, then, so that you will not become destitute.—Complaining and whining, even crying out in bodily pain, is unworthy of you. (6:436)

Dignity is inalienable but it remains always possible that its bearers will fail to *live up to it.* Dignity is an incalculable value but it cannot itself fulfill *needs* of a practical or financial kind and thus would seem to require a certain practical as well as moral independence. There will be no whining in the kingdom of ends, no beggars, lackeys, or parasites. Therefore, although dignity is precisely the name for the capacity to will and obey the moral law beyond all personal or subjective needs or interests, it would appear to be always in need of a certain calculation (thriftiness) to be and remain worthy of itself. Dignity would seem to require, in order to be (worth) itself, not just bodily discipline (in order not to whine or cry out in pain) but also such things as "rights" and financial welfare. Thus dignity, across this strange double structure of its coming to be recognized as such, is not exactly or entirely beyond *all* price.

Indeed, it turns out that, just as the priceless dignity that lifts us above the other animals supplements a merely natural being which already has a value, although merely a limited or calculable one, so the kingdom of ends itself proves in need of a certain supplement, which Kant provides by postulating a *sovereign* for such a kingdom. Kant does this in a manner, both rhetorically and conceptually, that seems to me both striking and strange. Kant has just been arguing that

> A rational being belongs as a *member* to the kingdom of ends when he gives universal laws in it but is also himself subject to those laws. He belongs to it as *sovereign* when, as lawgiving, he is not subject to the will of any other. (4:433)

But then, a few lines later, he says again that:

> A rational being must always regard himself as lawgiving in a kingdom of ends possible through freedom of the will, whether as a member or as sovereign. He cannot, however, hold the position of sovereign merely by the maxims of his will but only in case he is a completely independent being, without needs and with unlimited resources adequate to his will. (4:434)

And Kant finally stipulates that:

> Duty does not apply to the sovereign in the kingdom of ends, but it does apply to every member of it and indeed to all in equal measure. (4:434)

Between them, these passages seem to inscribe a strange economy in which a self-sufficient commonwealth already founded on the incalculable value (reason and morality) of which each member is a bearer nevertheless must be supplemented by a yet higher level of unconditionality or incalculability. Kant's point surely seems to be, and has been commonly taken to be, that *any* rational being belonging to this hypothetical "systematic union of various rational beings" (4:433) does so both as "member" and as "sovereign," both as subject to the moral law and as giving or willing that will. In the Kingdom of Ends, as Roger J. Sullivan writes, "each person is both ruler and subject" (Sullivan 85). But why would a kingdom or commonwealth essentially defined by the distributed universality of a rational and moral legislative capacity need a singular sovereign at all? Kant himself moves quickly past this point, and his commentators are largely silent as well: for example, Thomas E. Hill Jr. says that "The sovereign, who is presumably God or the holy will . . . can be ignored" (59).

I suggest, on the contrary, that for Kant to postulate this sovereign *of* a kingdom whose members are already joined on the basis of their incalculable mutual dignity is to tacitly concede the points I have sketched above. By imagining a "completely independent being, without needs and with unlimited resources adequate to his will," he seems to concede implicitly that mere dignity is not really priceless (that there is still a pricelessness beyond this one); and that, indeed, as we were seeing above, it remains subject to the calculations of need and a world in which resources are not necessarily adequate to one's will. As one might put it, dignity for Kant *is* sovereignty, constituted essentially to be the human subject's capacity to act wholly free from the sway of any needs or inclinations; and yet dignity is not sovereign, for it always confronts an ideal of unconditionality and autonomy beyond its own, a sovereign not even subject to the duty that otherwise binds all members of the kingdom of ends. It would thus appear that Kant's absolute sovereign is the kind, as Derrida famously argues in "Structure, Sign and Play," that must be located both "*within* the structure and *outside* it" (279). This, as Martin Hägglund argues, would be Kant's unconditional: that is, "a sovereign instance that is not subjected to time and space (e.g. god)" (19); and as such would be one evident place where Kantian ethics opens to a deconstruction. For Derrida, as Hägglund also suggests, what is unconditional is, on the contrary, "the spacing of time that undermines the very Idea of a sovereign instance" (19). Could "dignity" thus be understood as unconditional in *this* sense, as a certain shared condition of possibility for singular, mortal beings joined only in difference and dispersal in time and space, bound together *as* other instead of in the assumption that each Other is dignified insofar as he is like me?

Another way to put this would be to evoke the terms from Georges Bataille discussed in the preface, to suggest that Kant's kingdom of ends, a realm or commonwealth allegedly united by its common possession of an incalculable dignity, reveals itself as inscribed within a restricted economy, an economy of need and work, of investment and return. Correspondingly, the godlike singular sovereign, a being with infinite resources and yet no needs, can only be associated with a kind of general economy. One can still perhaps wrest something from Kant's own reasoning here by turning this economy inside-out and seeing that general economy could never be the place of the singular but only of the common or the commonwealth. What might be called Kant's ultimate vision of dignity as that which names a certain necessary *relation* to the other would here reemerge hand-in-hand with Kant's implicit acknowledgment of dignity's conditionality, making the latter not a flaw in Kant's argument but a place where it opens up to a rational deconstruction. In other words, Kant himself might be said to have shown, even if in an extremely roundabout way (and to adapt a famous passage from Marx and Engels), that only in community with others could individual dignity be possible. Only in community could a "general" abundance be realized in practice for restricted, singular, mortal beings—so that human dignity might finally be unconditionally and universally ensured. In the final chapter of the book, I return to more or less this same argument with regard to the question of a right to die.

## CHAPTER FIVE

# The Right to Die:
# Mapping a Contemporary Debate

In this chapter I return to the contemporary debate about a right to die. This debate, as we have already seen in part, is often envisioned by activists on both sides as a clash between two absolute positions. A more careful analysis reveals, by contrast, a precarious structure of argument both within each side's case and within the debate as a whole, a structure that turns on a set of relations between the conditional and the unconditional, between calculation and incalculability. To be sure, this debate has often been construed by relatively conservative thinkers in exactly this way: that is, as a clash of ideals and principles against mere expedience and practicality. For example, the columnist David Brooks wrote, in the final days of the controversy about Terri Schiavo:

> The core belief that social conservatives bring to cases like Terri Schiavo's is that the value of each individual life is intrinsic. The value of a life doesn't depend upon what a person can physically do, experience or achieve. The life of a comatose person or a fetus has the same dignity and worth as the life of a fully functioning adult.
>
> Social conservatives go on to say that if we make distinctions about the value of different lives, if we downgrade those who are physically alive but mentally incapacitated, if we say that some people can be more easily moved toward death than others, then the strong will prey upon the helpless, and the dignity of all our lives will be diminished.

By contrast, Brooks claims, social liberals "shift [the] arguments away from morality and on to process." While conservatives advance "a moral argument about the sanctity of life," liberals merely talk "about jurisdictions, legalisms, politics and procedures." As Brooks would map this debate, we have, on one side, an unconditional affirmation of the dignity and sanctity of life; and on the other side, nothing but the calculations of law and politics. Brooks himself prefers the former, though only with reservations. "The socially conservative argument," he claims, "has tremendous moral force," and its only weakness is that it "doesn't accord with the reality we see when we walk through a hospice," where we encounter "forms of existence that upon direct contact do seem even worse than death." The socially liberal argument is not only "morally thin," but eventually becomes "vapid mush," because

> Once moral argument is abandoned, there are no ethical checks, no universal standards, and everything is left to the convenience and sentiments of the individual.

Nevertheless, Brooks finally claims to have described merely "the clash of two serious but flawed arguments," and as his column closes, he pictures himself in "agonized" indecision "betwixt and between" them.

One must consider in more detail the opposition that Brooks seems at once to entertain and abandon, grasping first that this same opposition of calculation and incalculability structures not merely the debate as a whole, but also the cases on both sides of the question. To put it in schematic terms: each of the two sides *leads* with an argument that addresses an unconditional and incalculable value (and that is itself, *as* an argument, claimed to be unconditional); and then *adds* a second, supplementary argument that addresses a set of specific conditions and the consequent necessity to calculate among them. Further analysis reveals that even the leading arguments on both sides have a kind of internal fracture by which a logic of calculation undermines the incalculable principle on which the whole case is declared to depend.

In the pages that follow, I will illustrate this process with a series of brief examples from the discourse on both sides of this issue. It will be only then, only after the internal tensions and contradictions on each side have been unfolded, and a certain complicity of both sides with one another has betrayed itself, that this whole landscape of thought can reveal itself again as an opposition of calculation and incalculability, of the conditional and the unconditional. In other words, one might venture to say that this debate has the shape of a chiasmus, characterized by a pattern of symmetry within opposition; or even, more broadly, a kind of *fractal* structure, in which the logic or economy emerging in each of the two opposed arguments replicates itself once again *in* their mutual relation, and thus in the debate as a whole.

In the latter, however, the ultimate opposition at work will prove to be something more than Brook's simplistic and irresolvable "clash" of expedient practice and absolute principle. On the contrary, it will be the very thing that opens up this whole vexed landscape of thought to a deconstruction: a process that (as have seen in chapter 1) will require its own set of further reversals and displacements.

Before going on, I must stipulate that the very schematic summaries I go on to provide do not precisely describe the argumentative strategy actually pursued by any one particular text or thinker, and that my rhetoric of leading and supplementing, of before and after, is to be taken structurally rather than chronologically. Perhaps even to speak in this way of two "sides," and of cases simply *for* or *against* a right to die, necessarily risks reducing significant philosophic differences between different writers and within the debate as a whole. The necessity and usefulness of such risks will, I venture to hope, reveal itself as we proceed.

Those who count themselves generally in favor of a right to die encompass a rather broad philosophic and political spectrum ranging from strict utilitarians all the way to moderates, liberals, or libertarians. Nevertheless, the case for a right to die, I suggest, can finally be reduced to two fundamental arguments. It is argued, first and foremost, that a right to die is the *ultimate* instance of the autonomy and freedom of human beings, the final, absolute, and decisive expression of the reason wherein consists, as Kant famously argues, the incalculable value of human dignity. A right to die is the right to exercise such reason with regard to the time, place, and circumstances of death—either directly, by a conscious human subject, or insofar as the presence of such a subject persists in its own inscription: in the memories of friends and family, or, more formally, via "living wills" or "advance directives" that record and preserve the subject's express intentions. As Ronald Dworkin summarizes:

> People who believe that competent patients should be permitted to arrange their own deaths, with the assistance of willing doctors if they wish, often appeal to the principle of autonomy. They say that it is crucial to people's right to make central decisions for themselves that they should be allowed to end their lives when they wish. (190)

In the succinct formulation posted on billboards in several American states in the summer of 2010 by the Final Exit Network, a national right-to-die organization, advocates on this side of the issue affirm that what is at stake is always "My Life, My Death, My Choice."

This basic principle has also had a long-standing but measured success in American jurisprudence. In recent decades, several major Supreme Court decisions have affirmed the individual's autonomy with regard to end-of-life decisions, though only as balanced against what it also commonly claims to be the state's legitimate interest in the preservation of life. In other words, the law recognizes in this area only a kind of negative right: what William Rehnquist calls, in the majority decision in *Cruzan v. Director, Missouri Department of Health* (1990) "the right of a competent individual to refuse medical treatment" (278). No constitutional right to commit suicide or to have assistance in committing suicide, or indeed any "general and abstract 'right to hasten death'" (*Vacco v. Quill* 806) has yet been recognized. The law has also struggled with certain highly technical and yet profoundly consequential questions, such as whether a so-called feeding tube represents medical treatment or merely nutrition. But beyond all such ongoing specific questions, the case in favor of a possible "right to die" almost always turns on the question of autonomy and reasoned choice. As Supreme Court Justice John Paul Stevens writes in his dissenting opinion in *Cruzan*, an individual's "intense interest in self-determination in her choice of medical treatment" should outweigh "the State's general interest in life" (314).

Indeed, some thinkers go so far as to affirm that the right to die is, as M. Pabst Battin puts it, "a fundamental human right, on a par with rights to life, to liberty, to freedom of speech and worship, to education, political representation, and the pursuit of happiness" (271). Therefore, to summarize rather too quickly, it appears that the contemporary case in favor of a right to die at least *claims* to enfold an extremely broad constellation of legal, political, and philosophic traditions, including the "possessive individualism" of Anglo-American liberalism, the emancipatory ideals of the European enlightenment, the aspirations of American constitutional democracy, and a Kantian ethical vision of the incalculable "dignity" of the human person.

In popular discourse, however, and as we have again already glimpsed, it often appears as though this incalculable value of "human dignity" and autonomy is asked to *supplement* a distinctly different sense of dignity that also necessarily figures in the question of a right to die. Consider, for example, Brian Clark's *Whose Life Is It Anyway?*, the award-winning British play from 1972, which was filmed in 1981, revived on Broadway in 1980 and 2005 (with the protagonist now made female), and which remains today probably the best-known literary work to address this issue. At the end of the play, the protagonist, a sculptor who had been paralyzed from the neck down in an accident, is allowed to confront a judge in his hospital room in order to request legal permission to refuse the treatment necessary to maintain his life.

JUDGE: All right. You tell me why it is a reasonable choice that you decided to die.

KEN: It is a question of dignity. Look at me here. I can do nothing, not even the basic primitive functions. I cannot even urinate. I have a permanent catheter attached to me. Every few days my bowels are washed out. Every few hours two nurses have to turn me over or I would rot away from bedsores. Only my brain functions unimpaired but even that is futile because I can't act on any conclusions it comes to. . . . I choose to acknowledge the fact that I am in fact dead and I find the hospitals' persistent effort to maintain this shadow of life an indignity and it's inhumane.

JUDGE: But wouldn't you agree that many people with appalling physical handicaps have overcome them and lived essentially creative, dignified lives?

KEN: Yes, I would but the dignity starts with their choice. If I choose to live, it would be appalling if society killed me. If I choose to die, it is equally appalling if society keeps me alive. (79–80)

In this dialogue the word *dignity* transforms itself right before our eyes. When Ken claims that the preservation of his life under conditions of extreme disability constitutes an "indignity," the judge reminds him that other disabled people live "essentially creative, dignified lives." The term dignity here slips between two shades of meaning that both pertain to conditionality or calculation: in one, certain conditions of life are said to lack dignity; in the other, dignity lies, quite precisely, in victory over those conditions. But Ken then interposes the question of autonomy and choice, claiming the salient fact is the power to choose, not the reasons for the choice (even though he had himself begun by stressing precisely those reasons). The conditions that provoke Ken's choice are therefore both central to the decision and ultimately irrelevant to it. Thus, as opponents of a right to die frequently assert, this logic would appear to lead towards an affirmation of a right to suicide in general, even for people who are perfectly healthy. But what concerns us at the moment is rather how the incalculable value of one kind of dignity, dignity as sovereign choice, seems to supplement the other, merely conditional dignity, to plug the hole in the semantic structure within which these incommensurable senses vie for position.

For another vivid example, compare the case of Debbie Purdy, a British woman with multiple sclerosis who, in a case that continues to unfold at the time of this writing, sued the British government to be reassured that her husband would not be prosecuted for accompanying her to a euthanasia clinic in Switzerland. In a newspaper account from September 2009, Purdy explains:

> "When I was 20 and jumping out of airplanes, I thought being in a wheelchair would be unbearable," Ms. Purdy said. "But it's not. I thought asking people for help would be horrible and unbearable.
>
> "But what I consider dignity has changed, and what I consider unbearable and horrible has changed," she said. "Having a stranger pick me up off my bathroom floor, that's not undignified. What is undignified is having a stranger say that I have no control over my own life." (Lyall)[1]

As such examples make clear, even if "dignity" is defined as autonomy, it has at least two possible forms: it can refer to the capacity for "independence" in the physical or corporeal sense, the ability to walk, to talk, to perform basic acts of physical hygiene, and the like; but also to the freedom to choose, beyond all such conditions, whether to live or die. A similar double logic is evident in the thought of Peter Singer with regard to a possible right to die. Writing for a general audience in his 1993 utilitarian manifesto *Rethinking Life and Death*, Singer presents a series of case studies of patients who, like Ken in the play, seek assistance in dying because of various catastrophic disabilities. Singer's utilitarianism is grounded in what he calls the need to "de-sanctify" human life, and in an explicit calculation about the relative worth of individual lives. Nevertheless, Singer also concludes, closely echoing the play, that in such cases: "It is, after all, the patient's life, and as long as the patient is capable of reaching an informed decision, then who better to decide whether life is worth living?" (132). Here again, even without sharing the utilitarian logic of Singer's thought in general, one might still join him in believing that individuals should be considered sovereign over their own lives. Indeed, even if a hypothetical decision to seek death stems from a specific calculation about one's condition (a judgment that one's life is not "worth" living), the actual *act* of giving one's self death must, insofar as it expresses a truly free autonomy, wholly transcend all utilitarian calculation.

The second standard argument in favor of a right to die is that allowing hopelessly ill or severely disabled people to die will free up financial, medical, and human resources that could be used better elsewhere. The general coexistence of these two basic arguments is easy to demonstrate. Derek

Humphrey, author of the worldwide best-selling book and video *Final Exit*, which offers step-by-step practical instructions for ending one's life, declares in an online manifesto that such a right is "humankind's ultimate civil and personal liberty" ("Liberty and Death"). In his book *Freedom to Die* (2000), however, Humphrey also argues that it is "economics, not the quest for broader individual liberties or increased autonomy," that "will drive assisted suicide to the plateau of acceptable practice" (Humphrey and Clement 339). Conceding that such an argument may seem "politically incorrect," Humphrey nevertheless insists that

> People are beginning to question the common sense of keeping someone alive, at great societal and personal expense, who prefers to forgo the final hours or weeks of an intolerable existence. To what purpose? Might not money be better spent on preventative treatment, medicine for the young, educating the youth of the nation, or for that matter, the children in the patient's own family? Is there, in fact, a duty to die . . . ? (339)

His final question here echoes the title of a 1997 essay by John Hardwig that answers it in the affirmative. Indeed, Hardwig goes so far as to cite Kant's affirmation of a "human dignity" that "rests on the capacity for moral agency" (133) in order to argue not merely that we have the *freedom* to choose death, but rather, that we sometimes have a positive *responsibility* to do so—since, for example, "the lives of our loved ones can be devastated just by having to pay for health care for us" (123). As one would expect, the utilitarian case for a right to die also often stresses, as Peter Singer does, that "in a public health-care system, we cannot ignore the limits set by the finite nature of our medical resources, nor the needs of others whose lives may be saved by an organ transplant" (Singer 192).

Thus an argument based essentially on calculation and economic scarcity is called upon to supplement the affirmation of unconditional autonomy and dignity. As Hardwig's invocation of a quasi-Kantian "duty to die" indicates, the reason that exercises itself in economic calculation is itself the very ground of human dignity, so that these two quite distinct arguments might almost be further reduced to one: to a unitary affirmation of such reason. At the same time, however, if the choice to embrace death is driven by a rationally perceived need to conserve scarce resources, then does such a choice remain *free*? For Kant himself, as one can hardly forget, an action done from interest cannot be an expression of a free will. Indeed, Kant specifically suggests that any act of suicide can never be "consistent with the idea of humanity *as an end in itself*"; because a human being who "destroys himself in order to escape from a trying condition . . . makes use of a person *merely as a means*" (*Groundwork* 4:429). Thus this second argument in favor of a right to die, the argument from economic calculation, implicitly undermines the absolute principle that grounds its first and primary argument. On the one hand, the freedom to choose might be thought of, quite precisely, as the freedom to *calculate*; on the other hand, to echo the Kantian phrase, calculation assaults the holiness of human dignity by assigning it a price.

The case against the right to die, for all the evident ideological differences among those who maintain it, might similarly be reduced to two fundamental arguments. First and foremost, it is argued that (human) life is absolutely sacred under any of its possible conditions, and therefore (to cite the title of a manifesto issued in 1991 by the Ramsey Colloquium of the Institute on Religion and Public Life), there is an absolute ethical injunction "Always to Care, Never to Kill." As the manifesto declares:

> It is never permitted, it is always prohibited, to take any action that is aimed at the death of ourselves or others. . . . Our decisions, whether for or against a specific treatment, are to be always in the service of life.

Although the manifesto distinguishes between the moral, political, and medical aspects of this issue, it also makes clear that all three are merely subcategories of the absolute moral injunction "always to care." Therefore, no further elaboration of such an argument appears to be necessary, because the principle of the sanctity of (human) life is framed and deployed with a constitutive simplicity affirmed precisely as such. In other words, the very essence of the principle lies in its unconditionality as an absolute rule intended to predetermine all conceivable decisions in advance.

It is, however, all too easy to show that the doctrine of the sanctity of life, when placed within its inevitable theological frame, continues to involve and demand a logic of calculation. Here, for example, is Paul Ramsey himself summarizing the metaphysical context within which alone this principle of the sanctity of life could subsist:

> The immorality of choosing death as an end is founded upon our religious faith that life is a *gift*. . . . To choose death as an end is to throw the gift back in the face of the giver; it would be to defeat his gift-giving. . . . So also religious faith affirms that life is a *trust*. And not to accept life as a trust, to abandon our trusteeship, evidences a denial that God is trustworthy. . . . We are stewards and not owners of our lives. (*Ethics* 146–47).

This familiar rhetoric of trust and stewardship, emerging from a long tradition of "moral economy" and still familiar today from a wide spectrum of Christian discourse, can easily be shown to be, in the present context, entirely untenable. Ramsey's rhetoric indicates all too clearly how God's gift of life is understood to come *with conditions attached*, which is to say that it is, in the most rigorous sense, not a gift at all. This point, which gestures toward Derrida's well-known deconstruction of the figure of the gift in *Given Time*, need not be belabored here. But it remains necessary to observe how the calculative and conditional logic that always accompanies the principle of the sanctity of life undermines in advance the justice of such a principle as a guide for practical politics.

Consider, for example, how Ramsey goes on to suggest that the "decisions" made with regard to the end of (human) life must always be

> consistent with accepting life as a gift and a trust. None seizes dominion over human life and death. . . . Worthy or unworthy, we remain *trustees* making choices among the goods of life, and we do not lay claim to dominion, co-dominion, or co-regency over human life itself. (*Ethics* 148)

Yet it is all too easy to see that this claimed *abdication* of dominion over life would, in the context of law or politics, necessarily involve some human beings claiming and exercising dominion over the lives and deaths of others. Perhaps this is the very place where a hypothetical right to die necessarily entwines itself with a sovereign right to death, and where (as Agamben suggests in another context) the vegetative or comatose patient becomes one of several possible figures for the bare or naked life to which it is the ultimate vocation of sovereign power to reduce human beings (*Homo Sacer* 186).

If, therefore, the case against a right to die grounds itself in the unconditional value of (human) life, it also commonly makes one more argument in which, by contrast, the question of the relative conditions of life becomes central. This time, however, the argument takes the shape of what one might call a *refusal* of calculation. As I have briefly observed above, it is very commonly argued that any of the practices conceivably named under the rubric "a right to die," no matter how carefully limited, puts society on a "slippery slope" towards ethical, social, and political disaster, and particularly puts at risk the most vulnerable members of society: the disabled, the elderly, the poor, and so forth. The infamous programs of involuntary, government-controlled euthanasia that took place in Nazi Germany are commonly cited as the inevitable destination to which any instituted right to die must lead (see, e.g., Smith, *Culture of Death* 37–46). This argument in effect turns the secondary argument from the other side on its head. Precisely because medical resources are scarce, and because people may reasonably fear becoming an economic burden to their friends and family because of disease or age, to legalize "death on demand" will induce relatively healthy people to end their lives needlessly or prematurely. Thus a truly autonomous *right* to die would be a kind of luxury good, limited to the privileged. As Smith argues:

> Most leaders of the euthanasia movement . . . are people of the "overclass": well-off whites with a strong and supportive family or social structure who never believe they could be victimized or pressured into an early death. They want what they want (to be able to die) when and how they want it. They downplay the hardship that will follow for the poor, the uneducated, those without access to medical care, or the disabled, many of whom . . . view themselves as being in the crosshairs on this issue (*Forced Exit* 9).

Some advocacy groups for the disabled do strongly oppose any loosening of the laws against assisted suicide. One such group, Not Dead Yet (whose name, taken from a Monty Python film, further indicates the comic undertones of this debate), was founded as a response to the campaign of Dr. Jack Kevorkian, and claims in its mission statement that "legalized medical killing is really about a deadly double standard for people with severe disabilities."

On the surface of it, such "wedge" or "slippery slope" arguments, insofar as they refrain from shrill polemic about moral decline and emphasize, instead, a concern for the vulnerable members of an unequal society, have an undeniable force, especially when juxtaposed to the economic arguments in favor of a right to die. As I observed above, a choice constrained by economic scarcity is no longer a free choice; and in a society of radical economic inequality there appears every reason to fear that some individuals might feel pressured by financial need to end their lives. Yet this forceful rejoinder also subtly undermines the absolute principle which it intends to supplement. After all, if the principle of "always care" were to prevail, there would be no need even to formulate the second argument; and thus to formulate it at all is to concede a certain necessary limit to the principle as a sufficient guide to social practice. My point here perhaps necessitates a notion of something like what Fredric Jameson famously calls a "political unconscious," for in this case it is as though opponents of a right to die draw an absolute line of ethical prohibition precisely out of a certain secret fear that, in at least some cases, other lines almost certainly would have to be drawn. For example, legal scholar Yale Kamisar, formulating what he calls a "non-religious" case against a right to die, concedes that "the case for voluntary euthanasia is strong," at least for anyone with an incurable disease, intolerable pain, or a "rational desire to die." But we must fear the possibility of "abuse and mistake" and "the danger that legal machinery initially designed to kill those who are a nuisance to themselves may some day engulf those who are a nuisance to others" (Kamisar 86–87). Such a point necessarily moves the argument as a whole away from its original ground (the sanctity and incalculable value of life) towards the realm of process and procedures. Kass, similarly, goes so far as to acknowledge "a strong temptation to remove myself from life to spare my children the anguish of years of attending my demented self" (Kass 210); and further concedes that

> This is not to say that all reasons for promoting a "right to die" are suspect. Nor do I mean to suggest that it would never be right or good for someone to elect to die. But it might be dangerous folly to circumvent the grave need for prudence in these matters by substituting the confused yet absolutized principle of a "right to die," especially given the mixed motives and dangerous purposes of some of its proponents. (211)

Kass here seems to be simply claiming there is a "grave need for prudence" in end-of-life decisions, and that we must not "circumvent" such prudence, especially not by "substituting" a "confused" and merely "absolutized" principle for the clear and truly absolute principle of life's inviolable sanctity. But, of course, proponents of a right to die are calling precisely for prudence, calculation, and choice in end-of-life decisions. Isn't it therefore the principle of life's sanctity and its practical corollary "always to care" (which predetermines all decisions in advance) that actually circumvents the exercise of prudence? Or, to put it another way, Kass affirms the *general* prudence of sticking to absolute principle, and denies or eschews the *particular* prudence that might be exercised in a specific situation—even one in which, as he explicitly concedes, it might be "right or good for someone to elect to die." Thus the prudence affirmed here is one that renounces in advance any possibility of exercising itself, a prudence that chooses not to choose, and decides not to decide.

These brief examples suggest that the cases both for and against a right to die form a kind of chiasmus, a symmetrical crisscross of opposed yet analogous arguments. The debate *seems* to be one in which two figures of incalculable value, human dignity and the sanctity of life, confront one another. Yet, as we have already seen, these two figures can neither be forced into simple identity nor maintained as rigorously distinct. The alleged *sanctity* of human life can only lie in that which distinguishes us from all other natural beings: that is, in human *dignity*. The latter, similarly, refers to the incalculable and inviolable value of humanity, something that is itself, as such, commonly claimed to be "sacred." Thus the real *polemos* of this debate takes place beneath this clash of titans, in the realm of calculations and conditions. When those opposed to a right to die raise fears about the abuse of such a right with regard to the poor and the disabled, the force of this point is that it exposes how proponents of a right to die undermine their own affirmation of dignity by economizing it. As its opponents charge, the institution of a right to die could successfully conserve medical resources (assuming these remain constant) only if it includes some process of triage: a calculation by which lives are compared to one another in terms of their relative worthiness or eligibility for medical care. As many have already asked, how could such a process ever be squared with the vision of an incalculable and universally shared human dignity? Indeed, as we have seen, the very conditions in which the right to die would normally be exercised (pain, disability, imminent death) are necessarily those in which a certain dignity (in the secondary, material sense of the word) is lacking.The contradiction between death and dying as both the *loss* and the *achievement* of dignity sometimes produces strange convolutions of argument whose limit case might be something like Marjorie Casebier McCoy's 1974 book, *To Die with Style!*, which suggests one should plan one's death as though "rehearsing for a performance that is the climax of the drama of our own lives" (162).

But by the same token, when those in favor of a right to die raise these calculative arguments, reminding us that medical and social resources are, at least under the current state of affairs, always limited, they too expose a hidden contradiction in their opponents' case, though one that is not so easily stated and whose full analysis would take a separate discussion. As a brief illustration, consider how, in *Cruzan v. Missouri*—to date the most important US Supreme Court case on this subject—the majority affirmed that the state of Missouri, or any American state, may "assert an unqualified interest in the preservation of human life," even though it must weigh this "against the constitutionally protected interests of the individual" (281). In a footnote from his dissenting opinion, Justice William J. Brennan Jr. observes that this alleged state interest in preserving life

is not even well supported by that State's own enactments. In the first place, Missouri has no law requiring every person to procure any needed medical care nor a state health insurance program to underwrite such care. (314n15)

Brennan's ironic observation directs our attention to the cohabitation, in contemporary right-wing politics, of a classically liberal affirmation of market economics and a so-called social conservatism, a combination which, on the level of policy, means that conservatives tend to oppose both a right to die *and* any organized plan for universal health insurance.

The 2008 Republican party platform, for further example, in a paragraph briefly mentioned earlier entitled "Maintaining the Sanctity and Dignity of Human Life," states clearly that "we oppose euthanasia and assisted suicide which endanger especially those on the margins of society." In another section, the same document denounces the American health care system as one that "costs too much," and denounces any possibility of what it calls a "government takeover of health care" (Republican National Committee). Similarly, in an article from the *Wall Street Journal* from August 2009 that was widely discussed at the time of its appearance, the entrepreneur John Mackey observes that:

> Many promoters of health-care reform believe that people have an intrinsic ethical right to health care—to equal access to doctors, medicines and hospitals. While all of us empathize with those who are sick, how can we say that all people have more of an intrinsic right to health care than they have to food or shelter? . . . A careful reading of both the Declaration of Independence and the Constitution will not reveal any intrinsic right to health care, food or shelter. That's because there isn't any. This "right" has never existed in America.

Mackey's observations, which are entirely accurate in strict historical terms, might provoke an entirely separate discussion about the historical evolution of constitutional principles, or about the relationship of political versus economic rights in general. In the present context, more specifically, his observations compel us to question how an absolute injunction "always to care" could ever be reconciled with an ethics of the marketplace and a classically liberal economy of "haves" and "have nots." Indeed, one can only marvel at the uneasy relation still so often maintained between a "free market" capitalism (which, as Marx famously declares, drowns all "religious fervor . . . in the icy water of egotistical calculation") and a hypothetical quasi-religious ethic of absolute mutual *care*.

CHAPTER SIX

# Suicide and Sacrifice from Plato to Kant

Those in favor of a right to die often picture themselves as the rightful heir of enlightenment philosophy, not only by centrally affirming the "dignity" of individual moral choice, but also by envisioning the establishment of the right to die as a crucial step in the progress of human emancipation. Derek Humphrey writes, for example,

> Thanks to the work in the last century of a forceful right-to-die movement, a hidden reality has emerged about terminal suffering, indicating that the time has come for change. . . . With the inevitability of gradualness, as the idea takes hold amongst rising generations, reform will undoubtedly come. We who believe must ceaselessly work for it. ("Why I Believe")

As his rhetoric indicates, Humphrey understands the right to die as a kind of repressed truth gradually and inevitably brought to light, and thus (to echo the Kantian phrase), part of man's laborious emergence from a self-imposed immaturity.

Can such a narrative of enlightenment be rigorously maintained with regard to the history of evolving attitudes toward suicide in general? To be sure, the curious practices surrounding the act of suicide until the dawn of modernity (the desecration of the corpse, the burial at the crossroads, and so forth), might well seem to be survivals of primitive animistic beliefs. Correspondingly, a tradition of rational skepticism about suicide can be followed from texts such as Montaigne's "A Custom of the Isle of Cea" (1580), John Donne's *Biathanatos* (1608), and David Hume's "On Suicide" (1755), all the way to contemporary books such as Jean Améry's *On Suicide* (1976) or Thomas E. Joiner's *Myths about Suicide* (2010). Perhaps one could even construe this history, to adapt Foucault's phrase, in terms of a "repressive hypothesis" in which the freedom to die when and as one chooses that is affirmed in Stoic philosophy and even perhaps in the Hebrew scriptures (which record several acts of suicide with no apparent disapproval) largely yields to the prohibitions of Augustinian Christianity, only to reemerge in our own time as a crowning instance of human self-determination. But in the end it is difficult or impossible to impose a narrative of repression, enlightenment, or incremental progress on a history of thought marked most of all by ambivalence and inconsistency, a history that repeatedly circles back to revisit the same themes and entertain the same doubts. It is precisely this that will interest us here: how the general prohibition of suicide in Western thought maintains itself only in the face of certain acknowledged exceptions that thus appear as necessary as the prohibition itself.

Preeminent among those exceptions is the figure of self-sacrifice. As I'll try to suggest with a series of disparate examples, suicide seems to have been nearly unthinkable in Western thought except alongside a figure of sacrifice which then reemerges on *both* sides of the contemporary debate about a right to die. One cannot even define the word or concept of suicide without coming to terms in some way with a certain economy by which a being might willingly embrace death in the name of some value or purpose deemed to outweigh life itself. Across a very long tradition of thought and philosophic debate, the question has always been how to distinguish between suicide itself and a whole range of other acts in which, so to speak, a being *decides* for death without actually *desiring* death. As John M. Cooper observes, neither classical Greek nor Latin had even a single word to refer to suicide, so that classical writers used circumlocutions such as *e vita excedere,* to withdraw or retire from life (10, 32n1).[1] Greek and Roman philosophers also always distinguish between a "death that a person both intended and brought about" and a death seen merely as "an acceptable price to pay for the attainment of the goal being pursued" (Cooper 10). By contrast, the modern understanding of the act of suicide usually adapts the approach of Emile Durkheim, who in his celebrated study (1897) defines the term empirically as *"all cases of death resulting directly or indirectly from a positive or negative act of the victim himself, which he knows will produce this result"* (44; emphases original). For Durkheim, "an act cannot be defined by the end sought by the actor," so that to commit suicide and to sacrifice one's life for a purpose are indistinguishable:

The soldier facing certain death to save his regiment does not wish to die, and yet is he not as much the author of his own death as the manufacturer or merchant who kills himself to avoid bankruptcy? This holds true for the martyr dying for his faith, the mother sacrificing herself for her child, etc. (43)

Contemporary discourse follows Durkheim's usage in locutions such as suicide bomber, suicide attack, suicide weapon, and the like. Nevertheless, Durkheim can perform his empirical and theoretical reduction whereby all acts by which someone is literally the "author of his own death" are to be considered suicide only by naming the familiar instances that, as he implicitly concedes, at least *seem* to be not quite the same thing. As Derrida puts it, to give oneself death, to put oneself to death, means both

> dying while assuming responsibility for one's own death, committing suicide but also sacrificing oneself for another, *dying for the other*, thus perhaps giving one's life by giving oneself death, accepting the gift of death, such as Socrates, Christ and others did in so many different ways. (*Gift of Death* 10, emphases original)

Or, to put it another way, in Western thought and culture, self-sacrifice is the exception that troubles the prohibition of self-murder via a certain *economy* of life and death that, in a paradoxical and at times nearly laughable manner, seems always to be at once affirmed and forbidden.

Before returning to the contemporary debate, I therefore briefly consider a few outstanding examples of the philosophic approach to suicide, by way of illuminating the sacrificial economy that always seems to condition the question, and the case either for *or* against an individual right to die. An inevitable first example of this process is Plato, who unequivocally denounces suicide and assumes it is forbidden; and yet also, in one key passage, enumerates a broad series of qualifications and exceptions about precisely what kind of acts should be considered suicide in the first place. As Georges Minois observes, Plato's approach to suicide is by no means one of simple condemnation; rather, he opposes suicide only with "a degree of circumlocution" that may suggest "he himself had not quite made up his mind" (44–45). In the *Laws,* the Athenian asks, "what of him who takes the life that is, as they say, nearest and dearest to himself?" Such a person must "be buried ignominiously in waste and nameless spots" in solitary tombs "marked by neither headstone nor name" (873d-e).[2] This treatment, however, is to be reserved for

> the man whose violence frustrates the decree of destiny by *self-slaughter* though no sentence of the state has required this of him, no stress of cruel and inevitable

calamity driven him to the act, and he has been involved in no desperate and intolerable disgrace, the man who thus gives unrighteous sentence against himself from mere poltroonery and unmanly cowardice. (873c; emphasis original)

The first clause following the opening antithesis is perhaps intended to exempt Socrates from the charge of suicide, a possibility that later thinkers continue to debate. This instance is a surprisingly difficult one, for although Socrates was sentenced to die by the power of the state, in some sense he did give himself death. As R. G. Frey observes, Socrates' jailers "did not have to hold him down and pour the hemlock down his throat"; and, at least as he is depicted in Plato's *Phaedo*, Socrates seems to embrace death quite willingly. By a rigorously empirical definition along the lines of Durkheim, Socrates would have to be considered the author of his own death, and hence a suicide. Indeed, as Frey suggests, such questions, which might seem at first merely academic or historical, open up to much larger ones. To the possible objection that "Socrates died a noble and dignified death and suicide is ignoble and undignified," Frey replies, "the fact that Socrates died a noble and dignified death does not show that he did not commit suicide, but rather that suicide need not be ignoble and undignified" (108). In passing, one might note another instance of the supplementary logic that seems to haunt the question of dignity: for why does Frey find it necessary to say that a suicide such as Socrates' might be both noble *and* dignified? But in any case, here is the question that always remains at stake in the debate about a right to die: that is, can the act of suicide ever, in any circumstances, be an act *of* dignity? Can the act of giving one's self death be, not merely dignified, not merely an act done *with* dignity, but an absolute expression of dignity as the self-declared essence of humanity?

Even if we lay the difficult instance of Socrates aside, as categorically different from the other things Plato names in the passage above, the clauses that follow seem to articulate so broad a spectrum of further possible exceptions to the law against suicide that one might question what possible motivation for suicide has *not* been included. Cooper concedes that "Plato's language, though it appears to be carefully chosen, is not completely clear," and goes on to paraphrase the basic point, choosing his own language with equal care, as:

Anyone who commits suicide when his judgment is unclouded by grief, depression, or other severely distorting emotions, because he considers that morally neutral bad things, such as pain, disease, the absence of interesting work to do, or the inability to do it, etc., so outweigh any good that his life can bring him that it is better not to go on living it, will be judged to have shown cowardice and a reprehensible unwillingness to take action against these evils and their effects on his life. (19)

As this summary suggests, Plato's point seems to be that anyone who, with clear mind, makes a certain *calculation* about the relative value of life and death, will be *judged* (by the law and by ethics) to have acted out of a reprehensible combination of laziness, effeminacy, and cowardice, or what Benjamin Jowett gives, in his translation of this passage, as "sloth or want of manliness."

But is this a just judgment, or does Plato's carefully phrased argument raise as many questions as it answers? For one thing, and although this will not be my primary point here, any consideration of Plato's schema would have to account for the way it is implicitly but unmistakably grounded in an assumed structure of gender difference, ascribing suicide in the end to something that might be translated as effeminacy or "unmanly" cowardice. More broadly, is there really so clear a distinction between a "clouded judgment" (which exempts one from responsibility for suicide), and various other "morally neutral bad things" such as pain or disease? If intolerable disgrace or shame clouds the mind, then surely intolerable pain might do so as well, and it is not self-evident that the moral neutrality of the latter should be the deciding factor in an ethical judgment. Couldn't the case be argued at least equally well in the other direction—that is, couldn't one suggest that to kill one's self to escape responsibility for a moral transgression is *more* cowardly than to do so to escape "bad things" such as pain or disease that are not one's own fault? Moreover, as David Gallop observes, "the charge of cowardice . . . is plainly inapplicable to altruistic self-sacrifice, to self-destruction on behalf of a worthy cause, and to the taking of one's own life to avoid morally worse alternatives" (Gallop 1975, 84). Acts of self-sacrifice, whatever else one says about them, and whether or not they are considered suicide, cannot possibly be called cowardly. For that matter, can *any* act of suicide be essentially construed as an act of *cowardice*? Without belaboring a painfully literal point, it appears that more or less any conceivable method by which human beings might put themselves to death requires at least a certain strength of mind, an audacity or steely resolution. Isn't it at least as likely, as Plato himself concedes elsewhere, that for most of us, there is "a child inside" who is "afraid of death, as if it were a bogeyman" (*Phaedo* 77e); and that it is this, as much or more than any fear of what life could give, that often makes cowards of us all?

Notwithstanding such questions, one might be less ready to laugh at Plato's radically qualified prohibition of suicide were it not that Plato himself repeatedly imagines that response in the other celebrated passage, from the *Phaedo*, where he again addresses the subject. This dialogue, which takes place in prison on the last day of Socrates' life, is best known for its discussion of the immortality of the soul; but the prelude for this argument is a brief consideration of suicide. These are the two horns of a dilemma that haunts this dialogue and that forces it to confront a kind of gallows humor. For Plato wants to argue that a philosopher should be willing or even eager to die, and yet still should not ever presume to *give* himself death. The first proposition is stated strongly and repeatedly. As Socrates puts it, "the man who has truly spent his life in philosophy . . . is hopeful that, when he has died, he will win very great benefits in the other world" (64a). Therefore, to die (citing the summary of Edith Hamilton and Huntington Cairns) is to enter "not into death, but into new life, 'life more abundantly'" (Hamilton and Cairns 40). The modern editors' slightly incongruous Christian figure (taken from John 10:10), whose applicability in the context might be doubted, has the virtue here of directing our attention to the sacrificial economy that is unmistakably central to Plato's argument in the *Phaedo*.

In itself, however, the doctrine of the immortality of the soul cannot and does not account for a prohibition of suicide. If anything, as Socrates' friends point out at the beginning of the dialogue, it makes such a prohibition even more difficult to justify. Socrates, who has stated clearly that a philosopher should be willing to die, or even seek and welcome death, mentions only as a kind of reluctant afterthought that this should not include doing "violence to himself" because "they say it's forbidden" (61c). But how, Cebes asks, "can it both be forbidden to do violence to oneself, and be the case that the philosopher would be willing to follow the dying"? (61d). Socrates first tries to pass the buck and answer one question with another. "'Why Cebes, haven't you and Simmias heard about such things through being with Philolaus?'" (61d), he asks, the latter a Pythagorean philosopher in whom the real Plato was apparently interested.[3] No, Cebes says, he has never heard anything specific about why suicide is morally unacceptable. "Well," says Socrates, "maybe you will hear."

What they do hear, however, is a sentence that Plato scholars have called "intractable" (Gallop 1975, 79), "notoriously difficult" (Miles 250), and "one of the most obscure statements in all the dialogues" (Dorter 11), a *locus vexatis* that can be translated only by deciding about certain semantic and philosophical ambiguities that are impossible to resolve once and for all.[4] Here is how Gallop gives the passage in his 1998 translation of the *Phaedo*:

Perhaps, though, it will seem surprising to you if this alone of all rules is unqualified, and it never happens, as in other cases, that sometimes and for some people it is better for a person to be dead than alive; and perhaps it seems surprising to you if those people who would be better off dead may not without sin do themselves a good turn, but must await another benefactor.

In response to this, writes Plato, "Cebes chuckled," and "'Hark at that now,' he said, speaking in his own dialect" (62a).

One is almost tempted to think that Cebes' joke, which has attracted relatively little interest from Plato's commentators, might have been provoked by the grammatical and logical difficulties of Socrates' strangely convoluted sentence. Paul Stern suggests that "Cebes utters an expletive in his native dialect, perhaps in the way that we revert to slang in the face of unfathomable or troubling truths" (Stern 23). But exactly what "truth" that has yet been broached should seem so troublesome? As Cebes' initial questions already indicate, there might be something troubling, something strange or surprising, about either of two things Socrates has briefly mentioned, and also about their combination. That is, it might be surprising to think (as Socrates puts it slightly later) either that "the right practice of philosophy" is "the cultivation of death" (80e–81a), or that suicide should be forbidden, or especially, that *both* of these together should be true. Does philosophy truly consign humanity to a state of such passive impotence, in which we must cultivate and embrace death (and accept it willingly in whatever shape it may come, including even the sentence of the state), and yet have no right to take it or have it by our own decision?

Of course, the note of comedy that emerges here might be a response, not to anything troubling that has been said so far; but, on the contrary, to the cheerful willingness with which Socrates confronts his own imminent death. Cebes' joke itself might be thought to have been provoked, at least in part, by the previous line, in which Socrates seems to imagine, wittily or sarcastically, that someone who puts another person to death, as Athens is now doing to him, should be regarded as a "benefactor." In fact, the dialogue as a whole is punctuated by several incidents of this kind of gallows humor. For example, Socrates laughs slightly later when he realizes that his friends are hesitating to raise objections to his argument about the soul's immortality because they fear that in his "present misfortune" he might "find it unwelcome":

Dear me, Simmias! I'd certainly find it hard to convince other people that I don't regard my present lot as a misfortune, when I can't convince even you two. (84d)

One might suggest, however, that Socrates willfully misunderstands the reticence of his friends, who almost certainly do not fear to offend him through simple disagreement with his point. Socrates has been arguing that death is no misfortune because a philosopher should be confident "that there is something in store for those who've died" (63c); and surely it is this that provokes the reticence of his friends, who might reasonably hesitate, whatever they really think, to dash the hopes of immortality being so confidently expressed on the very brink of death. Socrates laughs again, near the end of the dialogue, when Crito asks "in what fashion are we to bury you," because, as he explains, "Crito imagines I'm that dead body he'll see in a little while," and has already forgotten "the great case I've been arguing all this time, that when I drink the poison, I shall no longer remain with you, but shall go off and depart for some happy state of the blessed" (115e). Socrates' joke here turns on the metaphysical opposition of body and soul, and, so to speak, invites a laughter that takes flight to some more blessed realm. Still, the joke also partially escapes such transmigration insofar as it necessarily also reminds us that, regardless of the fate of Socrates' soul, his friends are indeed shortly going to have to make some sort of arrangements about a corpse.

Both rhetorically and structurally, therefore, the *Phaedo* is a kind of comedy that represents apparent misfortune transformed to happiness. Indeed, Socrates has long been understood to embody the figure of the *eiron*, that typical figure of classical comedy (already identified as such by Aristotle) who, as F. H. Cornford puts it, "masks his cleverness under a show of clownish dullness" (120). The essential character of the *eiron*, as Wylie Sypher elaborates,

> is incarnate in Socrates, who was "ignorant," and who also had the disposition of the "buffoon" or "fool," the features of the comic spirit itself, the coarse, ugly mask of the satyr or clown. (255)

The *Phaedo* evidently locates itself at this nexus of tragedy and comedy, in the anticipation of the feast that follows the sacrifice, the resurrection that recuperates loss into gain and death into abundant life. This of course is why, as Socrates insists, his friends should "be of good cheer" (115e). But the general comic structure of the dialogue does not yet explain or account for the curious detail, in the earlier scene, by which Cebes reverts to "his own dialect" as he "chuckles" and, with a sort of sarcasm or friendly derision, says something like "Hark at that now" (Gallop), "Guid sakes, yes!" (Hackforth), or "Doan Zeus knoweth" (Brann et al.). Doesn't this untranslatable gesture of studied naïveté, of strangeness within familiarity, so reminiscent of the punch line of a myriad of jokes, convey a pointed note of comic skepticism about the philosophic aspiration to cultivate death? Doesn't the irony here even threaten to overflow or confound Socrates' own? Here, I recall the distinction outlined in my preface between a certain comedy (the divine comedy of loss and redemption that Socrates explicitly invokes) and a certain laughter that escapes the closure of the former even as it emerges from it. In this case, Cebes declares, indirectly, and in the mere form of a comic exclamation, that it is somehow all too obvious that what Socrates has just said is "surprising" (Gallop), "strange" (Dorter and Tredennick), or "astonishing" (Warren 95). It seems to be here, and here alone, that the dialogue allows to erupt, for the briefest of moments, a sovereign laughter that refuses the paradoxical catch-22 by which humanity, precisely *because* it has the dignity to rise above life and choose death, must be, precisely as such, enjoined against suicide as the greatest of crimes.

Even in the rest of the dialogue, an uncertainty about this strange, surprising, and wondrous point seems always to be part of Socrates' (or Plato's) point. Socrates says that it may seem "surprising" that *"this* alone of all rules is unqualified" (emphasis added). But, as James Warren asks,

> what is this "this"? Various candidates have been proposed, including the injunction not to commit suicide, or the proposition that it is better to be alive than dead, or simply "death" itself. In essence, however, the exact referent does not alter to any great extent the overall meaning of the passage. (95)

Socrates clearly is speaking of some surprising or strange relation between an "unqualified," an unconditional or absolute rule, and a field of human experience in which decisions and judgments are otherwise always qualified and conditional. The sentence as a whole is constituted by what Gallop calls "two 'if' clauses" that state two distinct but related things that may or may not be true. Socrates says, of either or both of these two things, that *if* they are true, they *may seem to be* strange or surprising. But it is not even clear whether the surprising thing is a conditional or an unconditional. Is Socrates saying that it is surprising that even the question of life and death is merely conditional, and that, as Murray Miles paraphrases, "while life is usually better than death, death may yet be better for some people at some times" (Miles 253)? Or is Socrates, on the contrary, suggesting that, *precisely because* everything else in human life and experience is qualified and conditional, it is surprising to realize that *this* alone, the matter of life and death, is absolute, unconditional, unqualified by circumstance; so that "life and death [are] . . . the only exceptions to the rule that circumstances may make a difference" (Miles 254)? In either case, such difficulties, which will not be resolved here, must at least partially explain why this sentence seems to do no more than instantiate in its own texture a radical uncertainty about the relation of life and death: a *double* uncertainty that even leaves open the question *of* the question, the question of whether one is ever so much as *allowed to decide* to be or not to be.

Similarly, and although Socrates clearly accepts that suicide is forbidden, the justification of such a law is left at best partially explained before the dialogue goes in a different direction. What little Socrates does say on this subject includes another set of textual problems. Essentially, Socrates gives two possible reasons for the prohibition of suicide, one highly specific, the other somewhat more general; and he indicates his own preference for the second one. Both reasons essentially turn on a particular figure or metaphor. Socrates says, first:

> The reason given in mysteries on the subject, that we human beings are in some sort of prison, and that one ought not to release oneself from it or run away, seems to me a lofty idea and not easy to penetrate. (62b)

As many commentators suggest, Socrates is apparently referring to some esoteric Pythagorean or Orphic doctrine about the nature of the soul (Cooper 15; Dorter 19; Gallop 1975, 83; Minois 44). The problem is that the word translated here as "prison" might also mean something like "guardhouse" or "garrison," so that the linguistic and historical evidence leaves us finally uncertain whether Socrates is referring to "a post in which we are *under* guard (in effect, therefore, in a kind of prison), or one where we are *serving* as guards" (Cooper 34n7). The image of the soul as imprisoned in the body has analogues in other passages from Plato (*Cratylus* 400c and *Gorgias* 493a; see Gallop 1975, 83). Taking the passage in this way might also recall the *Crito*, in which Socrates refuses to escape from his literal prison because, he suggests, he had implicitly contracted to obey the laws of Athens by spending his life there and never choosing to emigrate (51d–53a). Gallop, acknowledging this possible parallel, also points out that it cannot really be applied to the question of suicide, because "there could be no comparable 'emigration' from life, and hence no analogous opportunity to opt out of the 'contract'—except through suicide itself" (1975, 84).

On the other hand, there is also evidence for the other reading of the figure, in which we have been placed in the world as sentries or guards, so that suicide would be a kind of desertion or dereliction of duty. Cicero wrote, in what became a very famous and frequently cited passage from *De Senectute,* that "Pythagoras bids us stand like faithful sentries and not quit our post until god, our Captain, gives the word" (20:73). In the Renaissance and later, this would survive as a conventional figure frequently cited in discussions of suicide. Montaigne, for example, writes that "many hold that we cannot abandon this garrison of the world without the express command of him who has placed us in it" (253); and, as we will see in a moment, Kant in the *Lectures on Ethics* claims that "men are stationed here like sentries, and . . . must not leave our posts." A certain laughter might tempt one to ask: from exactly *whom* or *what* is humanity being asked to guard the world? Insofar as this military metaphor eventually associates itself with a prescriptive ethics and the Christian doctrine of "the church militant," it would appear that human beings are in effect being asked to guard themselves *from* themselves. And in any case, whether humanity is imagined as a prisoner or as a guard, he remains subject either way to an imagined structure of sovereign power.

Socrates himself, however, seems in any case not very interested in such esoteric visions, which, he says, are "lofty" and "not easy to penetrate." His second justification for the prohibition of suicide substitutes a different metaphor:

> ". . . still, Cebes, this much seems to me well said: it is gods who care for us and for the gods we human beings are among their belongings. Don't you think so?"
>
> "I do," said Cebes.
>
> "Well, if one of your belongings were to kill itself, without your signifying that you wanted it to die, wouldn't you be vexed with it, and punish it, if you had any punishment at hand?"
>
> "Certainly."
>
> "So, perhaps, in that case, it isn't unreasonable that one should not kill oneself until God sends some necessity, such as the one now before us."
>
> "Yes, that does seem fair," said Cebes. (62b-c)

This is the point where the dialogue moves from the question of suicide to the question of the soul's immortality. Cebes suggests that human beings are in the service of the gods, who are "the best directors there are," so it would be "irrational" to choose to leave their service; and this provokes Socrates to posit his own belief that, after death, he "shall enter the presence . . of other gods both wise and good" (63b). His listeners ask him for proof of this, and the rest of the dialogue is devoted to this question. Plato's argument against suicide thus comes to rest by simply affirming that human beings do not own their own lives. As Gallop observes, Plato's reasoning here "prefigures the Christian orthodoxy that life is given, and may therefore be taken away, only by God" (1975, 84); a point which, as we have seen, persists all the way to contemporary debates about a right to die.

This is also the place, however, where a certain laughter completely overflows the dialogue's own comic structure and whatever might be imagined as Plato's intentions. For is it not obvious that Socrates' metaphor of masters and slaves applies quite differently in the two situations he compares? Imagined theologically, a human being who belonged to the gods could be punished for the act of suicide in some afterlife. But a slave or an animal who belonged to a human being would wholly escape from his master's power with a successful act of self-destruction. To be sure, Socrates' question is qualified: he asks Cebes that, if one of his "belongings" were to kill itself, "wouldn't you be vexed with it, and punish it, *if* you had any punishment at hand?'" (emphasis added)—or, as other translators give the line, "if you had some means of punishing it" (Brann et. al), or "if you had any means of doing so" (Tredennick). Socrates' point might thus be no more than a kind of thought experiment regarding the "as if" of an impossibility. Or perhaps the metaphor is deliberately asymmetrical, so that Socrates is asking Cebes simply to acknowledge his own *desire* to punish in this situation, as a way of suggesting how and why the divine sovereign might also have such an impulse. Such an analogy, however, finally does no more than underline the strangeness of the point being made. At work here appears to be a curious *fear* about a world in which an escape from all sovereignty and power might actually be available to all beings at every moment; or perhaps, rather, an equally misplaced *desire* for a sovereignty so absolute that no escape from it could ever be possible. The burst of laughter that cannot be restrained at this point, however, indicates precisely the space of that freedom and that escape. It is of course an old, old joke to suggest that the punishment for suicide is life imprisonment, and that the punishment for attempted suicide is hanging.

The entwined problems of suicide and sacrifice seem to remain the same sort of irritant in the work of later Western philosophers. In a brief and familiar passage from the *Second Treatise on Government*, John Locke illustrates how the ideas of suicide and sacrifice seem always to be bound together in a strange economy. Locke argues:

> though Man . . . have an uncontroleable [*sic*] Liberty, to dispose of his Person or Possessions, yet he has not Liberty to destroy himself, or so much as any Creature in his Possession, but where some nobler use, than its bare Preservation calls for it. (2:6)

Sacrifice is thus the exception that troubles a prohibition of self-murder that itself already constitutes the single absolute or freestanding exception to man's originary freedom, the only one prior to any relation of one human subject to another. Suicide and sacrifice are thus two limits of the natural right of corporeal and personal self-possession. In the first, a human being's natural freedom to dispose of himself meets its natural limit; in the second, human beings find themselves in exceptional situations (such as, Locke elsewhere specifies, "the state of war" (2:16-22), or instances of judicial execution) where some value "nobler" than the "bare preservation" of life demands a death. For Locke, human beings may not kill themselves most of the time precisely because they are the kind of being that can choose to lay down their lives in special situations, when death itself is amortizable in terms of "nobler use." Indeed, Locke is specifically envisioning situations in which not life, but death, has a certain utility; and in which this ultimate form of negativity, death itself, now has a positive value so great that it transcends not only whatever a living being would otherwise be capable of doing in that situation, but even the otherwise absolute prohibition of murder and self-murder.

Therefore, as Leon R. Kass has rightly pointed out, Locke's liberalism cannot be seamlessly integrated into a contemporary case in favor of a right to die (Kass 213-15). Kass reads the pages in which this passage appears as erecting a plausible framework of natural law on secular grounds, so that the prohibition of man's "quitting of his station" is simply a "corollary of the . . . right of self-preservation" (214). I suggest, on the contrary, that Locke's argument is wholly grounded in this double structure of exception. Locke argues that human beings have a positive right of self-possession—a *"State of perfect Freedom* to order their Actions, and dispose of their Possessions, and Person as they think fit"—which, however, is inseparable from, and entirely contingent upon, both a *negative* obligation of self-preservation and a *positive* obligation to self-sacrifice. What is the glue that holds together this strange triangle of freedom and obligation? Immediately following the passage above, Locke says:

> For men being all the Workmanship of one Omnipotent, and infinitely wise Maker: All the Servants of one Sovereign Master, sent into the World by his order and about his business, they are his Property, whose Workmanship they are, made to last during his, not one anothers Pleasure. (2:6)

Kass, wanting to uphold the argument as an essentially secular one, sees the theological language of this passage as a kind of detour, a moment of carelessness. But this familiar Christian figure of humanity as the servants and property of God, whose problems we have begun to glimpse above, is inescapably necessary within Lock's argument. The logic or economy instantiated in such a figure alone underwrites *both* of the two limits to the right of self-possession: the *prohibition* of suicide and the *obligation* to self-sacrifice—and it does so precisely by linking them in a double structure of opposition and analogy.

A human being's right to destroy "any Creature in his Possession" in the name of "nobler use" obviously includes the consumption of animals as a means of subsistence. Such a right, in practice, is by no means exceptional but absolutely general; and with it (as Locke knows as well as we do), humanity licenses itself to exploit and consume all other natural life on earth. Everything is thus at stake in the word "nobler," which seems both to state, and aspire to transcend, the process of calculation that governs the argument. Under this word Locke claims to think *value* and *use* together, to state the constitutive link that binds politics, law, and carnivorous sacrifice, the courtroom, the battlefield, and the slaughterhouse. But to focus momentarily on the last example, precisely as Locke does not invite us to do, is to see how only within an assumed theological structure could a concept of "nobility" govern all the practices that are thereby licensed under the scriptural command to subdue the earth. Locke *opposes* the "bare Preservation" of life to the "nobler use" to which a life can be put, yet human beings consume other creatures precisely so as to preserve their lives. So the "nobler use" that supposedly outweighs the mere preservation of life is in this case itself no more or less than the preservation of (human) life. Locke's adjective thus stands guard, so to speak, at the brink of a vast semantic and ethical abyss. Although a whole range of practices by which human beings kill animals—foxhunts, cockfights, bullfights, game hunting, and so forth—have indeed sometimes been referred to as "noble" pursuits, would it ever be possible, in any conceivable context, to refer to a meatpacking plant or a factory farm as "noble"?

My final philosophical example for the moment is from Kant, whose refusal to imagine an ethical place for suicide we have briefly encountered before. In the *Groundwork*, and indeed as the very first example after the formulation of the categorical imperative, Kant stipulates:

> Someone feels sick of life because of a series of troubles that has grown to the point of despair, but is still so far in possession of his reason that he can ask himself whether it would not be contrary to his duty to himself to take his own life. Now he inquires whether the maxim of his action could indeed be-

come a universal law of nature. His maxim, however, is: from self-love I make it my principle to shorten my life when its longer duration threatens more troubles than it promises agreeableness. The only further question is whether this principle of self-love could become a universal law of nature. It is then seen at once that a nature whose law it would be to destroy life itself by means of the same feeling whose destination is to impel toward the furtherance of life would contradict itself and would therefore not subsist as nature; thus that maxim could not possibly be a law of nature and, accordingly, altogether opposes the supreme principle of all duty. (4:422)

Whatever one's ultimate judgment on the categorical imperative itself, one may venture to suggest that this first example is at least a problematic one. In summarizing this portion of the *Groundwork*, more than one commentator (see, for example, Robert Johnson in the *Stanford Encyclopedia of Philosophy*) has passed by this first example and gone on to the second one: someone who wants to borrow money despite knowing that he will be unable to pay it back. It seems much easier to see why, in this second example, the implicit maxim (one should borrow money even if one cannot repay it) could never be generalized into a universal law, for it would make borrowing and lending impossible. But the example of suicide, despite Kant's explicit reference to the possibility of shortening the "duration" of a life, seems to be posed in obstinate denial of the essential finitude of "natural" existence. In a moment I will consider another passage from the *Lectures on Ethics* where Kant seems to distinguish radically between a "life" considered in some total sense, as though in retrospect, and the mere "prolongation of the years of [a] life." Given, as Kant is recorded as saying, "nature has already decreed that [all mortal beings] will some day die," and that the span of any life is known in advance to be finite, could it not be articulated as a universal maxim that the inevitable terminus of that life should be subject to moral decision? Such a maxim would obviously not make the *living of life* in its finitude impossible. Conversely, as we have seen in chapter 5, it is evidently possible to use the categorical imperative (as John Hardwig does) to argue in the reverse direction that there might sometime be a positive ethical "duty" to die.

In any case, the economy at play in Kant's point about suicide is finally a straightforward one: it involves a calculation in which the "priceless" value of the human being regarded as a person outweighs the "market value" of the human being regarded as mere natural life. Thus the only possible exception Kant explicitly acknowledges here is one readily answerable in terms of such a calculation. He asks about a few special circumstances such as "having limbs amputated in order to preserve myself, or putting my life in danger in order to preserve my life, and so forth," which, says Kant, belong to "morals proper" (4:429). In *The Metaphysics of Morals* (the volume dedicated to morals proper), however, Kant adds little except to reiterate that such examples "cannot be counted as a crime against one's own person" (6:423). Kant does elaborate the point further in the earliest set of the student notebooks (from 1784–85, about the time of the publication of the *Groundwork*), published as the *Lectures on Ethics*:

> Thus a man can have his foot amputated, for example, insofar as it impedes him in life. So to preserve our person, we have disposition over our body; but the man who takes his own life is not thereby preserving his person; for if he disposes over his person, but not over his condition, he robs himself of that very thing itself. (27:370)

In the first instance (the amputation of a diseased member), a calculable amount of violence is perpetrated against the body in order to preserve the person of which it is the bearer; but in the second instance (suicide), calculation undoes itself by encountering absolute loss, expenditure without return, an entire disposition of the disposer by himself. But even as Kant argues for the preservation of one's life in *any* circumstances, he seems constrained to imagine, and yet hold at bay, the possibility of some exception. Both in the *Lectures* and in *The Metaphysics of Morals*, Kant even evokes the ancient classical and Christian prohibition of suicide as "a violation of duty to God, as one's abandoning the post assigned him in the world without having been called away from it" (6:422). He insists, however, that this is not the essential point, which is that suicide violates our duty to *ourselves*. He even concedes that

> It seems absurd to say that a human being could wrong himself. . . . Hence the Stoics thought it a prerogative of his [the sage's] personality to depart from life at his discretion (as from a smoke-filled room).

But, says Kant,

> There should have been in this very courage, this strength of soul not to fear death and to know of something that a human being can value even more highly than his life, a still stronger motive for him not to destroy himself, a being with such powerful authority over the strongest sensible incentives, and so not to deprive himself of life. (6:422)

Here again is that strange paradox (a catch-22) in which, this time, to have the very courage and capability required to rise above the fear of death is to be obliged to preserve one's life.

In the same volume, Kant appends to his discussion of suicide four "Casuistical Questions" of which the first pertains to the question of sacrifice:

> Is it murdering oneself to hurl oneself to certain death (like Curtius) in order to save one's country?—or is deliberate martyrdom, sacrificing oneself for the good of humanity, also to be considered an act of heroism? (6:423)

It appears from evidence elsewhere that self-sacrifice is indeed the one exception to the moral law against suicide that Kant is willing to entertain, even if only reluctantly and with multiple qualifications. In the same *Lectures on Ethics* text cited above, Kant is recorded speaking at some length about the suicide of Cato:

> Suicide can also come to have a plausible aspect, whenever, that is, the continuance of life rests upon such circumstances as may deprive that life of its value; when a man can no longer live in accordance with virtue and prudence, and must therefore put an end to his life from honourable motives. . . . Cato . . . killed himself once he realized that, although all the people still relied on him, it would not be possible for him to escape falling into Caesar's hands; . . . One must certainly admit of this example, that in such a case, where suicide is a virtue, there seems to be much to be said for it. (27:370)

Leaving the judgment on this case open for the moment, Kant then turns to the case of Lucretia who, he says,

> ought rather to have fought to the death in defence of her honour and would then have acted rightly, and it would not have been suicide either. For to risk one's life against one's foes, and to observe the duty to oneself, and even to sacrifice one's life, is not suicide. (27:371)

If self-sacrifice distinguishes itself from suicide, it seems to do so only insofar as it takes place in a situation (such as battle) in which the outcome is not foreknown. As Kant goes on to say, "The sovereign can certainly oblige the subject to risk his life against the foe for the fatherland, and even if he loses his life in doing so, it is not suicide, but depends on fate" (27:371). In this hypothetical case, a soldier might anticipate the possibility, or even the probability (though not the absolute certainty) of his own death in battle and yet still be prepared to risk his life for a higher purpose (or at least, as Kant's formulation seems to concede, feel that he is obliged to do so by the claim of duty to the sovereign's command).

This instance and Kant's evocation of "fate" seem to evoke the philosophical question of the "Doctrine of Double Effect" (DDE) that, as P. A. Woodward defines it, distinguishes between "intentional production of evil . . and foreseen but unintentional production of evil" (Woodward 2), a question to which we will briefly return later. But this is not Kant's immediate point at the moment, which is, rather, that suicide is never acceptable if it is done out of any rational *calculation* about one's specific conditions, or what Kant later calls "mere interest or private aims" (27:376). Because Lucretia did not abandon herself to her own desires, and did not act out of personal interest, she therefore had not really lost her honor. Thus, it would have been acceptable for her to risk death and indeed, even to die while defending her honor, but not to decide, on the basis of a calculation, to sacrifice her person to her conditions: that is, to commit suicide because of a calculative judgment that her honor had in fact been lost. A few pages later Kant finally returns to the first example, this time concluding definitively that, "if Cato, under all the tortures that Caesar might have inflicted on him, had still adhered to his resolve with steadfast mind, that would have been noble; but not when he laid hands upon himself" (27:374).

Although his basic position on suicide is thus unmistakably clear, Kant nevertheless returns to the subject repeatedly in this extended passage from the *Lectures*. Just before his final judgment on Cato, Kant acknowledges that

> it is very flattering to a man to have the freedom to remove himself from the world if he so wishes. Indeed, there even seems to be something moral in it, for anyone who has the power to depart from the world when he pleases need be subject to nobody, and can be bound by nothing from telling the harshest truths to the greatest of tyrants. (27:374)

Now, as we have seen, for Kant, a suicide done out of interest is not a sacrifice. A soldier in a war who receives wages might be said to fight for interest but, Kant says, "that is not a private aim, but for the general benefit" (27:377). Yet as Kant himself tells the story, it appears that Cato, the great republican, was also acting quite precisely for the general benefit as he saw it. According to Kant, Cato knew that

> it would not be possible for him to escape falling into Caesar's hands; but as soon as he, the champion of freedom, had submitted, the rest would have thought: If Cato himself submits, what else are we to do? (27:370)

A man with the power to end his own life when he chooses is "subject to nobody." In such an instance, an individual right to die seems to confront a sovereign right to death as the latter's absolute limit. Only a few lines later, however, Kant stipulates unequivocally that this kind of suicidal self-sacrifice cannot, in fact, be reconciled with the categorical imperative:

> Suppose it were a general disposition that people cherished, that suicide was a right, and even a merit or honour; such people would be abhorrent to everyone. For he who so utterly fails to respect his life on principle can in no way be restrained from the most appalling vices; he fears no king and no torture. (27:374)

Therefore, in no more than a page of Kant's lecture, the argument changes in three related ways: (1) the hypothetical instance of sovereign power under consideration shifts from what Kant calls tyranny to what he calls kingship (although both are attended by violence and constraint); (2) a figure of death as both the absolute instance of individual autonomy *and* as the corresponding limit of state sovereignty shifts from something that briefly appears to be "moral" to something "abhorrent"; and (3) the valence of suicide itself shifts from heroic *resistance* (Cato) to *sedition* (the man whom no fear of king or torture can restrain from vice). It is a little disconcerting to see how quickly Kant, having just imagined the right to die as a potential political force, a uniquely privileged form of resistance to sovereign power, then repositions it as a kind of nihilism, an opponent of sociality itself. Indeed, the next paragraph returns to the classical image we observed above, declaring that a suicide

> arrives in the next world as one who has deserted his post, and must therefore be seen as a rebel against God. . . . Men are stationed here like sentries, and so we must not leave our posts until relieved by the beneficent hand of another. He is our proprietor, and we are his property. (27:375)

Kant also once again stipulates, however, that the moral law ought to bind all rational beings simply as such, and that, therefore, "suicide . . is impermissible and abhorrent not because God has forbidden it; God has forbidden it, rather, because it is abhorrent" (27:375). Nevertheless, it seems clear that, for Kant, an already merely hypothetical and exceptional right to die is—or rather, *ought to be*—finally overmastered by the sovereign right to death.

In one of his last published books, *Anthropology from a Pragmatic Point of View*, one finds Kant still worrying the question of suicide in a somewhat equivocal manner. He initially observes—seemingly contradicting, at least in part, some of the points we have just seen him making—that the possibility of considering suicide as a courageous act "is not a moral question but merely a psychological one" (156, §77). Here, Kant distinguishes again between two possible kinds of suicide. The first is an act of suicide "committed merely in order not to outlive one's honor"; the second is one that involves, in contrast, "a mental disorder stemming from anguish." The first kind, he writes, "seems to be a kind of heroism" by which a human being manages "to look death straight in the eye and not fear it"; while the second kind, on the contrary, must be considered "cowardice." Plato too, as we recall, writes in the *Laws* that suicide should be considered an act of "unmanly cowardice" *unless* it is done from certain highly specific motives, such as intolerable despair. Kant's distinction, as he goes on to suggest, may be observed in practice as indicated by the specific method by which a person attempts to put himself to death. For example, "if the chosen means are sudden and fatal without possible rescue" like a pistol shot to the head, "then we cannot contest the courage of the person"; but "if the chosen means are a rope that can still be cut by others" and so forth, "then it is cowardly despair." Finally, echoing the observations cited just above about suicide as a potential mode of resistance to tyranny, Kant writes that

> Although suicide will always remain horrible, and though by committing it the human being makes himself into a monster, still it is noteworthy that in times of public and legally declared injustice during a revolutionary state of affairs . . . honor-loving men . . . have sought to forestall execution by law through suicide. (158)

That the example of tyranny Kant has in mind in this case is that of a "revolutionary state of affairs" might be said to compound the ethical and political ambiguity I observed just above. But what I highlight once again is, rather, the apparent ambivalence with which Kant repeatedly worries about the possibility of suicide as a positively honorable act, an ambivalence even faintly discernable in the way he writes in closing here that "I do not *desire* to defend the morality of this act" (158, emphasis added).

Finally, consider how, at the end of the same section of the *Lectures on Ethics* discussed above, Kant is recorded suggesting that

> If a man can preserve his life no otherwise than by dishonouring his humanity, he ought rather to sacrifice it. He then, indeed, puts his animal life in danger, yet he feels that, so as long as he has lived, he has lived honourably. It matters not that man lives long (for it is not his life that he loses by the event, but only the prolongation of the years of his life, since nature has already decreed that he will some day die); what matters is, that so long as he lives he should live honourably, and not dishonour the dignity of humanity. (150)

Here, Kant seems to speak of a "life" that is neither simply the "person" it bears (and that the self must respect *as* the humanity in its own person), nor simply what is called the "animal life." This appears to be "life" understood in a kind of narrative sense, as an ethical or subjective unity, coherence, or reputation ("honour") that in principle transcends its literal embodiment in time and space. For any individual being, since "nature has already decreed that he will some day die," merely to lose some years of an already-finite number of them is to leave untouched this unity that may be called the "life"—just as it leaves untouched the person's honor or reputation, provided that he lived and died with both. When a finite being embraces death to avoid dishonor, Kant says: "it is not his life that he loses by the event, but only the prolongation of the years of his life." Thus, even while repeatedly prohibiting suicide in the strongest possible terms, Kant leaves open the possibility of *choosing death* for at least two different reasons. First and most obviously, he states clearly that someone who sacrifices his life for others, for the state or the "general benefit," is not a suicide. But he also seems to imply or suggest, without ever quite stating it, that one might embrace death in order to *preserve* the coherence and incalculable singularity of a "life" in the sense of a transcendent self-presentation of the subject to itself and to others, both *in* but also *beyond* the literal time and space of its embodied existence. In other words, let us venture to conclude, Kant concedes the possibility of a few paradoxical situations in which one might sacrifice one's "life" for the sake of one's "life." Thus sacrifice remains the single exception to the general prohibition of self-murder, but only insofar as it is brought back under the horizon of that very calculation that Kant otherwise refuses to entertain with regard to these matters of life and death.

## CHAPTER SEVEN

# Sacrifice and the Right to Die

To return to the contemporary debate, we can now see more clearly how it recapitulates the philosophic one, in a manner, however, that compels revision of my schematic summary of both sides. Previously I suggested that each side leads with an argument based in incalculable value ("human dignity" or the "sanctity of life"), and then supplements that value with a calculative argument that, on both sides, assumes the unavoidable scarcity of *care* itself. A new look allows us to see that in fact calculation governs the whole discursive and conceptual field on this issue, bringing the two opposed sides into a paradoxical near-identity. The contemporary debate also recapitulates the philosophic tradition insofar as it too, and on both sides, seems at once to require and renounce a figure of sacrifice, as the signal exception that either troubles the prohibition of suicide, or, on the contrary, recuperates and redeems the death chosen by right as one that somehow answers to the life it ends. In the contemporary debate, sacrifice thus remains the paradoxical site where a calculative economy infects that very unconditionality that is otherwise being invoked above all (and that thus remains as yet unthought across the entire debate). The logic of sacrificial calculation at work in this debate will also prove unmistakably to locate itself at the intersection of the (sovereign) *right to death* and the (individual) *right to die*.

In its concept and its history alike, sacrifice embodies in itself the economy of calculation and incalculability that seems to structure this entire debate: it is the very site of that momentous displacement by which, as has been noticed so often both from within and from without Christian discourse itself, God becomes no longer merely the receiver but himself the *victim* of a sacrificial expiation. This displacement is a central instance of what

Jean-Luc Nancy describes as a progressive "sublation" or "spiritualization" of the sacrifice that continues into modernity and beyond with thinkers such as Hegel, Bataille, Girard, and others (*Finite Thinking* 61). Even from within the Judeo-Christian tradition, according to recurrent theological suspicions and programs of reform, a sacrifice can only truly be itself insofar as it transcends the economistic reduction denoted by the formula of *do ut des* ("I give that you may give"). The history of the sacrifice, if one can speak of such a thing, takes the shape of a series of repeated ruptures (such as the Reformation insistence on "god's free gift of grace") by which the sacrifice is claimed to be purified again of the economism to which it always seems to fall prey. Western thought thus seeks to position the sacrifice between, on the one side, pure loss or waste (what Bataille calls "unproductive expenditure"), and, on the other side, a pure transactional economism in which (like the gift in a so-called gift economy) the sacrifice becomes no more than a calculable *price* to be paid for whatever it is we receive from it. As Derrida writes, "The sacrifice proposes an offering but only in the form of a destruction against which it exchanges, hopes for, or counts on a benefit, namely a surplus-value or at least an amortization, a protection, and a security" (*Given Time* 137). Or, as he puts it elsewhere, the sacrifice "recaptures with one hand what it gives with the other" (*Glas* 259).

This process, and thus a certain inescapable laughter, are irreducibly inscribed in the temporal logic of deferral which grounds all notions of "economy," including the economy of the sacrifice. Derrida observes that the scriptural story of the sacrifice of Isaac (itself commonly taken as allegorizing a prior displacement from human to animal sacrifice) involves a tragic double bind. Abraham can prove his faith to God only by sacrificing, though not rejecting, ethics itself: in order for his sacrifice to take place, as Derrida writes, "the ethical must retain all its value; the love for his son must remain intact, and the order of human duty must continue to insist on its rights" (*Gift of Death* 66). Although God will not really allow (or compel) Abraham to kill his son, Abraham must still go all the way, to the very *instant* in which the knife is raised: his sacrifice thus "remains irreducible to presence or to presentation" and "belongs to an atemporal temporality, to a duration that cannot be grasped" (*Gift of Death* 65). Christianity, so to speak, reinscribes this tragic double bind as a *comedy* in which, however (as I argue in the preface), a certain laughter always threatens to overflow the frame (the cosmic drama of sin and redemption) that is intended to contain it. In this case, God must be affirmed at once for the irreplaceable singularity of His sacrifice ("God so loved the world, that he gave his *only* begotten Son") *and* as the source of an inexhaustible plenitude through whom "all things came into being" (John 3:6, emphasis added; John 1:13). In other words, before or beyond the explicit comedy by which, in the Christian doctrine, Christ's sacrifice is followed by his triumphant resurrection, would always be the laughableness of a sovereignty that demands to be honored for its gift of debt, and for a self-sacrifice that actually takes place only in the brief deferral prior to an absolute recuperation—a sacrifice that thus has to *undo* itself in order to *be* itself. How or where could one venture to express the infinitely subtle yet inescapable suspicion that God, having taken on the burden that He imposed on us, might be, precisely as such, buying our redemption on the cheap and thus in the strangest possible way outwitting both humanity and Himself? Exposed as this impossible combination of scarcity and abundance, of implicit calculation and incalculable plenitude, the divine comedy is subtended by a mocking laughter that it always strives, but fails, to appropriate in its entirety.

This laughter seems to emerge alongside a figure of sacrifice that itself emerges paradoxically on both sides of this debate, where, among other things, it provides a site in which to locate the invisible link between a sovereign right to death and a (proposed or prohibited) individual right to die. Accordingly, in this section I move back and forth between disparate examples by way of further sketching a contradictory logic shared by otherwise quite different approaches to this issue. To do this will again be to risk entering the field of ideological conflict that I am trying to keep at arm's length, because I include a few texts from the discourse of early twentieth-century eugenic theory, a line of thought commonly conceded to have inspired and guided the Nazi programs of involuntary euthanasia a few decades later. This obviously risks seeming to agree with polemicists on one side of this issue, who, as we have seen, commonly observe a continuity or substantive affinity between these historical instances and contemporary discourses in favor of a right to die. Let me therefore state clearly in advance that I intend to suggest no such thing. As I acknowledged earlier, such "slippery slope" arguments have an unmistakable force when they expose how a utilitarian logic, applied to life and death decisions, might affect the weaker or less privileged members of a radically unequal society. Yet these necessary and legitimate concerns are commonly joined to sweeping historical and theoretical reductions, by which it is claimed, for example, that any institution of anything that might assist elderly, ill, or severely disabled people to choose death (even merely through counseling, for example) will lead inevitably to the involuntary state-sponsored extermination of anyone judged "unworthy" of life. Such overhasty claims merely foreclose in advance any possibility of ethical decision and responsibility. If anything, one must on the contrary begin by grasping that these two sets of discourse and practice (that is, the fascist project of eugenics, forced sterilizations, and involuntary euthanasia on the one hand, and the contemporary "right to die" movement on the other) are in one sense absolutely *opposed*. The former affirms above all the state's biopolitical command of life and death; the latter affirms, or at least claims to affirm, the right of individuals to control and determine their own lives and deaths. If there are lines of connection between these two, it is not because they are somehow simply the same thing, nor because the former influenced or inspired the latter, but rather because, as I have been suggesting throughout, this whole discursive field seems to be organized around the play of certain shared figures and a quasi-sacrificial logic.

I have already briefly mentioned Samuel D. Williams' "Euthanasia" (1870), commonly identified as the first modern text directly to advocate physician-assisted suicide, and perhaps the first to use the word "euthanasia" to denote not merely a "good death" but "the active shortening of life" (Lavi 42). Williams was an "obscure teacher" who belonged "to the equally obscure Birmingham Speculative Club," a group of professionals who met to discuss social problems in the northern English city, but his essay was widely reprinted and discussed in the medical community and elsewhere in the last decades of the nineteenth century (Dowbiggin 49–50). As we have seen, Williams begins by observing how the alleged doctrine of the sanctity of life is in practice "thrown to the winds, the moment national or political passion grows hot or even when mere material interests are seriously threatened" (Williams 215). Further, Williams observes,

> The very medical attendant who would revolt from the bare idea of putting a hopelessly suffering patient to death outright, though the patient implored him to do so, would feel no scruple in giving temporary relief by opiates, or other anæsthetics, even though he were absolutely sure that he was shortening the patient's life by their use. (216).

Suppose a man in great pain with only a month to live could have his pain relieved by drugs that will also shorten his life by one week. Most patients and most doctors, says Williams, regardless of their beliefs about the sanctity of life, would not hesitate to take or give the drugs in this situation. This distinction between "temporary relief" and a "death outright" remains a crucial sticking point across a wide range of subsequent debate. Although he acknowledges that medical attendants observe such a distinction absolutely, William himself asserts that anything that limits, shortens, or curtails the magnitude of a life necessarily breaks with any absolute principle of life's sanctity:

> Is it not clear that if you once break in upon life's sacredness, if you curtail its duration by never so little, the same reasoning that justifies a minute's shortening of it, will justify an hour's, a day's, a week's, a month's, a year's; and that all subsequent appeal to the inviolability of life is vain? You have already violated it, and rightly violated it; and the same reasoning which justifies what you have already done, will justify further violation. (217)

Williams' approach thus begins and ends with the simple empirical observation that neither "nature" in general nor human beings in particular ever really treat life as inviolable. And, for Williams, this is the way it should be: life is something

> to be used freely and sacrificed freely, whenever good is to be won or evil avoided by such sacrifice or use; the man who is ever ready to face death for others' sakes, to save others from grinding pain, has always been reckoned a hero; and what is heroic if done for another is surely permissible, at least, if done for oneself; the man who could voluntarily give up his life to save another from months of slow torture, would win everybody's good word; why should he be debarred from taking a like step when the person to be rescued is himself? (217)

Just as nature in general is "prodigal" with the lives of its innumerable beings, so any individual being has a right to use or sacrifice his life when (to echo the Lockean phrase) any value more than its bare preservation might call for it. Let me note in passing that Williams' argument is posed entirely in terms of a temporal economy that we have glimpsed briefly in Kant and that will come up repeatedly in several other texts. In the terms of this economy, the value of life itself has to be understood (to use Ronald Dworkin's terms) as an "intrinsic" rather than an "incremental" value, a value not to be judged by its mere quantity or magnitude. As Kant had put it, what matters with regard to judging a life is not the mere "prolongation of [its] years." For Williams, accordingly, it seems obvious that one should choose a quick painless death rather than "months of slow torture," or choose sacrifice over "grinding pain."

Williams' rhetoric, however, seems to force the ideas of *use* and *sacrifice* into virtual identity. Just so, his argument as a whole seems similarly to be suspended between his commitment to a kind of "general economy" of natural prodigality and human self-sacrifice on the one hand, and an economy of quasi-utilitarian calculation, an ethos of productivity, on the other hand. The only reason life might actually be called sacred, he writes, is "in so far as the word may signify the duty laid on each man of using his life nobly while he has it" (215); and similarly, the only question to be raised about euthanasia should be: "is the motive weighty enough to justify the sacrifice? For it is certain that life ought not to be sacrificed lightly" (217). Williams makes clear that he continues to oppose suicide in general, and that the only circumstance he envisions as making the choice of death reasonable is to avoid pain and suffering. Since "there are few duties . . . higher than that of diminishing . . . pain" (218), the giving one's self death in this circumstance is almost a duty as well as a right. Correspondingly, Williams sees the right to die as linked conceptually to the sovereign right to death, though he inverts the relationship of these two as it is commonly envisioned in theological or philosophic discourse on suicide. For Kant, as we have seen, suicide would be the expression or manifestation of an absolute individual sovereignty that, for good or ill, insults the preeminence of earthly or divine sovereignty. For Williams, conversely, the evident fact that states and sovereigns often require individuals "to face death for others' sakes" ought to license an individual right to "rescue" one's self from pain by embracing death. An assumed sovereign right to death and a proposed individual right to die are understood to be analogous rather than opposed, and society's acquiescence to the former becomes the best argument for the latter.

Notwithstanding this point, which marks a certain limit case, the idea of a right to die is perhaps more commonly understood as one of many possible instances of an emergent biopolitics that, as many have argued, transforms or even supersedes the classical model of sovereignty as the right to death. This is not the place, however, for anything like a full account of the development of eugenic theory and practice in the first decades of the twentieth century, nor of the Nazi programs of involuntary euthanasia, sterilization, and racial extermination, a history that has been documented at length elsewhere. Even the briefest of accounts, however, must begin by acknowledging that the Nazi regime drew heavily on eugenic research and legislation in the United States that continued at least until the brink of the Second World War (see, e.g., Black and Kühl) and that American exponents of "scientific racism" (writers such as William Shockley, J. Philippe Rushton, Richard J. Herrnstein, Charles Murray, and others) have continued to emerge right up to the present. For my limited purposes here, a few brief citations will be sufficient to indicate how, as Henry Friedlander observes, a "comparison of the death of worthy individuals in the service of their nation and the survival of pampered inferiors was a staple of eugenic argumentation" (Friedlander 15). Or in other words, the discourse of eugenics is itself thoroughly pervaded by an unmistakable sacrificial logic.

For example, Adolf Jost's *Das Recht auf den Tod* (1895), as its title suggests, justifies euthanasia and eugenic legislation in terms of a sovereign right to kill that all states already exercise in military conflict, declaring that "[t]he rights to death [are] the key to the fitness of life" (cited Lifton 46). Many commentators have observed the general prevalence in eugenic discourse of what Roberto Esposito calls a "vitalist conception of the state," a vision of the nation as "a whole that is inhabited by men and which behaves as a single individual both spiritual and corporeal" (16). The sovereign right to death is extended to a broader process of sociopolitical "hygiene," seen as necessary to safeguard the health of a state and a society conceived in explicitly organic terms, and capable accordingly of either health or disease. As Esposito and others also suggest, "Nazism carries the biopolitical procedures of modernity to the extreme point of their coercive power" by transforming them paradoxically into a full-fledged "thanatopolitics" (Exposito 111) that demands not only the extermination of the racial Other but even a suicidal self-sacrifice of the German nation itself (116). A rhetoric of sacrificial calculation is, however, equally central in German and American eugenic discourse of the early twentieth century. Karl Binding and Alfred Hoche's much-discussed *Permitting the Destruction of Unworthy Life* (1920), begins by contrasting the "sacrifice of the finest flower of humanity" that occurs in war and "the meticulous care shown to existences which are not just absolutely worthless but even of negative value" and "to whom death would be a release" (246). Their words were echoed (if they did not influence) the majority decision in *Buck v. Bell* (1927), in which the United States Supreme Court upheld the constitutionality of laws mandating the involuntary sterilization of alleged mental defectives. In his opinion, Justice Oliver Wendell Holmes declares, in lines which remain one of the most frequently cited utterances of this whole disquieting history, that

> We have seen more than once that the public welfare may call upon the best citizens for their lives. It would be strange if it could not call upon those who already sap the strength of the State for these lesser sacrifices, often not felt to be such by those concerned, in order to prevent our being swamped with incompetence. . . . Three generations of imbeciles are enough. (*Buck v. Bell* 207)

Holmes' point is a double one, and it has a kind of self-cancelling structure. He first suggests that a state which calls upon some citizens to give their lives in war can surely ask other citizens for a different kind of sacrifice (sterilization); and then he turns around to say that the latter is not really a sacrifice anyway, since it is "often not felt to be such by those concerned." Holmes' lines themselves were frequently cited or echoed by other subsequent writers. In one notorious example, an influential pamphlet entitled "Human Sterilization," published in 1934 by the Human Betterment Foundation, a eugenic organization in California, was in the following year mailed "to German racial hygienists and Nazi administrators" (Kühl 43). The pamphlet paraphrases Holmes' lines in the process of reaffirming that

> In time of war . . . the state calls on the fittest of its citizens to lay down their lives for the common good. In time of peace, shall it not be able to call on some of the most unfit of its citizens, not to sacrifice their lives, but to make a far lesser sacrifice,—one which, in most cases is regarded by them not as a sacrifice at all, but as a benefit to themselves. (7)

Comparing the paraphrase with the original, one sees clearly how this characteristic discourse tends at once to evoke a figure of sacrifice and to bring it back under the horizon of calculation. This time it is argued directly that eugenic sterilization both *does* and *does not* involve sacrifice. Or, that is, eugenic sterilization involves a sacrifice that will be even more profitable (if one can put it that way) than the sacrifices demanded by state sovereignty: because it will be a "benefit" even to those who make it, and because it will be not just a "lesser" sacrifice (achieving its aim with less expenditure of value) but, here again, finally no sacrifice at all. The figure of sacrifice occupies of kind of self-cancelling position in a discourse that seemingly seeks both to appropriate and economize its ethical heroism.

The strangeness of this figural economy is perhaps most evident in Binding and Hoche, whose little book, scarcely more than a pamphlet, has had an extraordinary historical and interpretive afterlife. This text comprises two essays: the first, written by Binding, considers the legal argument for euthanasia; the second, written by Hoche, considers the medical implications. At a climactic moment of the first essay, Binding asserts that to ask the question of an individual life's value is to raise "an uneasy feeling." This unease stems, as we have partially seen in the lines cited above, from the radical contradiction of costs and benefits manifest in the apportionment of duty and care by society and the state. Of a hypothetical observer of such things, Binding writes,

> It hurts him to see how wastefully we handle the most valuable lives (filled with and sustained by the strongest will to live and the greatest vital power), and

how much labor power, patience, and capital investment we squander (often totally uselessly) just to preserve lives not worth living. . . . Reflect simultaneously on a battlefield strewn with thousands of dead youths, or a mine in which methane gas has trapped hundreds of energetic workers; compare this with our mental hospitals, with their caring for their living inmates. One will be deeply shaken by the strident clash between the sacrifice of the finest flower of humanity in its full measure on the one side, and by the meticulous care shown to existences which are not just absolutely worthless but even of negative value, on the other. (246)

The source of the uneasiness and pain is, therefore, the contrast between the *sacrifice* of soldiers in the battlefield or laborers in a mine (the "*most valuable*" of lives, "*filled* with . . . the *greatest* vital power," "the *finest flower* of humanity in its *full measure*"), and the *waste* of labor and capital in mental hospitals, where a "meticulous care" is squandered on lives no longer capable of contributing to society.[1] The beings on whom the care is wasted, Binding claims, do not merely *lack* the normal value possessed by living beings; rather, they are bearers of a "negative value," beings

to whom death would be a release, and whose death would simultaneously free society and the state from carrying a burden which serves no conceivable purpose, except that of *providing an example of the greatest unselfishness*. (246, emphases added)

Here again is that vision of a sacrifice that is not a sacrifice, of a gift of death that can be twice economized, benefiting both those who give it and those who receive it.

But why does Binding add that final clause highlighted above, which is by no means necessary to the point being made? Binding seems to go out of his way to remind the reader that to care for helpless and hopeless beings might itself be construed as a form of sacrifice ("an example of the greatest unselfishness"), just as the vision of "a battlefield strewn with thousands of dead youths" can be construed, as Binding himself does, as an image of "how wastefully we handle the most valuable lives." He thus seems to obscure the very contrast whose painful clarity was supposed to lead to only one possible conclusion. A certain gallows humor or laughter also prompts one to ask: what do the dead youths and energetic workers actually have to do with the argument? In essence, Binding speaks of a contradiction between the *care given to worthless lives*, and the *death given to worthy lives*; and he proposes that we resolve this contradiction by giving the worthless lives death instead of care. But if we do away with the worthless people instead of caring for them, will this mean that soldiers and miners will no longer have to be sacrificed? Or if there were no war and better provisions for mining safety, would the care given to worthless lives seem less wasteful? On the one hand, it apparently does not cross Binding's mind that the schema he proposes be fully inverted, so that, in other words, we give care *instead of* death to the worthy beings. On the other hand, he assumes the operations of a quasi-Hegelian spiritual economy in which all negativity (here, quite literally the giving of death) can be recuperated as value, and in which indeed, the very same act is at once a cost-saving measure *and* a sacrifice.

Much of the rest of Binding's essay enumerates in some detail the regime of calculation he envisions would govern the administration of euthanasia: for example, procedures for the "competent objective verification" (251) of those to be euthanized, including who will be entitled to serve as the "petitioner" in requesting death (the patient himself, the doctor, a close relative, and so forth). Near the end, however, he declares, as though in final summary or conclusion, that

> No one can have a *right to kill*—even less a *duty to kill*—not even the petitioner. *The act of euthanasia must be a consequence of free sympathy for the patient.* (252, emphases original)

This assertion seems to once again risk a certain laughter. Since Binding's essay presents itself to us as a specifically legal discussion of euthanasia, it is not obviously immediately clear why he should so strongly renounce the terminology of right. Moreover, since this declaration follows an enumeration of the particular conditions that should be required as a condition for involuntary euthanasia, Binding can only mean that no one has an *absolute* right to kill, and that euthanasia should only be permitted on the basis of particular conditions, such as those he describes. Yet even as he says this, he also insists that the killing itself, as an act, must be somehow *unconditional*, that it must spring from a *"free* sympathy." The economy of Binding's argument has come full circle: he asks that the waste of care, which now pains us by its contrast with heroic sacrifice, be displaced by a different kind of sacrifice, a gift given without conditions. Earlier, Binding had said that the question evoked by the shocking contrast of sacrifice and waste, the question about the possibility of *valuing* lives, and of declaring some lives to be valueless—arises "from nothing but the deepest sympathy" (246). As we just saw above, the same is said to be true of any justifiable act of euthanasia itself, in which, Binding insists repeatedly, the "agent" always "proceeds out of sympathy and in order to spare the comatose patient a fearful end—not to rob him of life." And yet, in the final lines of his essay, we find Binding deploring once more how,

> Applying endless time, patience, and care, we labor to preserve lives of negative value, for whose extinction every reasonable person must hope. *Our sympathy grows beyond its proper bounds and becomes a horror.* (254, emphases original)

This emotion of sympathy or compassion is, therefore, at once the cause of the problem, the source of the painful contrast that allows one to see the problem, and the solution of the problem. That solution must therefore involve the most precise calculation and calibration of this crucial emotion, of which we apparently must have *enough*, but not *too much*, and which must be constantly both solicited and kept in check.

Something similar happens in Hoche's essay, which begins by observing that many forms of medicine, such as surgery, involve what he calls " professional acts of wounding the body," and that "in all surgical procedures, one tacitly counts on a certain percentage of fatal outcomes." His point seems to be that surgeons always at least "wound" people and sometimes might be said to kill them, yet their actions are entirely legal and legitimate, because "the higher legal good of restoring the majority to health makes the sacrifice of the minority necessary" (256). That one must sometimes hurt in order to heal is an ancient proverbial commonplace, and we have previously seen more than one instance of the commonplace image of an amputated limb as an example of a permissible violence against the self. But the sacrificial logic of this instance, which is intended to set up an argument for allowing surgeons and other physicians to administer death *directly*, is at least strained. Even though one may know in a general way that all doctors lose some patients, can one really say that the patients they lose have been "sacrificed" for the sake of the patients who survive?[2] This seems to be a statistical logic masquerading as a sacramental or sacrificial one. Hoche's figure also seems to clash with the stringent impulse of calculation that otherwise drives his argument. Hoche too finds it "painful to think" about institutions filled with "idiots" where "whole generations of caretakers grow old next to these empty human shells" and where "incredible capital is withdrawn from the nation's wealth for food, clothing, and heating—for an unproductive purpose" (260-61).

Hoche thus insists that, with regard to mental and physical defectives, "we must calculate the return on our investment"—in both an economic *and* a moral or ethical sense. Under the status quo, we are confronted by an apparent contradiction "between the individual's subjective right to exist and objective expediency and necessity." He thus envisions what he calls "a higher civil morality" to replace what he calls "alien perspectives" (i.e., what he has previously specified as "religious ideas, sentimental feelings, and so on") that

> have caused us to forget that the civil organism is a whole, with its own laws and rights, in just the same sense that an independent human organism is a whole—a whole which, as we physicians know, *sacrifices* and casts aside individual parts or segments that have become worthless or even harmful. (261, emphasis added).

For Hoche, the state functions via a sacrificial economy in which some individuals must always die for the sake of the general good, to stanch the bleeding-away of resources from the "civil organism" as a whole. Even in its own terms, however, there is something paradoxical about Hoche's invocation of this figure of sacrifice, for as we will continue to see, it is impossible that he can be envisioning the deaths to be administered to "empty human shells" as "sacrifices" in the full sense of the word. On such beings, on what he calls "mentally dead" persons, even sympathy itself is wasted, because, as he puts it (managing to turn the point into a kind of pun), "where there is no suffering (*Leiden*) there can be no sympathy (*Mitleiden*)" (263). By contrast, he declares that

> We are overcome by justified sympathy when we read how, on their return from the South Pole, in the interest of the life of the rest of the party, Scott and his companions silently accepted the sacrifice of one comrade who voluntarily left the tent to freeze outside in the snow.
> A small part of this heroic mood of soul must enter us before we could consider acting on the possibilities sketched theoretically here. (264)

And then finally, in the final lines of the essay and the book, Hoche declares that "a new age will arrive—operating with a higher morality and with great sacrifice—which will actually give up the requirements of an exaggerated humanism and overvaluation of mere existence" (265).

This is one more place where, quite apart from all the other ethical and political critiques so justly raised against this text, laughter threatens to dislocate every other mode of analysis. For Hoche actually seems to claim that the people who will someday put into effect the policies he proposes (that is, the people of the "new age" who will administer the fatal drugs to mentally or physically incompetent people) will be doing so out of the same "heroic mood of soul" as possesses the man who sacrifices himself for his comrades (represented here by the reference to Lawrence "Titus" Oates, a member of Robert Scott's ill-fated expedition to the South Pole in 1912).[3] But who or what will these people be sacrificing, and for what cause or end? The object of this sacrifice cannot be the literal proposed victims, those worthless beings whose lives are no more than burdens both to themselves and to society. One cannot sacrifice that which is valueless. No, it can only be, as the analogy itself seems so improbably to suggest, that those of the new age will be sacrificing, in a certain sense, "themselves": their "exaggerated humanism," the overgrown sympathy that had impelled them to care for the hopeless. But because the giving-up of this old-fashioned and overgrown sympathy is *required* for the success of these proposals—because in fact these proposals are entirely *about* giving up these things—this is a "sacrifice" that is anything but, that is wholly governed and justified by calculation.

In the rest of this chapter I suggest that this spurious or incomplete sacrificial logic pervades the contemporary debate about the right to die. It would perhaps not be surprising to find a similar kind of sacrificial rhetoric deployed by those opposed to a right to die, given how many of their key arguments are either implicitly or explicitly theological. In practice, however, a figure of sacrifice emerges regularly on all sides of this issue. In contemporary Christian discourse about euthanasia and the right to die, the figure of sacrifice is once again the singular exception that troubles the prohibition of self-murder, even as it also seems to ground an argument that otherwise frankly accepts the necessity of calculation in end-of-life decisions. For example, the "Declaration on Euthanasia" issued by the Congregation for the Doctrine of the Faith of the Catholic Church (1980) asserts that suicide is "equally as wrong as murder," and should be considered, among other things, "a rejection of God's sovereignty" and

> a refusal of love for self, the denial of a natural instinct to live, a flight from the duties of justice and charity owed to one's neighbor, to various communities or to the whole of society.

Nevertheless, the text goes on:

> one must clearly distinguish suicide from that sacrifice of one's life whereby for a higher cause, such as God's glory, the salvation of souls or the service of one's brethren, a person offers his or her own life or puts it in danger.

In the terms of this argument, to put it very schematically, sacrifice distinguishes itself from suicide along the axis of the positive and the negative, and not merely in terms of the ultimate moral judgment that must be made about either. Sacrifice is permissible and legitimate because it involves a certain transaction in which life is offered or risked "for a higher cause," and in which the loss of life can therefore be recuperated as a positive value, as glory, salvation, service, or the like. Suicide, by contrast, involves rejection, denial, and a flight from duty. In self-sacrifice, a being *chooses* death without *desiring* it; but in euthanasia, a being *desires* death without having the right to *choose* it.

For severely ill or disabled patients at the end of their lives, accordingly, this text offers a choice between limited or attenuated versions of, respectively, sacrifice or the "right to die" in the full or proper sense. On the one hand, a dying person may understand his experience as a kind of symbolic sacrifice:

> suffering, especially suffering during the last moments of life, has a special place in God's saving plan; it is in fact a sharing in Christ's passion and a union with the redeeming sacrifice which He offered in obedience to the Father's will. Therefore, one must not be surprised if some Christians prefer to moderate their use of painkillers, in order to accept voluntarily at least a part of their sufferings and thus associate themselves in a conscious way with the sufferings of Christ crucified.

On the other hand, patients do have the right to control the conditions of their dying to some extent:

> it would be imprudent to impose a heroic way of acting as a general rule. On the contrary, human and Christian prudence suggest for the majority of sick people the use of medicines capable of alleviating or suppressing pain.

The voluntary acceptance of a pain and suffering that might otherwise be alleviated is a kind of ideal (like celibacy) to which most people, however, are unsuited.

Therefore, as articulated here, Catholic doctrine freely accepts the necessity of calculation about the conditions and options of health care at the end of life. There are times when it is entirely permissible to reject a possible treatment; one makes a judgment on such matters

> by studying the type of treatment to be used, its degree of complexity or risk, its cost and the possibilities of using it, and comparing these elements with the result that can be expected, taking into account the state of the sick person and his or her physical and moral resources.

And, similarly, if one should refuse a particular treatment that might extend one's life but is also risky, expensive, or painful,

> such a refusal is not the equivalent of suicide; on the contrary, it should be considered as an acceptance of the human condition, or a wish to avoid the application of a medical procedure disproportionate to the results that can be expected, or a desire not to impose excessive expense on the family or the community. (Congregation for the Doctrine of the Faith)

The process of calculation and decision envisioned here encompasses both qualitative and quantitative terms and considers both the "physical" and "moral" resources that might be available. Up to a certain point even such matters as the imposition of "excessive expense" on the whole community (the kind of thing often observed, as we saw above, by advocates of a right to die) may be permissibly considered in making end-of-life decisions.

It is also claimed, however, that all such permissible and even necessary calculations must always be subordinated to an unconditional principle grounded in an incalculable value. As William E. May summarizes,

> Although it is always gravely immoral to kill a person because of his or her alleged bad quality of life, the condition of a person's life can be used in judging whether a particular medical treatment is "proportionate" or "disproportionate." (45)

May insists that there is nothing "proportionalist" about this argument—in other words, there is no hint of a utilitarian logic—precisely because "the *Declaration* had *previously* [emphasis added] affirmed unambiguously the existence of an absolute moral norm prohibiting an intrinsically evil act, namely, the norm absolutely proscribing the intentional killing of an innocent human being" (45). Therefore, among all the possible conditions of the process of dying, the only thing one may never calculate or decide is the precise *instant* of death. One may decide about the place or conditions of one's dying: one might choose to die at home or in a hospital, to receive this treatment but not that one, and so forth. But one may not *hasten* death, not even by a moment; or, that is, one may not hasten death *directly*, since one may do other things, such as taking painkillers, that may indirectly, as a secondary or side effect, hasten death. In the economy of this argument, an absolute or unconditional principle makes possible, by *preceding* it (temporally, conceptually, and ethically), a process of calculation that it thus both anchors and limits.

As we previously observed, the "Declaration" itself claims it is imprudent to take "a heroic way of acting as a general rule." Their word is perhaps not the most felicitous one in the context, because the phrase "heroic measures" is also used in legal and medical terminology to describe a relatively risky treatment undertaken as a last resort. As used in the "Declaration," a "heroic" approach abandons the calculations and decisions otherwise licensed above, faces the event of death and dying in a deliberately passive manner, and embraces suffering in order to share in the incalculable value of the divine sacrifice. This idea seems to compel a certain set of questions, though ones that can be raised at all only with a certain reticence. Because the divine sacrifice could never be equaled by a mere human being, one can do no more than *share* it. Moreover, the suffering of a dying human being is not *necessary* to the process of redemption, because a person is not required to embrace his suffering, and because, as Milton famously writes, "God doth not *need* / Either man's work or His own gifts." So, for the singular finite being facing death, wouldn't the actual process of dying, mediated as it must be by the practical concerns and decisions envisioned above, always involve a certain unavoidable calculation, at once moral and physical, spiritual and sensible, by which one would determine, *by* suffering it, exactly how much pain can and will be borne before the release of death? Given the weakness of the flesh, must we not imagine that even the most heroic of people might eventually have to abandon—one might even say *sacrifice*—some amount of what their suffering *might* have shared and signified? The two potential modes of "heroism" that might be at issue at the end of life (risky and difficult medical treatment versus the sacrificial embrace of suffering) are thus themselves locked in a strange relation, a relation neither of opposition nor of identity. If the "heroic" person were to accept a "heroic" treatment, one which involves considerable pain but might result in some degree of recovery, would this still be to share the divine sacrifice, or not? Might one even venture to ask why God would even ask for, or be pleased by, the subsequent repayment of a tiny amount of the "superabundant" sacrificial value which He had already given for our sakes? These are, no doubt, questions of the utmost awkwardness, but they necessarily arise from the double economy (calculation grounded in and limited by incalculability) that informs this argument at every level.

One thus need not raise any objections to these specific recommendations about end-of-life decisions to suggest that the figure or logic of the sacrifice always remains in this context at least slightly incongruous. The figure of sacrifice as loss, as a gift of death, does not really suit an alleged regime of care driven by the injunction to preserve and prolong life to its uttermost. Such a regime must in principle privilege accumulation over expenditure, and dedicate itself at most to the incremental prolongation and conservation of sacrificial *life*. Yet a certain figure of sacrifice often continues to anchor an argument that is otherwise predicated on an economy of deferral and a certain deliberate misrecognition. Robert P. George, for example, argues that the "key distinction" in the question of a possible right to die is that

> between what traditionally has been called "direct killing," where death (one's own or someone else's) is sought either as an end in itself or as a means to some other end, and accepting death or the shortening of life as a foreseen side effect of an action or omission whose object is something other than death—either some good that cannot be achieved or some evil that cannot be avoided without resulting in death or the shortening of life. ("Terminal")

George gives two examples of this distinction:

> A soldier jumps on a grenade that has been rolled into the camp in a life-sacrificing effort to save the lives of his comrades in arms. Because he did not intend his own death, though he foresaw and accepted it, no one regards this as a suicide. It was a side effect of his (heroic) attempt to save the lives of others.
>
> More immediately relevant is the case of a patient suffering from a painful condition who takes palliative drugs of a type that he knows will result in his dying sooner than he would otherwise. Again, he does not intend his own death, though he foresees and accepts it, and no one regards this as suicide. ("Terminal")

Let us grant George his distinction between "accepting death" and "direct killing," and consider more closely these two examples of the former: the soldier sacrificing himself to save his comrades, and the dying patient who accepts painkillers even though they hasten death. This pair of examples is very commonly invoked throughout this whole discourse, yet the analogy between the two instances is at least a difficult one: if they are like from one point of view, they might seem to be near opposites from another. The first instance would typically involve a death willingly embraced or aggressively seized as a fatal necessity; the second instance would typically involve a death deferred past the point where it would have been welcome. One might therefore question whether the two examples complement one another or whether, on the contrary, the first one might be used against the second. If the soldier can be understood as willingly *embracing* a death that cannot be avoided, then couldn't even direct, voluntary euthanasia be understood in the same way (especially since the analogy between the two cases has already been affirmed)? Should it not be possible at least to imagine a (human) being who embraces death willingly, even joyously or heroically? Perhaps the link between the terminal patient on drugs and the heroic soldier who sacrifices his life is actually to be found simply in the strange relation that seems always to link a possible individual right to die and an assumed sovereign right to death.

At any rate, the second instance, the use of pain-relieving drugs by terminally-ill patients, is, as we have seen, very commonly cited as a fundamental exception to the general prohibition of any action that might be regarded as *choosing death*. The "Declaration on Euthanasia" recalls a declaration by Pope Pius XII:

> In answer to a group of doctors who had put the question: "Is the suppression of pain and consciousness by the use of narcotics . . . permitted by religion and morality to the doctor and the patient (even at the approach of death and if one foresees that the use of narcotics will shorten life)?" the Pope said: "If no other means exist, and if, in the given circumstances, this does not prevent the carrying out of other religious and moral duties: Yes." In this case, of course, death is in no way intended or sought, even if the risk of it is reasonably taken; the intention is simply to relieve pain effectively.

As we have already seen, a doctor may thus give a narcotic drug to relieve pain despite foreseeing that the same drug will hasten the patient's death; the key point is claimed to be that the doctor *intends* only the former, not the latter. This argument of course exemplifies the so-called Doctrine of Double Effect (DDE): that is, the distinction, first formulated by Aquinas, "between the intended, and the merely foreseen effects of a voluntary action," and which remains in our times "absolutely essential to Christian ethics" (Anscombe 256). Any consideration of such an argument would have to begin by asking whether it really can be made in such complete indifference to any of the twentieth-century philosophical, linguistic, or psychoanalytic critiques of consciousness, the subject, and self-identity in general. This argument assumes a *sovereign* subject whose decisions are the result of *intentions* that can be determined precisely both by their own subject and by others. This argument envisions such a subject, however, within a situation that seems to involve a certain *méconnaissance* or "misrecognition" in Pierre Bourdieu's sense: that is, the process operative in complex social situations in which "a subjective truth and a quite opposite objective truth . . . co-exist" (Bourdieu 107). In the case of the "gift economies" that anthropologists have described in preindustrial cultures, an outside observer might conclude their participants were merely exchanging generous gifts in the expectation of getting even larger gifts in return; yet, as Bourdieu argues, it is essential to the working of the system that its participants themselves refuse to recognize or acknowledge any such possibility.

In the kind of situation under consideration here, let us envision that a physician administers painkillers to a dying patient. The physician declares and perhaps even believes that he is doing so *only* to relieve pain. He also knows with near-certainty that the same drug will bring his patient's death sooner, but this is merely an acceptable side effect and not, it is argued, the object of any independent intention of its own. Still, such a side effect could be acceptable only if the patient's prognosis was hopeless, if his or her days were, as we put it in common language, *numbered*. Suppose, therefore, one asked the doctor whether in his judgment it would be generally a good thing (for this patient in particular, or in any sense at all) if death came relatively sooner rather than later, and he acknowledged that it would be, because the patient was in severe pain and because his condition was absolutely hopeless. In such a case, how could it be rigorously determined by any one, including the doctor himself, that this other good thing, this other value or desirable end that will almost certainly be brought about by his decision, was absolutely *no part* of his intention, that it did not in the slightest way shape, influence, or determine that decision? Even in the explicit terms of this argument, the positive value that governs the whole transaction, the value that makes it possible to accept as ethically legitimate the hastening of death, is the relief of pain. But death itself, in a whole range of familiar Christian discourse, is also commonly figured as a release from pain. Death, for a Christian, is a passage to a new and more abundant life where all souls "shall hunger no more, neither thirst any more," and where "God shall wipe away all tears from their eyes" (Revelation 7:16–17). It thus appears, even within the argument itself, difficult to distinguish absolutely between *relieving pain* and *hastening death*, especially since both always are conceded to remain available as the possible objects of desire, intention, or decision.

In response, it is commonly observed by the advocates of this position that, if there were some other method that would relieve the patient's pain without hastening death, the doctor would use it. This, it is claimed, proves that the doctor's intention can be rigorously determined to be *only* the former and not the latter. Since there seems to be no such method available as of the time of this writing, this hypothetical instance indicates clearly enough how these ethical issues always in principle must intersect with technical, scientific, and medical ones. But even if one concedes this point and accepts that acts have an "intention" that can be wholly known, an intention wholly free of any unconscious, partial, or ambivalent determinants, the argument would still depend on a somewhat precarious temporal logic. A delay between the administration of a drug and its potential effects is in one sense determined by the various physical mechanisms of the body: the speed of the drug's absorption, the progress of the patient's disease, and so forth. But in this case the delay or deferral is also absolutely necessary to the ethical argument. In the terms being argued here, one obviously could not administer a drug known to cause *instant* death and claim *only* to be relieving pain. Indeed, since the very same (narcotic or opiate) drugs commonly given to *alleviate* the pain of terminal illness can also, at higher dosages, cause death directly, even the amount of such drugs administered must always be precisely calibrated. The permissible hastening of death is thus made possible only by a process of careful calculation and measurement, and, even more so, by the imagined or anticipated interval between a certain "now" and a certain "instant," the instant or moment of death itself. There must be an interval between the alleviation of pain and death so that the former may not *be* (or at any rate may not *appear*) as the direct or immediate cause of the latter. This interval or deferral is all important. It alone makes possible the abdication of causality and the preservation of the purity of an intention, in the same way that one prays or sacrifices to God with the definite hope of His blessing, but without daring to demand or expect it as a direct, immediate, or instant effect of the sacrifice or the prayer. This logic or temporal economy corresponds to (or inverts) the sacrificial logic briefly described above. In the one, the sacrificial victim must be resurrected, but not *too soon*; in the other, the suffering patient may hasten death—but only *so much*.

Therefore, the figure of self-sacrifice, in the discourse of those *opposed* to any right to die, plays more or less the same role it does in the philosophic tradition as I described it above: a unique and privileged instance of "accepting death" that may accordingly be exempted from the strictures against suicide itself. But a sacrificial logic, in a less obvious or explicit form, seems if anything more fundamental within the discourse *in favor* of a right to die. Most advocates of a right to die rely on secular modes of inquiry and reasoning; and the fundamental arguments on this side—the affirmation of individual freedom on the one hand, and of socioeconomic calculation on the other—would not necessarily seem to invite a logic or rhetoric of the sacrificial. But however surprising on the surface of it, the case for the ethical legitimacy of a right to die proves once again to involve a process of calculation anchored and limited by an incalculable and unconditional value.

To show this I consider a constellation of arguments centering on *Cruzan v. Director, Missouri Department of Health*, perhaps the most important (though not the most recent) Supreme Court decision touching on the question of a right to die. Of particular interest, as exemplifying what might be called a "liberal" position on this issue, will be the dissenting opinions by Justices William Brennan and John Paul Stevens, and the broadly similar arguments of Ronald Dworkin, whose *Life's Dominion* remains today, nearly twenty years after its publication, one of the most influential liberal approaches to the issue. The majority decision in *Cruzan*, as with many other controversial decisions, did not entirely please partisans on either side of the issue. In this case, the parents of Nancy Cruzan, who had been in a persistent vegetative state for seven years following an auto accident in 1983, had sued the state of Missouri to be allowed to remove their daughter from life support. Missouri's statute required there be "clear and convincing" evidence of Nancy's own wishes in the matter, and the state Supreme Court would not accept the "substituted judgment" of her family in place of such evidence (nor the family's testimony about Nancy's beliefs). The Supreme Court upheld the constitutionality of the state law, which had the practical effect at the time of preventing the family from removing Cruzan's feeding tube, and was therefore initially understood to be a defeat for those in favor of a right to die. Yet the *Cruzan* decision also clearly affirmed, and arguably for the first time in American law (citing the summary of William Colby, lawyer for the Cruzan family), "a constitutional right to liberty for competent people to refuse medical treatment" (*Long Goodbye* 323). In retrospect, therefore, as many have already suggested, *Cruzan* might be said to have established at least a partial "right to die" as a principle in American law. Indeed, more evidence was eventually discovered as to Nancy Cruzan's own beliefs and intentions, and the courts in Missouri did finally allow her life support to be withdrawn.

To speak very schematically, the *Cruzan* decision turns on two interrelated questions involving calculation, which are then implicitly anchored and linked by what is called, in *Cruzan v. Harmon* (the Missouri Supreme Court decision upheld in *Cruzan v. Director, Missouri Department of Health*), the "sanctity of life": something understood as an incalculable value. As usual, however, we will also find that the concept of the sanctity of life deployed in the reasoning of the decision has been always-already hollowed out by a certain calculation. The two questions are closely linked in the events of this case, but are also, as matters of law or theory, separate and distinct. The first question would be: what are the basic rights, liberty, and autonomy of the person and the citizen with regard to end-of-life decisions? The second would be: how does one determine the intentions of a subject who is no longer able to communicate or act on them? With regard to the first, the court basically reaffirms what they acknowledge to be an already established principle that "a competent person would have a constitutionally protected right to refuse lifesaving hydration and nutrition." They also stipulate that this individual right must be balanced against the State's interest in the preservation of life in general. But in the strict letter of the majority decision (and notwithstanding certain remarks to the contrary in the dissents), this state interest in life seems to be envisioned primarily as a practical (legal and political) commitment to safeguard the persons of its citizens from unwanted intrusion of any kind, whether it be the literal violence of theft and battery, or any form of medical treatment imposed on an unwilling patient. In other words, at least in the context of euthanasia, the principle of autonomy and the state's interest in preserving life might even be thought to *cooperate*, because the state, in protecting a citizen from unwanted medical treatment, and attempting to preserve the purity of each citizen's decision as to the end of his or her life, might be said to be fostering and preserving that citizen's autonomy as well. At any rate, in many or most of the practical situations that commonly come into play at the end of human life, an individual right to accept or refuse treatment would usually serve in practice as a kind of de facto right to die; although, to be sure, only a limited or negative right. In a case involving, for example, something like the situation in the play referenced earlier, *Whose Life Is It Anyway?*—that is, a fully conscious and competent person who, because of disastrous physical disability, chooses simply to *refuse* some treatment that was necessary in order to keep him alive (and who can communicate this choice as a competent legal subject)—this court would presumably be compelled to rule in favor, just as the fictional judge ruled in the play.

The second question, however, is one that emerges because the Cruzan case, by contrast, involves a subject no longer competent to decide or act for herself. This situation raises difficult questions of epistemology and communication. Even granted that an individual has the personal liberty to refuse medical treatment and thus choose to die, how do we determine intentions that cannot be stated by the subject at the very time they must be realized? This need has been answered practically in the form of "living wills," "advance directives," and the like, which record and document in written form the subject's intentions at a previous moment, and which are officially recognized in law in most American states. To be sure, a myriad further questions continue to attend such practices, which constrain an individual subject to do something that always remains, in some strict sense, impossible: to state in advance the intentions and desires he or she shall have at some future point and under entirely different conditions. Nevertheless, in cases like Cruzan's, this epistemological or subjective question would remain to be confronted no matter how firmly established was an individual right to die. Even or *especially* from a point of view that values individual autonomy, one might well join the majority in rejecting the idea that Cruzan's parents should be allowed to decide for her, and in judging that "there is no automatic assurance that the view of close family members will necessarily be the same as the patient's." In the light of the many recent scholarly and theoretical critiques of the family, whether from Marxist, feminist, or queer points of view, one will also probably be forced to agree with Justice Rehnquist's refusal to grant "a constitutional requirement that a State must recognize the primacy of [family] relationships in a situation like this" (286).

The *Cruzan* decision as a whole also, as we have briefly observed, affirms a general state interest in life, and in what the Missouri decision calls the *sanctity* of life. In the Supreme Court majority decision, by contrast, the words "sacred" or "sanctity" do not appear, and the concept seems to recede into the background, to the point where one might question whether it is necessary to the final decision as rendered, at least in any conceivable practical terms. But insofar as any concept of the sanctity of life might be said to be affirmed in this decision, it proves to be a difficult concept to define or elaborate. The Missouri Court had ruled specifically that "the state's interest in life embraces two separate concerns: an interest in the prolongation of the life of the individual patient and an interest in the sanctity of life itself" (419). This formulation seems to suggest a distinction between the individual and the species, so that to affirm life on the individual level is to prolong it, and to affirm life on a collective or general level is to affirm its sanctity. In the present context, we also recognize another pairing of calculation and the incalculable. The Missouri Court explicitly understands the question of prolonging life as involving a subtle and complex calculation of time and conditions. In a passage cited from another decision in which still more previous citations are embedded, the Missouri Court argues that, with regard to preserving or prolonging the life of a patient, the State's interest . . . is very high when "human life [can] be saved or where the affliction is curable." That interest wanes when the underlying affliction is incurable and "would soon cause death regardless of any medical treatment." The calculus shifts when the issue is not "whether, but when, for how long, and at what cost to the individual that life may be *briefly* extended." (419; citations omitted)

So the prolongation of life is the product of a complex calculus in which the likely span of that life and its current conditions must both be factored. By contrast, the court suggests, "the state's concern with the sanctity of life rests on the principle that life is precious and worthy of preservation without regard to its quality" (419). This formulation, by which in the name of justice the state refuses to judge or calculate the *quality* of a life in terms of its fitness to be protected and preserved, is of course a familiar rubric that unites the two fundamental arguments opposed to a right to die as I formerly summarized them: it denotes at once an alleged commitment "always to care," and gestures towards the specter of an involuntary euthanasia in which lives would routinely be judged in this way. But, with regard to the state's second concern: how, exactly, does a state protect or preserve the sanctity of life in general except by securing, preserving, and prolonging the lives of its citizens? The Court finally observes, at the end of this passage, that "any substantive principle of law which we adopt must also provide shelter for those who would choose to live—if able to choose—despite the inconvenience that choice might cause others" (419). This is precisely the point we have marked before in which a "conservative" argument serves as a forceful rejoinder to the implicit contradiction of their opponents' side. Yet this very argument again betrays, in turn, its own inconsistency: for example, in the choice of the word "inconvenience" to denote what would actually have to be a fundamental social commitment to universal health care. As Brennan observes in a footnote to his dissent in *Cruzan v. Director, Missouri Department of Health* (and as we briefly cited earlier), how can any state be said to "provide shelter for those who would choose to live" if it has no "state health insurance program to underwrite such care" (note 15)? So the State's interest in the sanctity of life must be said to be, and in every sense of this expression, a *calculated* one.

The dissenting opinions of Justices Brennan and Stevens in *Cruzan*, however, are memorable not so much for their consideration of either of these questions (that is, the basic right to refuse treatment or the determination of the subject's intentions), as for a somewhat different point. The majority decision, as we have seen, upholds the state law requiring "clear and convincing evidence" of the individual's wishes. It does so first by arguing that, because "the choice between life and death is a deeply personal decision," the state "may legitimately seek to safeguard the personal element of this choice through the imposition of heightened evidentiary requirements" (281). In formulating this particular point, Rehnquist seems to go out of his way to emphasize it as a matter of protecting the autonomy of the individual; and the explanation he gives here seems already adequate in itself to support his basic point about evidence. But Rehnquist goes on to claim that it is also appropriate to place the burden of proof "on those seeking to terminate an incompetent individual's life-sustaining treatment," because the "risk of an erroneous decision" is greater for them:

> An erroneous decision not to terminate results in a maintenance of the status quo; the possibility of subsequent developments . . . at least create the potential that a wrong decision will eventually be corrected or its impact mitigated. An erroneous decision to withdraw life-sustaining treatment, however, is not susceptible of correction. (284)

This is the point to which Brennan and Stevens object most strongly. In his dissent (joined by Justices Marshall and Blackmun), Brennan maintains strongly that "an erroneous decision in *either* direction is irrevocable," and that "an erroneous decision not to terminate life-support" is as much of an injustice as the reverse. Such a decision, Brennan declares

> robs a patient of the very qualities protected by the right to avoid unwanted medical treatment. His own degraded existence is perpetuated; his family's suffering is protracted; the memory he leaves behind becomes more and more distorted. Even a later decision to grant him his wish cannot undo the intervening harm. (320)

At issue in this critique is thus a remarkable vision of "life" envisioned paradoxically from two entirely different temporal points of view: first, as a set of traces distributed across a span of time, but also, and above all, as a singular and coherent "memory" that can be apprehended in an instant, all at once. This memory, which is not the same thing as the subject's own memory, is a kind of generalized and impersonal synthesis of that subject's total being as it existed across a span of time and as it is subsequently left "behind"; and it is something that presents itself even (or perhaps *especially*) in the relative or radical absence of its subject. When the set of temporal traces constituting a life in the first sense is "protracted," when certain things are added to it at its end, it permanently changes the "life" in the second sense, the life as this general or collective trace of itself. This, it is argued, is as irreversible and as fatal as death itself. We previously saw a passing hint of something like this argument in Kant's distinction between the "life" and the mere "prolongation of . . . years," which seems to leave open the possibility of "sacrificing" the latter for the former, of exchanging a certain span of mere animal life for the "life" in this higher sense: as a coherent and consistent ethical unity. When Brennan declares, at the end of the preamble of his dissent, that "Nancy Cruzan is entitled to choose to die with dignity" (302), it seems to be this that he has in mind. After all, as we have already seen, the decision does theoretically preserve the autonomy of Nancy's choice (and hence her "dignity" in this sense); and, conversely, "dignity" in the sense of a corporeal soundness or uprightness had vanished long before the case had even entered jurisdiction. So the "dignity" with which Nancy Cruzan might be allowed to die seems to refer not merely or simply to the conditions of her dying, but, rather, to the soundness and uprightness, the ethical coherence and subjective unity of Nancy's "life"—now, however, reborn in its own absence as "memory," as an object of commemoration. This is the very thing that the conditions of her dying, if rightly calculated and managed, are said to be able to preserve.

Justice Stevens, in his solitary dissent, seems to go even farther in the same direction. The early pages of his text strongly affirm the principle of autonomy in end-of-life decisions, and Stevens seems to assume that, for a person in Cruzan's condition, a desire to terminate life is almost inevitable. He cites, for example, previous legal decisions in which invasive medical procedures were judged to be "offensive to human dignity" (342). Therefore, and this point must again be emphasized in the light of the permutations of the concept of "dignity" that we have considered in the first section, Steven envisions this increasingly common situation at the end of life as one in which "dignity" in multiple senses is in peril. Dignity, either in the sense of a physical uprightness and a "dignified" deportment, *or* in the developed, quasi-Kantian sense of humanity's moral freedom and autonomy, is precisely absent in cases of this kind, cases whose central subjects are often (citing one of Brennan's citations) "in a sedated or comatose state; betubed nasally, abdominally and intravenously; and far more like manipulated objects than like moral subjects" (329). But something else, something that absolutely transcends any good that might be directly experienced or possessed by the subject in question at the moment of decision, is also in mortal peril. As Stevens writes,

> the right to be free from unwanted life-sustaining medical treatment . . . presupposes no abandonment of the desire for life. Nor is it reducible to a protec-

tion against batteries undertaken in the name of treatment, or to a guarantee against the infliction of bodily discomfort.

Rather, he suggests, this right is ultimately grounded in a particular metaphysical or transcendent determination of human finitude:

> death is not life's simple opposite, or its necessary terminus, but rather its completion. Our ethical tradition has long regarded an appreciation of mortality as essential to understanding life's significance. It may, in fact, be impossible to live for anything without being prepared to die for something. Certainly there was no disdain for life in Nathan Hale's most famous declaration or in Patrick Henry's; their words instead bespeak a passion for life that forever preserves their own lives in the memories of their countrymen. From such "honored dead we take increased devotion to that cause for which they gave the last full measure of devotion." (343-44, footnotes omitted)

In this striking passage, the sacrificial figure that had been merely implicit in this argument up to now emerges so explicitly and in so elaborate a form as to raise a slightly uneasy feeling—although one whose source is quite different from that of the unease that otherwise haunts this debate and often seems to inaugurate the arguments on both sides. For one thing, Stevens' evocation of Patrick Henry is, if one considers it more closely, at least problematic, because the Cruzan case involves a person who is asking for both liberty *and* death, for the liberty to choose death. Stevens also manages to appropriate for his argument the same figure of the heroic, self-sacrificing soldier that is commonly evoked on the other side of this debate. In the passage from Robert P. George above, the self-sacrificing soldier corresponds by analogy to the dying patient who merely "accepts death"; but here in Stevens' dissent, the very same figure now corresponds to the dying patient who embraces directly his or her positive right to die. The self-sacrificing soldier thus seems to serve as the inevitable exemplum of two symmetrically opposed arguments. George's dying patient and dying soldier are analogous because they both accept death without desiring it; Stevens' dying patient and dying soldier are analogous because they both embrace or seize death in the name of something that they both believe will live on after them.

If anything, however, the figure of the heroic soldier might be said to be more necessary for Stevens' argument. Stevens' evocation of Nathan Hale in particular reveals the underlying sacrificial logic of his whole argument, by which a proposed right to die is understood, above all, as the liberty to sacrifice "life" for the sake of something that one may as well go ahead and call "dignity," now using this crucial term to denote what is otherwise called the honor, the life, or the memory. This life-as-dignity or dignity-as-life serves as the unconditional value that here again anchors an assumed process of calculation and decision (what Brennan had called "the patient's calculus," the process through which the patient's autonomy is specifically exercised by either accepting or rejecting treatment). The "dignity" of an individual "life" understood in this way must in principle transcend any of the conditions or particulars of the life in some more literal or practical sense. Such dignity, itself transcended only by "human dignity" in its ultimate, absolute, and universal form, demands expression and preservation even in the radical absence of dignity in virtually any other conceivable sense of the word.

This argument, unfolded like this, demands question at two points, the first relatively small and the second relatively large. First, doesn't it somewhat curiously rejoin the Christian vision considered earlier, in which suffering at the end of life completes a person's "life" in the sense of a journey or pilgrimage of salvation, whose absolute and perfect fulfillment would be a final sharing of the divine sacrifice? At least, so to speak, a Christian who thinks in this way would seem to fulfill this vision of a "life" completed by its end at least as well as the dying person who chooses to die out of a calculation that days of indignity will sully the memory he or she leaves behind.

The second question would pertain to Stevens' evocation of Lincoln's Gettysburg Address, in which the national and military sacrifice is envisioned as directly, and almost literally, *productive.* In the economic figure from Lincoln that Stevens cites, the "honored dead" are said to have given "the *last full* measure of devotion," a measure at the very limit both of quantity and time. In this context, however, the two adjectives do not entirely cooperate. Lincoln does not presumably mean to say merely that these heroes gave "the last *full* measure," as though someone might later give less; nor that they gave "the *last* full measure," as though such giving has now stopped. Rather, what these honored dead gave was a *full* measure precisely because it encompasses the *last,* or in other words because what they gave was the full account of all they could ever give, namely, their lives and their deaths. Then, this gift or sacrifice, in its fullness and finality, *produces* in those who receive it an "*increased* devotion to that cause for which" this gift of death was given. Just so, Stevens also suggests, the instances of national sacrifice that he cites "bespeak a passion for life"; and this passion, manifest paradoxically in the act of embracing death, "preserves their own lives in the memories of their countrymen." The situation envisioned is thus a virtual displacement or secularization of the sacrificial formula of *do ut des* ("I give that you may give"), in which it is now said that one heroic American gives his life precisely so that others will later give theirs.[4]

Therefore, this argument (in a manner once again strangely similar to the Christian arguments considered earlier) also depends on a precarious temporal economy. Stevens begins by asserting that the event of dying crucially shapes a "life" considered specifically as an object of *commemoration*. Thus the precise details of how Nancy Cruzan dies, he writes, "will affect how that life is remembered" (344). Stevens also reproaches the majority for separating Cruzan's "life and liberty," that is, her literal existence (the "life" that is protected by the state), and her "dignity" in the sense of her ability to choose and act autonomously. On the contrary, Stevens writes in response, "absent some theological abstraction, the idea of life is not conceived separately from the idea of a living person" (347). But Stevens himself also unmistakably separates the "life" from the life, insofar as the former can—or perhaps *can only be*—apprehended as a "memory" in the radical absence of the being who lived it. Thus in the end Stevens can only invert the sacrificial logic that he discovers in the majority opinion, so that whereas the majority decision is, in his view, all too willing to sacrifice Nancy's dignity for the sake of her life, Stevens himself seems to be perhaps too willing to sacrifice her life for the sake of her dignity. Or, at least, this symmetry indicates, one more time, the secret, invisible, and yet unmistakable complicity that links the arguments on both sides of this debate.

To be sure, I am reading these texts and the *Cruzan* decision in general so far against the grain as to have seemingly discovered a more fundamental or more forceful (if not more rigorous) concept of the "sanctity of life" in the dissents than in the majority decision they oppose. As we have seen, the majority in *Cruzan v. Harmon*, which was upheld by the Supreme Court, does identify the sanctity of life as one of two concerns constituting the state's general interest in life. Ronald Dworkin, whose *Life's Dominion* was first published three years later, suggests that Rehnquist's *Cruzan* decision

> amplified the Missouri court's claim about the sanctity of life: he said that Missouri, as a community, had legitimate reasons for keeping Nancy Cruzan alive, even on the assumption that remaining alive was against her own interests, because the state was entitled to say that it is *intrinsically* a bad thing when anyone dies deliberately and prematurely. (12)

In formulating this summary, Dworkin seems to choose his words carefully. Although it is perhaps true, for example, that Rehnquist "amplified" the Missouri court's claim about the sanctity of life in the sense of unfolding it or expatiating upon it, in my view, as I suggested above, he cannot be said to amplify it in the sense of enlarging or developing it; if anything, he seems to reduce or diminish it. But regardless of how one construes the majority decisions, it remain striking that the arguments of Brennan, Stevens, and Dworkin should all at least *equally* depend on a certain unconditional value of a "life" that, as the latter acknowledges, might be called, almost interchangeably, either its sacredness or its dignity.

As I observed in chapter 2, *Life's Dominion* is in fact framed by a single central observation: that "we" share "a fundamental idea . . . that individual human life is sacred" (13). One can suspend judgment on such a claim in its empirical sense, or even grant it, and still necessarily observe a disjunction between this empirical claim and the even larger theoretical questions that necessarily subtend it. In *Life's Dominion*, Dworkin's central argument is presented as one that simply *prevails*. That is, if Dworkin himself maintains that human life is sacred, which he finally must be said to do, for much of the book he does so only indirectly, in the form of what he claims to be a belief already universally shared (and yet whose universality is itself universally misunderstood). For example, in a chapter audaciously entitled "What is Sacred," Dworkin recites a whole variety of beliefs that he claims "we" accept with regard to the essential inviolability of the value of human life, which he relates to widespread ideas about artistic and natural creation in general. He then goes so far as to suggest:

> It is not my present purpose to recommend or defend any of these widespread convictions about art and nature, in either their religious or secular form. Perhaps they are all, as some skeptics insist, inconsistent superstitions. (81)

Rather, he explains, his intention is simply to show us that the arguments both in favor and opposed to a right to die are alike grounded in a fundamental belief in life's sanctity, a conclusion to which we have also been led here, though via a rather different path. But we are thus forced to question the ultimate ground of Dworkin's whole exposition of a case for a right to die, by which he specifically claims to "redesign our explanation" of this vexed question as a way to cut through the prevailing conflict, even as he also begins and ends by directly affirming a sanctity of life—that, however, he also renames "dignity" (e.g., 238-39). Among the generally held convictions that Dworkin refers to in his discussion of sanctity is the general idea that works of art are "intrinsically valuable," something that "must be respected and protected," not for any conceivable subjective or instrumental value they might also possess (not even because they provide "pleasurable aesthetic experience") but absolutely in themselves (71). The instance of art is related to the instance of the sanctity of life both by analogy and by the intimate causational relation of one to another as forms of natural and human creativity; and the two are also implicitly linked via the vision of life as having a coherent narrative or "aesthetic" structure in itself. Yet the very category of the aesthetic he deploys here would be difficult to reconcile with a history of modern and postmodern art characterized by an impulse of negation and repeated attempts to destabilize the "work" of art—from the Futurist call to destroy all "masterpieces" to Duchamp's "readymades," to the self-destroying machines and immaterial "objects" of Yves Klein, Jean Tinguely, and many others. This again is not necessarily to contradict, as an *empirical* claim, that works of art are often (or commonly, or by many people) believed to be the bearers of intrinsic value. But it is to observe that this is a vision of aesthetic value (as intrinsic and inviolable) that is often resisted from *within* the very domain of modern and contemporary aesthetic practice. Moreover, the evident fact that the aesthetic has always involved myriad hierarchies of social value and status is precisely what makes it the very site where the process that Pierre Bourdieu famously calls "distinction" is so often negotiated and performed, which raises further questions about this attempt to reclaim the aesthetic as the paradigm or analogue of an intrinsic value also attached to life itself.

In *Life's Dominion* as a whole, however, this vision of the "life" as analogically related to the work of art is more than an explanatory example or comparison. This analogue is the place where Dworkin allows what I have called here a logic of sacrificial calculation to pervade his argument. He identifies "three distinct issues" that "come together in decisions about euthanasia," namely, "the patient's autonomy, his best interests, and the intrinsic value or sanctity of his life" (26). The division between autonomy and interests is an important one in practical and legal terms. In the case of a demented or unconscious patient there could conceivably be a conflict between, on the one hand, the patient's "best interests" as determined by someone who has the legal right (what Dworkin proposes to call "the right to beneficence") to decide for her; and, on the other hand, the patient's own "precedent autonomy when competent" (22), as recorded either in the memories of friends and family or in some formal legal document. But Dworkin's three-part division is readily reducible to one between calculation and incalculability. The first two of his terms, although crucially separated in practice, nevertheless pertain entirely to the ground of "the patient's calculus," to the possible process of decision that might come into play at the end of life. The third term, as Dworkin repeatedly acknowledges, pertains to incalculable value, to incalculability itself. For Dworkin too, therefore, the incalculable value of "sacred" life both *makes possible* and *demands* the exercise of calculation either through a direct autonomous act, or via a determination of the subject's "best interests" when that subject is incapable of acting on them. Dworkin further suggests, however, that

> We can properly understand none of these issues . . . until we better understand why some people want to remain biologically alive so long as they can, even in appalling circumstances, and why others in such straits want to die as soon as possible. . . . We must ask . . . about the *retrospective* meaning of death or the diminution of life, about how the last stage of a life affects its overall character. We understand how one life can be more pleasant or enjoyable or full of achievement than another. But the suggestion that a period of unconsciousness or dementia before death might make that life worse as a whole than if death had come sooner introduces a very different kind of standard for judging lives; it judges lives not just by reckoning overall sums of pleasure or enjoyment or achievement, but more structurally, as we judge a literary work, for example, whose bad ending mars what went before. (27; emphasis original)

Here, it seems to me, the figural and conceptual economy we have been tracing emerges with peculiar clarity. If, as Dworkin himself specifies, even a "period of *unconsciousness*" before death "might make [a] life worse as a whole," then this very judgment, this calculation as to the diminution or worsening of a "life," can only be made in the absence of the being whose life and whose "life" are at stake; for this being would be able to calculate about such matters only in anticipation of them, and only in terms of a future perfect that in principle cannot encompass all the conditions that may actually attend the anticipated moment.

Moreover, the ethical or subjective economy envisioned here is always one in which less can be more. An incalculable singular thing (the "life") outbalances any other possible calculus, any "reckoning" of the "sums of pleasure, enjoyment or achievement" that might have been experienced in the life. One might venture to suggest that this is the point in which this argument passes from those hints in Kant (who similarly imagines a "life" whose preservation outweighs the mere prolongation of years) to a quasi-Hegelian economy in which the negativity of death is wholly superseded in the production of a "life" that can only exist at all *after* it has been terminated and completed by (a certain kind of) death. Indeed, Dworkin goes on to acknowledge that the idea "that lives can be judged in that structural way," evaluated as though they were works of art and literature, presupposes an even more basic premise: that we are ethically responsible *for making something worthwhile of our lives*, and that this responsibility stems from the same, even more fundamental idea that I argued is at the root of the abortion controversy as well, the idea that each separate human life has an intrinsic, inviolable value. (27, emphases added)

Thus, an argument addressing a possible right to die finds itself compelled to appropriate both life and death in an ethos of productivity. In the terms of this argument, we have a responsibility to "make something worthwhile of our lives" in two distinct senses, both by living it in a productive way (by *making something* of it) and also by avoiding a death whose conditions might irretrievably mar that life notwithstanding anything contained in it otherwise or any mere prolongation of its years.

Dworkin's argument as a whole thus once again divides precisely on an axis of calculation and incalculability. On the one hand, what he means by "the sacred," as we have seen, is a value that is *intrinsic* rather than *incremental* (70), so that to believe in the sacredness of life does *not* entail a belief "that there should be as much human life as possible" (70). On the other hand, our common belief in the sanctity of life, he says, means specifically that we regret any "waste of nature's *investment*," which means "not that nature is a conscious investor but that even unconscious natural processes of creation should be treated as investments worthy of respect" (79). For Dworkin, this vision of life as a process of precarious but productive investment, something always susceptible to what he calls "waste" or "frustration," is the very thing that unites both sides of the debate about the right to die. It is not the *loss* of life, he argues, but merely the *waste* of it that we deplore. Therefore, those opposed to such a right believe that "immediate death is inevitably a more serious frustration than any option that postpones death, even at the cost of greater frustration in other respects"; whereas those in favor believe "a choice for premature death minimizes the frustration of life and is therefore not a compromise of the principle that human life is sacred but, on the contrary, best respects that principle" (90). And since all lives are the product of two investments, one natural and one human, one side simply privileges the former and the other side the latter. According to Dworkin, in other words, both sides of this debate share not only a basic "concern for life's sanctity" but also this speculative commitment to regard life as an investment, a "sacred *responsibility*" (90, emphasis added). At the heart of this debate is therefore what he calls, in the book's conclusion, a "*sovereign* commitment to the sanctity of life" that governs our debate about these issues; and he says that "*dignity* . . is at the heart of both arguments" (238, emphases added). Dignity, sanctity, sovereignty: together again in a debate that, apparently, they simultaneously govern and yet are powerless to resolve.

Dworkin's argument, especially in the light of the Brennan and Stevens dissents which it echoes and intensifies, thus exemplifies the strange sacrificial economy that, as we have been seeing, seems to pervade the case in favor of a right to die, which seems to be able to think this "right," this crucial freedom, only in terms of the incalculable value that can be *recuperated* from death. This aspiration to *preserve* the incalculable singularity of the life by ensuring that its final act will complete and unify what went before, this recuperation of death into production, is really the mark of an incapacity that haunts the very possibility of thinking a right to die at every level. Indeed, one might say that the fundamental philosophic responsibility of *learning how to die* is the very thing most shirked in a discourse that claims to be bringing death within the compass of our sovereign decision. Perhaps this is why this logic of sacrificial calculation also seems to mark the place where the very *project* of establishing a sovereign right to die seems to confront the sovereign right to death in an opposition that remains, however, entirely unresolved, a mere aporia for which no resolution seems yet to beckon.

Let me offer some final illustrations of this problem with several brief concluding examples. On June 11, 1985, at the death of Karen Ann Quinlan (protagonist of the first major case about the right to die to emerge into national prominence), Paul Conrad published a cartoon in the *Los Angeles Times* (see figure).

The striking image seems to me to be one of those self-cancelling artifacts that contradicts the very thing it aspires to represent. For the cartoonist can only make his polemical point by showing Quinlan, newly be-winged and arching her body forward in ecstasy and freedom, as also still incongruously trailing a loose end of the techno-discursive knot in which she had been, for so long, so thoroughly tied up, and in which she continues to figure (as she so obviously does here). Moreover, the caption declares that Quinlan has been "finally *granted* the right to die." But in fact Quinlan's parents had been allowed to remove the respirator some nine years earlier; but she began to breathe normally on her own even when the machines had been removed, and survived in the same persistent vegetative state until she died from what must therefore, even if somewhat awkwardly, be called "natural" causes (Dowbiggin 122). So who or what actually *granted* her this freedom and this right? One might even suggest that the image, even more

Karen Ann Quinlan Is Finally Granted the Right to Die (Paul Conrad, *Los Angeles Times*)

FIGURE: Used by permission of the Conrad Estate

paradoxically, undoes the case for a right to die that we have just followed through Brennan, Stevens, and Dworkin. For Conrad represents Quinlan's life precisely *in* a certain recuperative aftermath of its mere embodied existence, as a triumph of "life" over death, of the spiritual over the technological, of the ecstatic instant over the mere prolongation of a weary life. But wasn't such a triumph supposed to be the very thing that had been made unavailable by the years of indignity which she nevertheless had to endure before the final "granting" (by whom?) of this right to die?

Twenty years later, the case of Terri Schiavo became the third watershed moment in the recent history of this issue, the occasion of an extraordinary and much-discussed sequence of legal and political decisions. After Schiavo's death on March 31, 2005, in an online polemic published on a Catholic church website, Keith Fournier railed in the strongest possible terms against what he claimed was the injustice of the multiple decisions that licensed the removal of her feeding tube. Fournier went so far as to argue that Schiavo should be considered a "martyr" in two different senses: first, because she is one of a "tradition of 'white martyrs,' those who live sacrificial lives that change the world"; and second, because her life was "taken away by the enforcers of a New Rome." Here is a particularly vivid example of how a certain underlying sacrificial logic seems often to push its way to the center of this debate in the most outlandish and illogical of ways. In this case, although even the precise details of Schiavo's life and death remain controversial, it is hard to see how either of these interpretations can be maintained according to any conceivable understanding of those events. In the first place, the court decisions that licensed the removal of Schiavo's feeding tube did so not by *enforcing* but by *renouncing* the state's power to overrule what was determined to be (whether rightly or wrongly) her individual choice to refuse treatment. That determination was, of course, bitterly contested by Schiavo's parents and by others opposed to the removal of life support. But regardless of how one determines what Schiavo's choice would have been, can she possibly be said to have chosen or embraced martyrdom? Suppose the cardiac arrest that placed her in a persistent vegetative state was an accident, as is almost certainly the case. Can death be martyrdom or sacrifice when it results from pure misfortune or mischance? Or suppose, on the other hand, that Schiavo made certain bad choices while alive that led, even if unintentionally, to her radical disability.[5] Can death be martyrdom or sacrifice when it results from youthful recklessness and negligence? Thus the one remaining possibility is to suppose that Schiavo would have chosen to persist in this vegetative state for the sake of some higher purpose: perhaps, let us say, to illustrate in her own person the principle of the sanctity of life. Then one could perhaps, just barely, understand hers as a kind of "white martyrdom." This phrase refers to those who give their lives, rather than their deaths, for someone or something, and is most commonly applied to those who nurse hopelessly ill people (such as Father Damien, the "apostle to the lepers" who was canonized by Pope Benedict XVI on October 11, 2009; see Henaghan). In this case, however, the obvious problem is that the term and concept of the "white martyr" would be more plausibly applied to the nurses who, had the story ended differently, would have tended to Schiavo's bodily needs day and night, possibly for years into the future.

Even more broadly, to claim that Schiavo embraced her severely disabled life as a sacrifice: would this not be to concede the very thing that must otherwise be denied in opposing the right to die? That is, doesn't such a claim concede that to avoid so debilitated and undignified a life would normally be considered a value, the very value, in fact, that Schiavo allegedly would be *sacrificing* by continuing to live?

A few days earlier, just before Schiavo's death, the distinguished scholar and theorist Eric L. Santner posted his own brief commentary on the affair on the website of his publisher, the University of Chicago Press. This time, and once again in strong terms, Santner denounced those opposed to a right to die as merely using the language of Christianity to "give cover to the radical intrusion of political power into the sphere of life." Thus the legal and political effort to keep Schiavo alive, something which its participants claim is motivated by an ethos of universal *care*, was in fact an unprecedented act of biopolitical domination. In one striking passage, however, Santner also conceded that

> one might ask why it matters at all whether Mrs. Schiavo is kept alive by a feeding tube. That is, if it is true that she is in a persistent vegetative state without awareness, without access to pleasure and pain, joy and sadness—and no credible evidence has been brought forward that would cast any doubt on this diagnosis—why should anyone care if her parents take her home and keep her alive artificially? Whom does it harm if this makes her parents happy? I think that many would respond that it harms the *soul* of Terri Schiavo to be so totally subjected to the will of others even if those others are her parents who no doubt love her (or politicians who at least claim to speak on her behalf). And what greater form of subjection is there than to have the will of others impinge directly on our life substance, our existence as living tissue? Those pleading for state intervention into Terri Schiavo's persistence as living tissue are pleading for the most radical form of domination one can imagine. And domination does damage to the human soul. I am tempted to say that the effort to keep Terri Schiavo alive is a kind of *soul murder*. (Santner, emphasis original)

But precisely what semirepressed or diabolical agency might it be that *tempts* Santner to the vision of "soul murder" at the culmination of an argument that does not seem to require it, and in which the concepts of *soul*, of *domination*, and of *murder* are being deployed in a manner that at least risks a certain laughter? This laughter does not emerge from the difficulty of imagining how a being "without awareness, without access to pleasure and pain, joy and sadness," a being with no capacity for cognition, recognition, or communication, a being who is a mere assemblage of what Santner frankly calls "living tissue," can be subjected to domination. Surely one can dominate even memories, even the dead, as arguably happens in every discourse that one might call "historical." This laughter therefore emerges, rather, from the converse possibility on which Santner also insists: that one might dominate or murder a "soul" by keeping its body alive. This formulation seems unthinkable outside of a whole chain of classical and Christian figures (from Pythagoras to Augustine and beyond), and therefore to be predicated on a *division* of body and soul that Santner seems at once to invert and to reaffirm. According to the classical formulation, as Augustine writes,

> the sanctity of the body does not consist in the integrity of its members, nor in their exemption from all touch; for they are exposed to various accidents which do violence to and wound them, and the surgeons who administer relief often perform operations that sicken the spectator . . . the sanctity of the soul remains even when the body is violated, the sanctity of the body is not lost; and that, in like manner, the sanctity of the body is lost when the sanctity of the soul is violated, though the body itself remains intact. (I:18)

Santner seems to be inverting this classical concept of the soul in order, so to speak, to reinstate it, though with a difference. The whole point of the classical concept was to make possible a kind of self (a "soul") that is impervious to the vicissitudes of the body. But Santner seems to envision a soul that is *resubjected* to the body: at once immanently complicit with and vulnerable to the body's suffering and yet still radically separate from it, a soul that can be harmed or murdered even (or *especially*) when the body to which is it linked can have no more real harm done to it. To attribute to Schiavo, to impose on her, this strange new *possibility-of-being-harmed*: is this not in its own way a kind of domination that is finally rather similar to the contrary project of *caring for* her tissue as a living instance and monument to the sanctity of life?

Finally, let me observe the emergence of this strange economy in one more text, John Protevi's *Political Affect*, which considers the Terri Schiavo case in some detail. This is not the place for a comprehensive rehearsal of Protevi's complex Deleuzian argument about the social interconnection of the body and mind in recent culture and theory. In his discussion of the Terri Schiavo case, Protevi contrasts what he calls a "Deleuzian jurisprudence" not founded "on privacy as control" or "on the subject as unified person" (137) to Giorgio Agamben's influential analysis, in his book *Homo Sacer*, of the figure of "sacred man" who can be killed but not sacrificed. In the latter, Agamben cites Karen Ann Quinlan as one of many disparate examples

in which a fatal cooperation of sovereign power and biopolitics reduces
singular beings to the status of what he famously calls "bare life" (186).
Protevi critiques Agamben's formulation in a variety of ways throughout
the book, in particular for its failure to accommodate the possibility of an
individual right to die. Here, we have approached from a very different
route something not entirely unlike one of Protevi's conclusions: that, with
regard to a right to die, "we remain trapped at the intersection of discipline
and biopower if we ground that right in sovereign rights of personal autonomy, which is the theoretical base of current American jurisprudence
on end-of-life issues" (127). I would also join Protevi, though for different
reasons, in suggesting that figures such as Quinlan or Schiavo do not seem
a particularly good fit with the paradigm of *homo sacer*. Protevi argues that
Agamben's thesis "cannot handle biopower," especially in end-of-life cases,
"because of its lack of purchase on real material change"—as opposed, that
is, to "incorporeal" matters such as the "change in juridical status" that
comes into play in such cases. For my own part, conversely, the figures
considered here seem, across a wide range of discourse and thought (and
whether they are maintained alive or granted a right die) always to remain
capable of being both murdered (see Santner above) *and* sacrificed; or, indeed, that these are figures who, as it were, can *only* be sacrificed.

It is thus a little uncomfortable to find Protevi, after these and other
useful observations, revealing a certain dependence on this same sacrificial
logic. Rather unexpectedly, and for the only time in the book, Protevi argues, still with Terri Schiavo in mind, that

> The glory of a personality, and the reason it trumps the organic system from
> which it emerges, is that it is free from automatic self-valuing and can value
> others, sometimes even to the extent of sacrificing its own organic system.
> Sacrificing. Making holy. In confronting biopower we have to preserve room
> for the sacrifice some might wish to make. (136)

The figure of sacrifice, already surprising in its sudden emergence, then
seems to shift in meaning rather bewilderingly in only a few sentences.
First, he suggests that to sacrifice one's self is a founding act of human
self-determination and a fundamental site in which individuals confront
biopower—a point that already seems to risk falling back on the very affirmation of personal autonomy that he strongly rejects elsewhere. Then,
however, he immediately further suggests that such an exercise

> is not even suicide but, to coin an awkward word for a strange situation,
> "organism-cide," the future targeting of the organism by the personality. It's

sacrifice, but not self-sacrifice, if by "self" we mean the coincidence of organism and personality. (136)

So this act, which he names with an acknowledged awkwardness, is not quite a sacrifice: it is simply a "targeting" of something which is valueless (or if anything, an impediment, a dis-value). Yet the targeting of this dis-value (which he insists should still be called a sacrifice) is nevertheless productive of *something*: a resistance to biopower and also a kind of fundamental altruism or sociality. For Protevi also imagines a Terri Schiavo who chooses to reject tubal feeding not out of concern for herself or her condition, but rather for "her loved ones—husband, parents, and siblings" (136). But if this is the case, then Schiavo's act was a sacrifice in the most classical sense of the word: for Schiavo would have embraced death for the sake of others, like a soldier jumping on a hand-grenade to save his comrades. And indeed, this finally seems to be exactly what Protevi has in mind:

> Should anyone say there is no evidence Terri Schiavo wanted to make such a sacrifice, I say there is no evidence she did not, and all the paternalistic speechifying about Terri's best interests robs her memory of the dignity of an other-directed motivation in not wanting to continue tubal feeding after the death of her person. (136)

So Terri Schiavo's hypothetical exercise of her right to die both *is* and *is not*—and yet again *is*—a sacrifice. Allowing Schiavo a right to die, and the liberty to exercise that right, to rephrase his conclusion in positive form, would recuperate her literal death in the preservation of the *dignity* of her *memory*.

In assessing Protevi's claims, especially his claim of Schiavo's possible "other-directed motivation," it is hard not to be reminded that Schiavo's parents fought bitterly against the removal of her feeding tube and tried their best for years to maintain her alive, which means, I suppose, that they strove to neutralize a sacrifice that was being made for their sakes. Yet the introductory letter on the foundation the Schiavos established in their daughter's name, a foundation dedicated to opposing the right to die, explains that

> Since Terri's death we have decided to carry her legacy of life and love forward so that her *sacrifice* will not have been in vain. (Terri Schiavo Life and Hope Network, emphasis added)

The striking fungibility of the figure of sacrifice in this context, its capacity to signify two bitterly opposed visions of life, should once again compel us to question the secret complicity of those positions. We would also have to ask, and of either the Schiavos or Protevi (whose argument insists on the root meaning of the word sacrifice), just *whom* or *what* has in fact been *made holy* here. Who has given, what has been given, to whom—and to what end? In all these sacrificial calculations of life and death, where does the sacred part come in?

## CHAPTER EIGHT

# A Debate Deconstructed

In mapping the contemporary debate about a right to die as a whole, I previously suggested that the positions on both sides, for and against, might be reduced to two fundamental arguments. In each case, an argument grounded in a vision of incalculable value (on one side, "human dignity," on the other, the "sanctity of life") was supplemented by an argument involving calculation and conditionality. Those in favor of a right to die first affirm the incalculable value of a "human dignity" that, already essentially defined as the possession of a faculty of reason, is claimed to be both *expressed* and *in that very expression preserved*, in the act of choosing and deciding on one's own death. To this affirmative declaration, however, is added an economistic argument about scarce medical resources and the need to conserve them, a rational, calculative vision of the social availability of *care* itself. If there are hopelessly ill people who might actually *choose* to die, it is argued, should they not be allowed to do so and free up resources that otherwise would be squandered uselessly or even harmfully? As we have seen, however, this supplementary argument actually undermines and contradicts the absolute principle of the primary argument. Even the incalculable value of a "death with dignity," the very thing affirmed above all on this side of the question, is always understood, via the incongruous figure of the *sacrifice*, as something that recuperates, conserves, or preserves a "life" itself understood as always-already in peril of being marred by the conditions of its ending. By the same token, those opposed to a right to die first affirm the sanctity of life as an absolute and unconditional value; and then suggest that, even if some extreme cases might *seem* to justify a right to die, to allow even these will put on us on a "slippery slope" towards a "culture of death." Thus the arguments on this side do not finally *abjure* calculation, but, rather, merely refrain from it *out of a calculation* that no code or process of decision making could ever master the incalculable possibilities unleashed by the establishment of this yet-unimagined new personal sovereignty over life and death. And, in any case, many voices on this side undermine even their fundamental principle of unconditional care—the very thing they also declare above all as absolute—by yoking it to an ethics of the marketplace within which its realization remains at best furtive and at worse impossible in principle.

Thus the entire debate now finally reveals itself (as David Brooks somewhat too-hastily argued in the column discussed in chapter 5) as an opposition of calculation and incalculability. Notwithstanding their other differences, however consequential these sometimes prove to be in practice, both sides in this debate assume that some incalculable value inheres in (human) life, and yet also that an unavoidable social scarcity will force us to calculate with the gift of *care*. To put it plainly, I suggest that what both sides in this debate share is the way they both *indicate*, without quite thinking it fully, how end-of-life decisions necessarily involve a *relation* of unconditional principle and rational calculation.

The discursive knot that presents itself here thus demands a deconstructive critique to unfold what remains unthought within it and to wager on the eruptive emergence of some new quasi-concept in which some such thought might find its opening. Derrida indicates, in his late book *Rogues*, some directions we might follow in what he acknowledges is a too-brief consideration of another vexed bioethical question: the possible therapeutic or even reproductive cloning of human beings. The "terrible dilemma of cloning," like the dilemma of a possible right to die, is one that necessarily unites concerns "of an ethical, juridical, political, and inseparably, techno-scientific nature—and precisely in the place where technicity, the great question of the technical and the logic of the prothesis, would be not accessory but essential and intrinsic to the problematic of reason" (*Rogues* 146). In noting this link between the technical and the question of reason in general, let me briefly digress to recall that other more general link between dignity and reason that emerged in chapter 4, and to observe that the principle or practice of reason plays a confusingly multiple role in the debate about a right to die. An ongoing project and practice of scientific reason, sometimes claimed as having wholly determined or brought to light the very question of a right to die, does unmistakably transform the process or experience of dying. As it does so, it gives more and more moments of decision or calculation, more and more moments where new treatments might be given or withheld, or where the prolongation of a life must, whether we like it or not, be at least *measured* against a certain "quality" of life. In other words, reason as calculation and technoscientific mastery here finds itself at least potentially opposed to itself in the form of a possible refusal, for whatever *reason*, to do all that might *reasonably* be done to ensure that life itself be preserved to its uttermost. At the same time, and over this same proliferating menu of end-of-life choices, reason as sovereignty—that is, sovereign power as the (legislative, executive, or judicial) exercise of reason—exerts its own incalculable force on this realm of individual decision, marking the very place where state sovereignty seems to transform itself into biopolitics. Reason as the sovereign and progressive aspiration to master the human condition; reason as the definitive characteristic of the dignity that inheres in (human) life; and reason as the faculty that can calculate mastery and measure, the very thing that, as Hegel writes in *The Philosophy of Right*, makes "the human being alone . . . able to abandon all things, even his own life" (37)—how is the line between all these to be drawn or calculated?

In the passage above, Derrida also refers to the inextricable link between technity in general and the logic of the *prothesis*, the logic of addition, doubling, or supplement—both of which would be obviously inseparable from the question of human cloning. One might perhaps have to question, however, whether such a logic is applicable at all to the question of a right to die; or whether, on the contrary, at stake here would be not only the incalculable singularity of dying itself, the one event that can never be shared, but also, at least in part, a sphere of potential freedom so limitless that it transcends technicity itself and remains urgently to be confronted in any and all possible conditions of (human) life. At work in the question of a right to die seems to be, on the contrary, a logic of subtraction or lack, of withdrawal or withholding—beyond all relief or cure, beyond all possibility of "resurrection, or redemption, for oneself or for anyone else" (Derrida, *Learning* 24).

Nevertheless, the arguments for and against the possibility of human cloning do seem to have a certain fundamental similarity to those about a right to die, and it is obvious that some contemporary thinkers (for example, Leon R. Kass) have been prominent participants in the debates about both issues. As Derrida writes,

> The proponents of cloning, and especially of therapeutic cloning, claim the
> rational necessity of not limiting theoretical and technoexperimental research

whenever the results can be calculated and the anticipated benefits pro-
grammed, even if this calculability risks, without any assurance, exposing us
to the incalculable. (146)

Derrida's brief summary can be conveniently illustrated by Gregory Stock,
who in the best-selling books *Metaman: The Merging of Humans and Machines
into a Global Superorganism* (1993) and *Redesigning Humans: Our Inevitable
Genetic Future* (2002) argues, among other things, that since genetic technologies such as cloning will inevitably be developed, we should embrace
them for their manifold benefits, confident that we can control them and
limit any possible abuses. As Stock suggests in a 2002 article,

> cloning has become a proxy for broader fears about the new technologies
> emerging from our unraveling of human biology. Critics . . . imagine that if we
> can stop cloning, we can head off possibilities like human enhancement, but
> they're dreaming. As we decipher our biology and learn to modify and adjust
> it, we are learning to modify ourselves—and we will do so. No laws will stop
> this.

For Stock, a constellation of actions associated with the faculty of reason
(self-modification, self-enhancement, learning, choice, decision, the will itself), and joining to constitute a kind of absolute sovereignty that "no laws
will stop," all cooperate to make the development of genetic technology
absolutely inevitable. But if we cannot stop this development in its tracks,
Stock argues, we can limit, control, and master it:

> Sure, a few interventions will arise that virtually everyone would find trou-
> bling, but we can wait until actual problems arise before moving to control
> them. These coming reproductive technologies are not like nuclear weapons,
> where large numbers of innocent bystanders can suddenly be vaporized. We
> have the luxury of feeling our way forward, seeing what problems develop, and
> carefully responding to them.

One might well consider further the way in which Stock seems to understand the process of human reason in terms of a kind of self-imposed auto-
necessity, by which the progress of human freedom in one of its manifestations simply cannot be curbed or restrained in any way, not even by any
other exercise of that freedom. For the moment, however, I observe merely
how Stock, just as Derrida summarizes, claims a "rational necessity" for
technoscientific progress, despite the (rational) knowledge that such progress can and will expose us to the incalculable: to "troubling" interventions

and as yet-unimagined problems. These, it is argued, can always be kept in check by another exercise of reason: by seeing, responding, and calculating. In this schema, therefore, an unconditional—the irresistible project of technoscientific reason—is understood to be anchored and limited by calculation (just as, one might conclude, the proponents of a death with "dignity" understand the incalculable value of the latter as preserved or made possible by a regime of legal and political policies and procedures).

By contrast, the opponents of cloning, as Derrida writes, fear its "limits would not be rigorously secured," and envision "the improbable programmation of countless armies of threatening clones in the service of an industrial, military, or market rationality, whether demonic or mad (for a certain reason can of itself become mad)" (146). In this contrasting but analogous schema, an incalculability is understood to inhere in the very project of cloning—that is, the application of a duplicative logic to the procreation or regeneration of the human being. This project reveals itself as but a subset (a kind of duplication) of a larger project of technoscientific reason whose ultimate future path cannot be foreseen or calculated. This reason is also understood as always having the upper hand, to the point that all the various modes of military, industrial, or market calculation are assumed to be in its service or at least its allies. Here again, as we have seen with the question of a right to die, one might say that the arguments on this side seem to abjure calculation; and yet in fact they merely anticipate and calculate in advance that no exercise of rational freedom could ever curb the incalculable possibilities that would be unleashed if even the most limited forms of therapeutic cloning were to be permitted. Further, as Derrida writes,

> One thus objects to all cloning in the name of ethics, human rights, what is proper to humanity, and the dignity of the human person, in the name of the singularity and *nonrepetitive* unicity of the human person, in the name of an ethics of desire or a love of the other—which we sometimes believe or try to make others believe, with an optimistic confidence, must always inspire the act of procreation. And, finally, one objects to cloning in the name of that incalculable element that must be left to birth, to the coming to light or into the world of a unique, irreplaceable, free, and thus nonprogrammable living being. (146–47)

It would again be easy to illustrate Derrida's schematic summary: for example, in the report of the President's Council on Bioethics on *Human Cloning and Human Dignity* (2002), written by a committee chaired by Leon R. Kass. The Council made nonbinding recommendations that human cloning either for reproduction or for biological research was unethical and ought to be legally prohibited, although to date no US law has been passed which forbids cloning altogether. Among other things, the Council argues that, with regard to human children,

> we do not, in normal procreation, command their conception, control their makeup, or rule over their development and birth. They are, in an important sense, "given" to us. . . . We treat them rightly when we treat them as gifts. (9)

In this "normal" process of reproduction and procreation, "the precise genetic endowment of each child is determined by a combination of nature and chance, not by human design" (10); so that each human life has a "unique, never-to-be-repeated character" (11). The child's birth is determined not by instrumental reason and deliberate choice but, rather, by an abandonment of those things:

> A child *is not made, but begotten.* . . . A man and woman give themselves in love to each other, setting their projects aside in order to do just that. Yet a child results, arriving on its own, mysterious, independent, yet the fruit of the embrace. Even were the child wished for, and consciously so, he or she is the issue of their love, not the product of their wills; the man and woman in no way produce or choose a *particular* child, as they might buy a particular car. (111)

By contrast, a hypothetical cloned child would be "at risk of living out a life overshadowed in important ways by the life of the 'original'"; and would find it hard to escape "parental attitudes that sought in the child's very existence to replicate, imitate or replace the 'original'" (115).

In such formulations, an appeal to the incalculable factors of chance, to the unprogrammable singularity of the individual, to the unconditioned and "general" economy of the gift, are obvious. Yet of course the whole *raison d'être* of this text in the first place is to formulate what it repeatedly specifies are "policy recommendations," and its authors declare that the general "challenge" presented by cloning is

> to determine what form to give to the tacit agreement between society and science, by which science promises freedom *within bounds,* and science affords us innovation, knowledge and power while respecting *reasonable limits.* (20; emphases added)

Thus, here again, all the incalculable determinants of human destiny must still somehow be fostered and preserved by calculative reason. Moreover, this text concedes that the incalculability of human procreation—the child as a "gift" given to a "man and woman" who "give themselves in love" (11)—is at most an aspiration or ideal that is always-already hollowed out with exceptions. Not only, as the authors concede in a footnote, are "many children . . . conceived in casual, loveless, or even brutal acts of sexual intercourse, including rape and incest" (111n), which means that human procreation cannot possibly be deemed to be essentially, exclusively, or absolutely a product of love; but also, a range of human activities from contraception to in vitro fertilization (IVF) already obviously interpose human choice and decision on the process of childbearing. Today, given the increasing prevalence of IVF and other reproductive technologies, the authors acknowledge, "it may become harder to see the child solely as a gift bestowed upon the parents' mutual self-giving" (111). Nevertheless, they suggest (and we will want to recall this point in the light of Derrida's account) that a child born from the use of IVF, since it will not be genetically identical to the parents, will still finally be the product of chance and not design.

One might suggest that, in either one of these positions on the cloning debate, a certain calculation is finally privileged or has the upper hand, as opposed to a figure of incalculability that is, quite precisely, bifarious or multifarious insofar as it takes the shape, by turns, of a sinister logic of duplication or multiplication. The latter itself is seen as threatening or potentially contaminating the incalculability of a "human dignity" that is constituted by the faculty of reason and that yet must abandon the exercise of reason as it might take hold of the conditions of its own production and reproduction. Addressing his final remarks to the second position, the ethical critique of cloning, Derrida suggests that it finally excludes two things from "rational examination":

> First of all, the fact that so-called identificatory repetition, the duplication that one claims to reject with horrified indignation, is already, and fortunately, present and at work everywhere it is a question of reproduction and of heritage, in culture, knowledge, language, education, and so on, whose very conditions, whose production and reproduction, are assured by this duplication. (*Rogues* 147)

The ongoing processes of culture, knowledge, education, and so forth, once admitted, have no simple limit predetermined for them in advance. At the very moment that thinkers opposed to cloning declare *thus far but no farther* (i.e., by accepting as ethical IVF but *not* reproductive cloning), they are already admitting reason and decision to the field and conceding that different lines might well be calculated and drawn. Further, this "prevailing

ethical axiomatic in the law and politics of the west" which seeks above
all to affirm the incalculable factors of chance, amorous attraction, genetic
indetermination, and so forth, has abandoned its own principle, abandoned
incalculability itself, just when such things might hypothetically be most
necessary. As Derrida explains,

> What is also, and especially, overlooked is the fact that this militant human-
> ism, this discourse concerned about ethics, about human freedom and human
> specificity, seems to assume that two so-called genetically-identical individuals
> will have identical fates, that they will be indistinguishable and subservient to
> the calculation that gave them birth. (147)

This thought thus ignores "what history, whether individual or not, owes
to culture, society, education, and the symbolic, to the incalculable and the
aleatory"; and by so doing betrays its own subservience to the calculation
that it at once enjoins and fears. Claiming to present itself as the ethical
critique of unbridled technoscience,

> this axiomatic actually shares with the axiomatic it claims to oppose a certain
> geneticism or biologism, indeed a deep zoologism, a fundamental but unac-
> knowledged reductionism. (147)

The dilemma of cloning therefore calls for "a systematic re-elaboration"
(148).

Derrida himself, however, does not provide a full re-elaboration in these
pages, but merely an initial formulation of the kind of protocol or strategy
of reading by which one might begin to approach such a thing. What he has
sketched, in effect, is an asymmetrical set of oppositions or hierarchies by
which a figure of reason as calculation and measure is set against a figure
of reason as the incalculable. This incalculable reason, however, presents
itself, by turns, as either the unconditionality of technoscientific progress
(whether affirmed or deplored), or as the definitive essence of that very
human dignity that is sometimes declared to be in danger from such progress. In any case, however, a systematic re-elaboration of the problem of
cloning would not and could not be some simple "solution" or "third way"
between the positions already mapped out; nor could it provide in advance
any ready-made set of specific policies and procedures. But it might bring
to light a new *relation* between the necessary claims of calculation and the
incalculable, precisely in the form of an *interruption* of the debate as it has
been constituted. When Derrida briefly suggests that an entire axiomatic
claiming to ground itself in the incalculable value of humanity—the un-

programmable mystery of its birth, either as species or as individual, the strange economies of gift and sacrifice by which his biological and subjective destinies are allegedly determined—is actually governed by a figure of calculation, he perhaps goes only as far as what he has called (as we saw in the introduction) the phase of *inversion* in a deconstructive analysis. In the subsequent phase of displacement, the violence of the hierarchy by which the two original terms had been related is both exposed and dissolved into a new openness. How, then, can we at least gesture towards the irruptive new "concept" that might thus be "kicked off" in the inversion and displacement of what have proven to be the violent hierarchies at work in this debate? It would involve a reason that calculates to the limits of (its own) calculability, a reason always also claiming the right and necessity of reasoning its own limitations; a reason that, as Derrida puts it in the final sentence of *Rogues*, can "let itself be reasoned with." At the very least, such a reason would allow us to recognize, in the event that "cloned individuals" should present themselves in person, that such individuals, like every being destined to birth and death in any conceivable sense of those words, would be as informed or determined by the sovereign incalculabilities of history, education, and chance as by "the calculation that gave them birth." Such beings would be *necessarily* subservient neither to the conditions of their own determination nor to the other operations of reason (in law, politics, religion, and so forth) that such an event would certainly inaugurate. And, in any case, would not such a birth and such an event also inevitably present itself, to those that determined or expected it, or even to those thus brought to life, as a *gift*? Perhaps it remains the case, as Derrida famously writes in another context, that we always turn our eyes away

> when faced by the as yet unnamable which is proclaiming itself and which can do so, as is necessary whenever a birth is in the offing, only under the species of the nonspecies, in the formless, mute, infant, and terrifying form of monstrosity. ("Structure, Sign and Play" 293)

Nevertheless, in the case of such a birth—or indeed, in the case of every birth—it would always be a certain *just reason* that would be most necessary, in order precisely to bid welcome to such an event and such a chance.

Is it, therefore, perhaps not so different after all, when it is a death, rather than a birth, that is in the *offing*? This word, used perhaps slightly unexpectedly by Alan Bass to translate Derrida's reference, in the famous passage above, to the anxiety or disquiet that emerges when "*une naissance est à l'oeuvre*," seems in the present context, and even if largely or entirely by chance, to be an almost excessively appropriate one. To begin with, through what the Oxford English Dictionary calls a "nonstandard, regional, or humorous" use (one especially conditioned by *Alice in Wonderland*), the word inescapably associates itself with a sovereign right to death ("off with his head!"). In more recent colloquial use, the word can also refer either to murder or to suicide, to the possibility of being "offed" or to having "offed" one's self. Etymologically, an "offing" originally meant the distance of open sea that either remains visible from an outlook on the shore, or to the requisite distance from the shore where a vessel must remain in order to avoid "navigational dangers" (OED, "offing")—or, that is, to prevent itself from "going aground." An "offing" is therefore a distance *away* from a certain safety that is at the same time a space *of* safety. In another context, Derrida calls our attention to how often the concept of *reason* itself is figured as "the bottom or the ground, the foundation, the groundwork"; a metaphor which consequently opens up a space "between the calculable and the incalculable, there where the *Grund* opens up into the *Abgrund*," where the grounds or foundations of reason are threatened by "the abyss, indeed by more than one abyss, including the abyss of translation between the different languages I have just juxtaposed" (*Rogues* 122)—an abyss whose edge I too have been navigating, not without many difficulties, throughout this book. An *offing* is, or at least concerns and locates itself within, a kind of *ground-work*. As a point or place that is not quite too far away to be seen, or, rather, just far enough so as to allow one to remain safely afloat, the *offing* seems to me also to figure "death" as it might be either feared or yearned for in the situations commonly envisioned under the question of a "right to die": a death that is at once too near or too far, and that is either (or both) the *source* of terror and pain and their absolute anticipatable limit. Finally, this death in the offing must also call to mind Bataille's appropriation of the Lucretian figure of the philosopher: "one who calmly looks from the shore at a dismasted ship." "I cannot imagine," Bataille writes,

> anyone so cruel that, from the shore, he could observe someone dismasted with a joyful laughter. The act of sinking, however, is something else: one can give oneself fully to this experience with a joyful heart. (cited Boldt-Irons 10)

The two possibilities that Bataille entertains and opposes here—an imminent death seen from a distance that gives it (to adapt Kant's famous phrase about the sublime) no dominion over us, and a death that might be, precisely when it is *in the offing*, to be somehow *offered* to one's self with joyous affirmation—will serve here to reframe the debate before us by refiguring the relation of calculation and incalculability at its heart.

The calculation that would necessarily be involved in any possibility of choosing death now reveals itself in the form of what Bataille called the "restricted economy" of singular beings, who are, as he puts it, "eternally needy" (*Accursed Share* 1:23). At the end of life, as at its beginning, the restricted, mortal being frequently is in need of what can only be called *care*. In the debate about a right to die, as we have seen, those who proclaim above all that we must "always care, never kill" often ally themselves to an ethos of market liberalism according to which this care is in practice to be distributed according to the vagaries of birth, employment and fortune. Among all the vexed permutations of this ongoing debate, the strangest of all, in my view, is the way in which so obvious a paradox could remain so relatively unthought on both sides.

So let me now say it plainly: only a state or society or community in which all necessary medical attention was absolutely guaranteed to all—and in which, therefore, anyone ever seeking to extend his or her life to the last instant of bare existence would be both entitled and practically able to do so—could be said to bring a practical rationality to the ethical principle of "always to care." If it is not possible here to formulate the myriad practical details that such a universal social project would involve, such a conclusion is nevertheless not to be grasped as "merely" theoretical, for it would be the absolute condition of possibility for realizing *in practice* anything like the incalculable principles (the "sanctity" or "dignity" of human life) centrally affirmed on *both* sides of this debate. Only in such a state or society would it be possible to ensure, at least to the limit of collective possibility, that no one need ever feel that his or her death is made necessary by anything other than mortality itself, nor fear that his or her "dignity" in either of its senses (bodily soundness versus the self-sovereignty of reasoned choice) might have to be sacrificed to the other. This would be calculating to the limits of calculability itself. In other words, at those unpredictable moments, perhaps made more common or more frequent by technoscientific progress, when one must decide on life or death, a set of procedures or programs to share and divide, to calculate and measure, would paradoxically make it possible to *abjure* all the other merely financial or practical calculations that might otherwise tip the scale in one direction or another.

The limit that such necessary calculation necessarily reaches—or, that is, the unconditioned or incalculable principle to which such calculation finally opens itself—would be something like Bataille's "general economy" of expenditure without return or reserve: the joyous negativity with which one might embrace the very limits of finitude by proclaiming "it is a good day to die." This absolute embrace or affirmation of death has always been, and must in principle always remain, *possible*. (Even my quotation—commonly claimed to have been declared by the Sioux warrior Crazy Horse at the outset of a famous battle that, nevertheless, he both won and survived—indicates both that there is nothing new about this willingness to declare for death, and also how a certain laughter can never be separated from it.) None of the philosophic labors expended to explain why killing one's self can *never* be justified has ever been able to spare us the ineluctable possibility that *someone* might commit to death by the act we call "committing suicide"; and even if we refrain from ever endorsing or approving or esteeming such an act, even if we continue to do all we can to prevent it, it will always in principle be "there," as a possibility always at least to be *entertained*.

Let us recall how those most opposed to any right to die claim that their opponents, whatever their announced programs, are actually advocating an absolute right to suicide ("death on demand") under any and all conditions. And then let us recall, correspondingly, how those in favor of a right to die commonly observe (as Samuel Williams did as far back as 1870) that if you are willing to *shorten* life at all (e.g., to alleviate pain) then what is the difference between such shortening of life and a positive *ending* of it? These two bitterly antagonistic arguments and mutual critiques both appear to be persuasive in their own terms. The opponents of a right to die are clearly correct to suggest that the other side's logic would lead towards an absolute right to suicide; but the proponents of a right to die are equally right (as I tried to show earlier) to observe the fatal illogic in this temporal scheme, especially when dealing with beings who are once finite *and* rational. As we have also seen, both sides necessarily concede (the one strongly and enthusiastically, the other hesitatingly and with many qualifications) that bodily weakness might sometimes make death welcome, even as it might make it practically impossible to *give death* to one's self. Thus the fundamental opposition at work in this question and this debate as a whole might be construed as one between the necessary and inescapable calculation that must be operative in any practical project of universal care (including the possibility of "assisted" suicide) and the incalculability of death embraced as absolute negativity without any recuperation as value, sacrificial or otherwise.

What, then, would be the irruptive quasi-concept that might emerge from the deconstruction, the inversion and displacement, of this opposition? This time we might venture to call it a *just care*—a mutual commitment to each other that, having on the one hand made possible the maintenance of life to its mortal limit, could, on the other hand, also make it possible to *think* or to *recognize* a decision *for death*. Perhaps the decision to die as we are envisioning it now could not precisely be understood as the product of a "right." But this decision and this death could finally be recognizable or thinkable at all only because another whole mechanism of right would have begun to be formulated and put to work. Given that it could never be made necessary by anything other than mortal necessity itself, and especially not by what Bataille calls merely *servile* reasons (of economy or need), such a death, beyond all reasons that might be given for it and in the utter secret of its coming-to-pass, can perhaps be defined at all only by saying it would be *absolutely anything but* a"sacrifice." In the debate as we have followed throughout, the positions on each side proved always to involve a process of calculation, a setting and debating of conditions, a process always claimed, however, to be anchored and grounded by an incalculable principle (dignity or sanctity) that then, however, proves itself to be groundless, always-already hollowed out by exceptions and by the very impulse of calculation it claims to govern and limit. So here, by contrast, it would be an incessant process of calculation and division that, at its very limit, makes possible an opening to incalculability, to that absolute secret that is universally shared only by *not* being shared, and hence to the chance that always remains of an unconditional escape from all conditions.

# Notes

PREFACE

1. Even to cite these dates with regard to the cases of the three individuals is to risk controversy. For example, the gravestone of Nancy Cruzan reads:

Departed: January 11, 1983
At Peace: December 26, 1990 (Colby, *Long Goodbye*, 391).

The same convention was used on Terri Schiavo's grave (Caplan et al., 345).

2. Dowbiggen observes how, in the last decades of the nineteenth century in the United States, "progressives became . . . receptive to previously heretical ideas such as eugenics and euthanasia" (7), and discusses activists such as Robert G. Ingersoll, Felix Adler, and, slightly later, Jack London, who publicly advocated for a right to euthanasia and suicide (10-21); the latter, for example, spoke of a personal "right to cease to live" (21). Lavi also documents at length the many debates about euthanasia among doctors and legislators in early twentieth-century America (see, especially 41-125).

3. Dowbiggin and Lavi discuss American eugenics in their accounts of the history of euthanasia; see also Black and Kühl.

4. Cf. Privitello, who similarly distinguishes in Bataille's thought between "the scoff" and a "sovereign laughter" that is associated with the "accursed share."

5. All quotations from *The Groundwork of the Metaphysics of Morals* and *The Metaphysics of Morals* are from *Practical Philosophy*, identified by volume and page of the "Akademie" edition.

6. Bataille writes, in *The Accursed Share*: "Changing from the perspectives of *restrictive* economy to those of *general* economy actually accomplishes a Copernican transformation: a reversal of thinking—and of ethics. If a part of wealth . . . is doomed to destruction or at least to unproductive use without any possible profit, it is logical, even inescapable, to surrender commodities without return" (1:25).

7. See Shershow, "Of Sinking" and *The Work and the Gift*.

8. The lines are from "A Satyr on Reason and Mankind" by John Wilmot, Earl of Rochester, about 1670.

9. For Derrida's critique of Nancy, see the former's reading of the latter's *The Experience of Freedom* in *Rogues* 42-55.

## CHAPTER ONE

1. On the "strategic wager," cf. Derrida and Ferraris 12-13.

2. Cf. "There Is No *One* Narcissism (Autobiophotographies)," from *Points*, where Derrida says that, for "interviews, live broadcasts, the organized appearance of what is called an author . . . I have never found a kind of rule or coherent protocol" (*Points* 197).

3. Cf. "Between Brackets I," where Derrida concedes his interviewer might think that "I am piling up the protocols in order to run away from an impossible question" (*Points* 10).

4. When Derrida refers to the "obsidionality of the triangle and the circle," he appears (either in French or English) to be punning on "obsidion," noun, a state of siege, and "obsidian," adjective and noun referring to the black volcanic stone proverbially famed for its hardness.

5. I borrow this phrase from K. J. Holsti's book of that title.

6. As a specific or "practical" example of the strategy abstractly outlined in such formulations, one might reference Derrida's description of Nelson Mandela as an "authentic inheritor," one who "conserves and reproduces, but also . . . respects the *logic* of the legacy enough to turn it upon occasion against those who claim to be its guardians, enough to reveal, despite and against the usurpers, what has never yet been seen in the inheritance" (Derrida and Tlili 16).

7. Here and occasionally elsewhere, I'm alluding indirectly to Derrida's discussion of the strangeness and force of the English and French words "remain" (*demeure*) and "henceforward" (*désormais*). See "Demeure," especially 100-102.

## CHAPTER TWO

1. Typography has been slightly modified, hyperlinks have been omitted, and the order of the second and third definitions has been reversed. Accessed May 21, 2012. http://wordnetweb .princeton.edu/perl/webwn?s=dignity&sub=Search+WordNet&02=&00=1&07=&05=&01=1&06 =&04=&03=&h=.

2. The opening sentence of this passage seems to echo Hume's famous essay "On Suicide," which asserts that "the life of a man is of no greater importance to the universe than that of an oyster."

## CHAPTER THREE

1. Cited from the transcript posted at Whithouse.gov on September 15, 2006. As Alan W. Wood observes, Bush misquotes the precise text of the Geneva convention, which actually prohibits "outrages upon personal dignity" (Wood 286-87, note 13). I have also slightly modified the published text to reflect the hesitation Bush clearly expresses in one moment of the video recording broadcast at the time.

2. Although initiatives by civil rights groups have made some progress in forcing international recognition that solitary confinement constitutes an assault on human dignity, the practice is not explicitly prohibited either in the Geneva Convention, or in the more recent International Covenant on Civil and Political Rights (1966; entered into force 1976).

3. The recent English translation I will be citing later gives the title as *Permitting the Destruction of Unworthy Life*, but the title is perhaps more commonly given as cited here.

4. Unless otherwise identified, I cite these various English Biblical translations from *The Bible in English*, Chadwick-Healey Literature Online. I have also consulted Green, *The Interlinear Bible*, Vine's *Complete Expository Dictionary*, and *The New Strong's Expanded Exhaustive Concordance of the Bible*.

5. For example, in Henry Home's *Elements of Criticism* (1762), and in Schiller's essay "On Dignity and Grace" (1793).

## CHAPTER FOUR

1. Passages from *De Officiis* will be cited by book and paragraph number; unless otherwise identified, I will be citing Miller's Loeb Library translation.

2. I cite the English text from the Fathers of the English Dominican Province edition; and the Latin from the online *Corpus Thomisticum.*

3. Unless otherwise identified, I cite the translation prepared by Pier Cesare Bori *et. al.* and published online under the auspices of the "Pico Project."

4. The Oxford editors provide no gloss to this line, perhaps because it can only refer to Italian humanist texts such as those of Manetti and Pico. As Copenhaver observes, Pico's texts were not reprinted very often in the early-modern period, though they would certainly have at least been available to Bacon. The available scholarship does not, however, document any clear evidence for Bacon's engagement with Pico's *Oration.* All references to *The Advancement of Learning* are from the Oxford edition.

## CHAPTER FIVE

1. Purdy won a judgment from the British House of Lords in July 2009 that obliged the Director of Public Prosecutions, Keir Starmer, to clarify if people would be prosecuted for helping others to commit suicide. On February 25, 2010, as reported in the *London Times*, Starmer issued revised guidelines which restated the government's opposition to "mercy killings," but seemed to affirm that someone (such as Purdy's husband) assisting a fully conscious patient who clearly wished to end his or her life would not be prosecuted (Gibb).

## CHAPTER SIX

1. According to the Oxford English Dictionary, the modern English word "suicide," which seems to be a seventeenth-century coinage based on Latin roots, is first recorded in 1651.

2. Unless otherwise identified, I will cite the text of Plato's *Laws* from A. E. Taylor's translation in Hamilton and Cairns, and the *Phaedo* from David Gallop's 1998 translation. The latter is a revised version of Gallop's 1975 translation, from which I sometimes cite the more extensive annotations.

3. According to Gallop, "Philolaus was a Pythagorean who survived the expulsion of the sect from southern Italy in the mid-fifth century B.C. and settled in Thebes" (Gallop 1975, 78; cf. Bluck 43n2), and from whom Plato had acquired notebooks (Gallop 1993, 84).

4. The passage was called a *locus vexatus* by R. D. Archer-Hind in his 1898 edition of the *Phaedo* (cited Dorter 11). On its extraordinary interpretive difficulties, see, especially, Gallop 1975, 79–83. After identifying five different possible readings, assessing each one on a variety of grounds, and even providing a chart that indicates their interrelationship in terms of symbolic logic, Gallop finally concludes that even so complex a schema "is too simple" to express the full variety of possible interrelations between the sentence's two major clauses. See also Dorter 11–19 for another detailed historical and textual account of the passage's difficulties.

## CHAPTER SEVEN

1. Lifton, similarly, cites the example of Dr. Hermann Pfannmüller, director of a Nazi euthanasia program for children, who "developed a policy of starving the designated children to death rather than wasting medication on them" (61–62). Lifton cites Pfannmüller's observaton: "'The idea is unbearable to me that the best, the flower of our youth must lose its life at the front

in order that feebleminded and irresponsible asocial elements can have a secure existence in the asylum" (63).

2. If a doctor were developing a new cure for some disease, and learned something crucial from a specific case in which the patient nevertheless died, one might perhaps say, in contemporary usage, that that patient had been a "sacrifice" to the cause of finding a cure. But Hoche seems to go out of his way to make his point in a general way, as referring to the patients that must sometimes be lost even by the best of doctors.

3. Oates is a somewhat qualified or ironic instance of self-sacrifice, since Scott and his four remaining companions perished on the journey home anyway.

4. I discuss the figure of national and military sacrifice, and elaborate this argument in more detail, in "The Time of Sacrifice."

5. For example, it has sometimes been suspected that she consumed alcohol and valium while already on a radical diet (see Caplan et al. 325).

# Works Cited

Agamben, Giorgio. *Homo Sacer: Sovereign Power and Bare Life*. Translated by Daniel Heller-Roazen. Stanford, CA: Stanford University Press, 1998.

Améry, Jean. *On Suicide*. Translated by John D. Barlow. Originally published as *Hand an Sich Legen* (Stuttgart: Klett, 1976). Bloomington: Indiana University Press, 1999.

Aquinas, Thomas. *Corpus Thomisticum*. http://www.corpusthomisticum.org/.

Aquinas, Thomas. *The Summa Theologica of St. Thomas Aquinas*. 2nd ed. Translated by the Fathers of the English Dominican Province. Originally published 1920. New Advent CD ROM 2.1. Denver, CO: Advent International, 2008.

Annan, Kofi. "Nobel Lecture." December 10, 2001. Accessed January 13, 2013. http://www.nobel prize.org/nobel_prizes/peace/laureates/2001/annan-lecture.html.

Anscombe, G. E. M. "War and Murder." In *The Doctrine of Double Effect: Philosophers Debate a Controversial Moral Principle*, edited by P. A. Woodward, 247–60. Notre Dame, IN: University of Notre Dame Press, 2001.

Augustine. *The City of God*. Translated by Marcus Dods. *Nicene and Post-Nicene Fathers*, 1st ser., vol. 2. Buffalo, NY: Christian Literature, 1887. Revised and edited by Kevin Knight. New Advent CD ROM 2.1. Denver, CO: Advent International, 2009.

Bacon, Francis. *The Advancement of Learning*. Vol. 4 of *The Oxford Francis Bacon*. Edited by Michael Kiernan. Oxford: Oxford University Press, 2000.

Bacon, Francis. *The Major Works*. Edited by Brian Vickers. Oxford: Oxford University Press, 2008.

Baker, Herschel. *The Dignity of Man: Studies in the Persistence of an Idea*. Cambridge, MA: Harvard University Press, 1947.

Bataille, Georges. *The Accursed Share: An Essay in General Economy*. Translated by Robert Hurley. New York: Zone Books, 1991.

Bataille, Georges. "Hegel, Death and Sacrifice." Translated by Jonathan Strauss. *Yale French Studies* 78, *On Bataille* (1990): 9–28.

Bataille, Georges. *Inner Experience*. Translated by Leslie Anne Boldt. Albany: State University of New York Press, 1988.

Bataille, Georges. *Oeuvres Completes*. 12 vols. Paris: Galimard, 1970–88.

Bataille, Georges. *Visions of Excess: Selected Writings 1927-1933*. Translated by Allan Stoekl. Minneapolis: University of Minnesota Press, 1985.

Battin, M. Pabst. "Suicide: A Fundamental Human Right?" In *Suicide: The Philosophical Issues*, edited by M. Pabst Battin and David J. Mayo. New York: St. Martin's, 1980: 267–85.

Benjamin, Walter. "Critique of Violence." Translated by Edmund Jephcott. In *Reflections: Essays, Aphorisms, Autobiographical Writings*. Edited by Peter Demetz. New York: Schocken, 1978.

Binding, Karl, and Albert Hoche. *Permitting the Destruction of Unworthy Life*. Originally published as *Die Freigabe der Vernichtung lebensunwerten Lebens* (Leipzig: Verlag von Felix Meiner, 1920). Translated by Walter E. Wright Jr. *Issues in Law and Medicine* 8.2 (1992): 231–65.

Black, Edwin. *War against the Weak: Eugenics and America's Campaign to Create a Master Race*. New York: Four Walls Eight Windows, 2003.

Bluck, R. S. *Plato's Phaedo*. London: Routledge and Kegan Paul, 1955.

Boethius. *Theological Tractates and the Consolation of Philosophy*. Translated by H. F. Stewart, E. K. Rand, and S. J. Tester. Loeb Classical Library, 1918. Reprinted Cambridge, MA: Harvard University Press, 1973.

Boldt-Irons, Leslie Anne. "Introduction." In *On Bataille: Critical Essays*. Translated by Leslie Anne Boldt-Irons. Albany: State University of New York Press, 1995.

Bondanella, Julia Conaway, and Mark Musa. *The Italian Renaissance Reader*. New York: Meridian, 1987.

Bontekoe, Ron. *The Nature of Dignity*. Lanham, MD: Lexington Books, 2008.

Borch-Jacobsen, Mikkel. "The Laughter of Being." *Modern Language Notes* 102, no. 4 (1987): 737–60.

Bourdieu, Pierre. *The Logic of Practice*. Stanford, CA: Stanford University Press, 1992.

Brooks, David. "Morality and Reality." *New York Times*, March 2, 2005, A27.

Brooks, Rosa. "Our Torturer-in-Chief." *Los Angeles Times*, September 22, 2006. Accessed January 13, 2013. http://www.latimes.com/news/la-oe-brooks22sep22,0,7510003.column.

Brownlie, Ian, and Guy S. Goodwin-Gill. *Basic Documents on Human Rights*. 5th ed. Oxford: Oxford University Press, 2006.

*Buck v. Bell*. United States Supreme Court. 274 U.S. 200. 1927.

Bush, George W. Executive Order 13440. "Interpretation of the Geneva Conventions Common Article 3 as Applied to a Program of Detention and Interrogation Operated by the Central Intelligence Agency." 72 FR 40707. July 24, 2007. The National Archives. Accessed January 13, 2013. http://www.archives.gov/federal-register/executive-orders/2007.html.

Bush, George W. "National Sanctity of Human Life Day, 2006: A Proclamation by the President of the United States of America." Accessed January 13, 2013. http://able2know.org/topic/67674-1.

Cancik, Hubert. "'Dignity of Man' and 'Persona' in Stoic Anthropology: Some Remarks on Cicero, *De Officiis* I, 105–107." In *The Concept of Human Dignity in Human Rights Discourse*, edited by David Kretzmer and Eckart Klein, 19–40. The Hague: Kluwer Law International, 2002.

Caplan, Arthur L., James J. McCartney, and Dominic A. Sisti, eds. *The Case of Terri Schiavo: Ethics at the End of Life*. New York: Prometheus Books, 2006.

Carlin, George. *Napalm and Silly Putty*. New York: Hyperion, 2001.

Cassirer, Ernst. "Giovanni Pico della Mirandola: A Study in the History of Renaissance Ideas." *Journal of the History of Ideas* 3, no. 3 (1942): 319–46.

Cassirer, Ernst, Paul Oskar Kristeller, and John Herman Randall. *The Renaissance Philosophy of Man*. Chicago: University of Chicago Press, 1948.

Chaucer, Geoffrey. *The Riverside Chaucer*. 3rd ed. Edited by Larry D. Benson. Oxford: Oxford University Press, 2008.

Cicero. *De Officiis*. Translated by Walter Miller. Loeb Latin Library. London: William Heinemann, 1928.

Cicero. *De Senectute*. In *On Old Age, On Friendship, On Divination*. Translated by W. A. Falconer. Loeb Latin Library. Cambridge, MA: Harvard University Press, 1923.

Clark, Brian. *Whose Life Is It Anyway?* Woodstock, IL: Dramatic Publishing, 1984.

Cohen-Almagor, Raphael. *The Right to Die with Dignity: An Argument in Ethics, Medicine, and Law.* New Brunswick, NJ: Rutgers University Press, 2001.

Colby, William H. *Long Goodbye: The Deaths of Nancy Cruzan.* Carlsbad, CA: Haye House, 2005.

Colby, William H. *Unplugged: Reclaiming Our Right to Die in America.* New York: Amacomo, 2006.

Colson, Charles W. "Introduction: Can We Prevent the 'Abolition of Man'?" In *Human Dignity in the Biotech Century,* edited by Charles W. Colson and Nigel M. de S. Cameron, 11–20. Downers Grove, IL: Intervarsity Press, 2004.

Congregation for the Doctrine of the Faith. "Declaration on Euthanasia." May 5, 1980. Accessed January 13, 2013. http://www.vatican.va/roman_curia/congregations/cfaith/documents/rc_con_cfaith_doc_19800505_euthanasia_en.html.

Cooper, John M. "Greek Philosophers on Suicide and Euthanasia." In *Suicide and Euthanasia: Historical and Contemporary Themes,* edited by Baruch A. Brody, 9–38. Dordrecht, the Netherlands: Kluwer Academic, 1989.

Copenhaver, Brian P. "Giovanni Pico della Mirandola." In *The Stanford Encyclopedia of Philosophy,* winter 2008 ed., edited by Edward N. Zalta. Stanford: Metaphysics Research Lab, Center for the Study of Language and Information, 2008. Accessed January 13, 2013. http://plato.stanford.edu/archives/win2008/entries/pico-della-mirandola/.

Cornford, Francis Macdonald. *The Origins of Attic Comedy.* London: E. Arnold, 1914. Reprinted New York: Doubleday, 1961.

*Cruzan v. Director, Missouri Department of Health.* United States Supreme Court. 497 U.S. 261. 1990.

*Cruzan v. Harmon.* Supreme Court of Missouri. 760 S.W.2d 408. 1988.

Derrida, Jacques. *Aporias.* Translated by Thomas Dutoit. Stanford, CA: Stanford University Press, 1993.

Derrida, Jacques. "Demeure: Fiction and Testimony." In *The Instant of My Death,* edited by Jacques Derrida and Maurice Blanchot and translated by Elizabeth Rottenberg, 15–103. Stanford, CA: Stanford University Press, 2000.

Derrida, Jacques. *Dissemination.* Translated by Barbara Johnson. Originally published as *La Dissémination* (Paris: Editions du Seuil, 1972). Chicago: University of Chicago Press, 1981.

Derrida, Jacques. "Différance." In *Margins of Philosophy,* 1–28. Chicago: University of Chicago Press, 1982.

Derrida, Jacques. "Economimesis." *Diacritics* 11, no. 2 (1981): 2–25.

Derrida, Jacques. "The Ends of Man." In *Margins of Philosophy,* 109–36. Chicago: University of Chicago Press, 1982.

Derrida, Jacques. "Force and Signification." In *Writing and Difference,* translated by Alan Bass, 3–30. Chicago: University of Chicago Press, 1978.

Derrida, Jacques. "Force of Law: The 'Mystical Foundation of Authority.'" In *Acts of Religion,* edited by Gil Anidjar, 230–98. New York: Routledge, 2002.

Derrida, Jacques. "From Restricted to General Economy: A Hegelianism Without Reserve." In *Writing and Difference,* translated by Alan Bass, 251–77. Chicago: University of Chicago Press, 1978.

Derrida, Jacques. *The Gift of Death.* Translated by David Willis. Chicago: University of Chicago Press, 1995.

Derrida, Jacques. *Given Time.* Translated by Peggy Kamuf. Chicago: University of Chicago Press, 1992.

Derrida, Jacques. *Glas.* Translated by John P. Leavey Jr. and Richard Rand. Lincoln: University of Nebraska Press, 1986.

Derrida, Jacques. *Learning to Live Finally: The Last Interview.* Translated by Pascale-Anne Brault and Michael Naas. Hoboken, NJ: Melville House, 2007.

Derrida, Jacques. "Letter to a Japanese Friend." In *Psyche: Inventions of the Other,* translated by

David Wood and Andrew Benjamin, vol. 2, 1-6. Stanford, CA: Stanford University Press, 2008.

Derrida, Jacques. *Margins of Philosophy*. Chicago: University of Chicago Press, 1982.

Derrida, Jacques. "Of Forgiveness." In *On Cosmopolitanism and Forgiveness*. Translated by Mark Dooley and Michael Hughes. New York: Routledge, 2001.

Derrida, Jacques. *Of Hospitality*. Translated by Rachel Bowlby. Stanford, CA; Stanford University Press, 2000.

Derrida, Jacques. *Of Spirit: Heidegger and the Question*. Translated by Geoffrey Benington and Rachel Bowlby. Chicago: University of Chicago Press, 1989.

Derrida, Jacques. "Outwork, Prefacing." In *Dissemination*, translated by Barbara Johnson, 1-59. Chicago: University of Chicago Press, 1981.

Derrida, Jacques. "Plato's Pharmacy." In *Dissemination*, translated by Barbara Johnson, 63-171. Chicago: University of Chicago Press, 1981.

Derrida, Jacques. *Points: Interviews 1974-1994*, edited by Elisabeth Weber and translated by Peggy Kamuf et al. Stanford, CA: Stanford University Press, 1995.

Derrida, Jacques. *Positions*. Translated by Alan Bass. Chicago: University of Chicago Press, 1981.

Derrida, Jacques. *Rogues: Two Essays on Reason*. Translated by Anne and Michael Naas Pascale-Brault. Stanford, CA: Stanford University Press, 2005.

Derrida, Jacques. "Structure, Sign and Play in the Discourse of the Human Sciences." In *Writing and Difference*, translated by Alan Bass, 278-93. Chicago: University of Chicago Press, 1978.

Derrida, Jacques. "The Villanova Roundtable." In *Deconstruction in a Nutshell*, edited by John D. Caputo, 3-28. New York: Fordham University Press, 1997.

Derrida, Jacques. *Writing and Difference*. Translated by Alan Bass. Chicago: University of Chicago Press, 1978.

Derrida, Jacques, and Maurizio Ferraris. *A Taste for the Secret*. Edited by Giacomo Donis and Davis Webb and translated by Giacomo Donis. Cambridge: Polity, 2001.

Derrida, Jacques, and Elisabeth Roudinesco. *For What Tomorrow . . . A Dialogue*. Translated by Jeff Fort. Stanford, CA: Stanford University Press, 2004.

Derrida, Jacques, and Mustapha Tlili. *For Nelson Mandela*. New York: Henry Holt, 1987.

Donne, John. *Biathanatos*. London, 1608.

Dorter, Kenneth. *Plato's* Phaedo: *An Interpretation*. Toronto: University of Toronto Press, 1982.

Dowbiggin, Ian. *A Merciful End: The Euthanasia Movement in Modern America*. Oxford: Oxford University Press, 2003.

Downing, A. B. "Euthanasia: The Human Context." In *Euthanasia and the Right to Death: The Case for Voluntary Euthanasia*, edited by A. B. Downing, 13-24. London: Peter Owen, 1969.

Durkheim, Emile. *Suicide: A Study in Sociology*. Originally published 1897. Translated by John A. Spaulding and George Simpson. New York: Free Press, 1951.

Dworkin, Ronald. *Life's Dominion: An Argument About Abortion, Euthanasia, and Individual Freedom*. New York: Vintage, 1993.

Dyck, Andrew R. *A Commentary on Cicero*, De Officiis. Ann Arbor: University of Michigan Press, 1996.

Eckert, Joern. "Legal Roots of Human Dignity in German Law." In *The Concept of Human Dignity in Human Rights Discourse*, edited by David Kretzmer and Eckart Klein, 41-54. The Hague: Kluwer Law International, 2002.

Emanuel, Ezekiel J. "The History of Euthanasia Debates in the United States and Britain." *Annals of Internal Medicine* 121, no. 10 (1994):793-802.

Emery, Giles. *The Trinitarian Theology of Saint Thomas Aquinas*. Oxford: Oxford University Press, 2007.

Esposito, Robert. *Bios: Biopolitics and Philosophy*. Translated by Timothy Campbell. Minneapolis: University of Minnesota Press, 2008.

Final Exit Network. Press Release, June 16, 2010. "Final Exit Network Right-to-Die Billboards Appear in California, New Jersey and Florida." Accessed January 13, 2013. http://www .ereleases.com/pr/final-exit-network-righttodie-billboards-california-jersey-florida-37003.

Foucault, Michel. *The History of Sexuality, Vol. 1: An Introduction.* Translated by Robert Hurley. New York: Vintage, 1978.

Fournier, Keith. "Terri Schiavo, Martyr." Catholic Online website. Published December 12, 2007. Accessed January 13, 2013. http://www.catholic.org/national/national_story.php?id=26167.

Frey, R. G. "Did Socrates Commit Suicide?" *Philosophy* 53, no. 203 (1978): 106-8.

Friedlander, Henry. *The Origins of Nazi Genocide: From Euthanasia to the Final Solution.* Chapel Hill: University of North Carolina Press, 1995.

Gallop, David, trans. *Plato: Phaedo.* Oxford: Clarendon Press, 1975.

Gallop, David, trans. *Plato: Phaedo.* Oxford: Oxford University Press, 1998.

Gasché, Rodolphe. *The Tain of the Mirror: Derrida and the Philosophy of Reflection.* Cambridge, MA: Harvard University Press, 1986.

Gemerchak, Christopher M. *The Sunday of the Negative: Reading Bataille Reading Hegel.* Albany: State University of New York Press, 2003.

George, Robert P. *The Clash of Orthodoxies: Law, Religion and Morality in Crisis.* Wilmington, DE: ISI Books, 2001.

George, Robert P. "Terminal Logic." *Touchstone* (online magazine) 19, no. 2 (2006). Accessed January 13, 2013. http://touchstonemag.com/archives/article.php?id=19-02-032-f.

Gerwith, Alan. "Dignity as the Basis of Rights." In *The Constitution of Rights: Human Dignity and American Values,* edited by Michael J. Meyer and W. A. Parent, 10-28. Ithaca, NY: Cornell University Press, 1992.

Gibb, Francis. "Terry Pratchett and Debbie Purdy Back New Suicide Guidelines." *London Times,* February 26, 2010.

Glick, Henry R. *The Right to Die.* New York: Columbia University Press, 1992.

Groscup, Jennifer. "Court Considers Prisoners' Rights." *Monitor on Psychology* 36, no. 4 (2005): 78.

Griffin, M. T., and E. M. Atkins, eds. *Cicero on Duties.* Cambridge: Cambridge University Press, 1991.

Guernsey, R. S. *Suicide: History of The Penal Laws Relating to It in Their Legal, Social, Moral and Religious Aspects, in Ancient and Modern Times.* New York, 1883.

Hägglund, Martin. *Radical Atheism: Derrida and the Time of Life.* Stanford, CA: Stanford University Press, 2008.

*Hamdan v. Rumsfeld.* 548 U.S. 557. United States Supreme Court. 2006.

*Hamdi v. Rumsfeld.* 542 U.S. 507. United States Supreme Court. 2004.

Hamilton, Edith, and Huntington Cairns, eds. *The Collected Dialogues of Plato.* Bollingen Series 71. Princeton, NY: Princeton University Press, 1961.

Hardwig, John. *Is There a Duty to Die? and Other Essays in Medical Ethics.* New York: Routledge, 2000.

Hegel, G. R. F. *Elements of the Philosophy of Right.* Translated by Allen W. Wood. Cambridge: Cambridge University Press, 1991.

Henaghan, John. *White Martyrdom.* Milton, MA: St. Columbans, 1946.

Higginbotham, John, trans. *Cicero on Moral Obligation.* Berkeley: University of California Press, 1967.

Hill, Thomas E, Jr. *Dignity and Practical Reason and Kant's Moral Theory.* Ithaca, NY: Cornell University Press, 1992.

Holden, Hubert Ashton, ed. *M. Tulli Ciceronis De Officiis.* Amsterdam: Adolf M. Hakkert, 1966.

Holsti, K. V. *Taming the Sovereigns: Institutional Change in International Politics.* Cambridge: Cambridge University Press, 2004.

Homes, Henry. *Elements of Criticism*. London, 1762.

Human Betterment Foundation. "Human Sterilization." Pasadena, CA: Human Betterment Foundation, 1934. Accessed January 13, 2013. http://www.eugenicsarchive.org.

Hume, David. "On Suicide." In *Dialogues Concerning Natural Religion*, edited by Richard H. Popkin, 97–106. Cambridge, MA: Hackett Publishing, 1999.

Humphrey, Derek. "Liberty and Death: A Manifesto Concerning an Individual's Right to Choose to Die." Accessed January 13, 2013. http://www.finalexit.org/liberty_and_death_manifesto_right_to_die.html.

Humphrey, Derek. "Why I Believe in Voluntary Euthanasia and Assisted Suicide." Euthanasia Research and Guidance Organization online website. Accessed January 13, 2013. http://www.finalexit.org/essay_why_i_believe.html.

Humphrey, Derek, and Mary Clement. *Freedom to Die: People, Politics and the Right-to-Die Movement*. New York: St. Martin's Griffin, 2000.

James I. *The True Lawe of Free Monarchies*. London, 1603.

*Jewish Study Bible*. Edited by Adele Berlin and Marc Zvi Brettler. Oxford: Oxford University Press, 2004.

Johnson, Barbara. "Translator's Introduction." In *Dissemination*, written by Jacques Derrida and translated by Barbara Johnson, vii–xxxiii. Chicago: University of Chicago Press, 1981.

Johnson, David E. "As If the Time Were Now: Deconstructing Agamben." *South Atlantic Quarterly* 106, no. 2 (2007): 265–90.

Johnson, Robert. "Kant's Moral Philosophy." In *The Stanford Encyclopedia of Philosophy* (summer 2010 ed.), edited by Edward N. Zalta. Accessed January 13, 2013. http://plato.stanford.edu/archives/sum2010/entries/kant-moral/.

Joiner, Thomas E. *Myths about Suicide*. Cambridge, MA: Harvard University Press, 2010.

Jost, Adolf. *Das Recht auf den Tod*. Göttingen: Dietrich,1895.

Jowett, Benjamin, trans. *The Dialogues of Plato translated into English with Analyses and Introductions by B. Jowett*. 3rd ed. Oxford: Oxford University Press, 1892.

Kamisar, Yale. "Euthanasia Legislation: Some Non-Religious Objections." In *Euthanasia and the Right to Death: The Case for Voluntary Euthanasia*, edited by A. B. Downing, 85–133. London: Peter Owen, 1969.

Kant, Immanuel. *Anthropology from a Pragmatic Point of View*. Translated by Robert B. Louden. Cambridge: Cambridge University Press, 2006.

Kant, Immanuel. *Lectures on Ethics*. Translated by Peter Heath. In *The Cambridge Edition of the Works of Immanuel Kant*, edited by Paul Guyer and Allen H. Wood. Cambridge: Cambridge University Press, 1997.

Kant, Immanuel. *Practical Philosophy*. Translated and edited by Mary J. Gregor. In *The Cambridge Edition of the Works of Immanuel Kant*, edited by Paul Guyer and Allen H. Wood. Cambridge: Cambridge University Press, 1996.

Kass, Leon R. *Life, Liberty and the Defense of Dignity: The Challenge for Bioethics*. San Francisco, CA: Encounter Books, 2002.

King, Martin Luther, Jr. *The King Papers Project*. The Martin Luther King, Jr. Research and Education Institute website. Accessed January 13, 2013. http://mlk-kpp01.stanford.edu/index.php/kingpapers/index.

Kretzmer, David, and Eckart Klein, eds. *The Concept of Human Dignity in Human Rights Discourse*. The Hague: Kluwer Law International, 2002.

Kristeller, Paul Oskar. *Renaissance Thought and Its Sources*. New York: Columbia University Press, 1973.

Kühl, Stefan. *The Nazi Connection: Eugenics, American Racism, and German National Socialism*. Oxford: Oxford University Press, 2002.

Lavi, Shai J. *The Modern Art of Dying: A History of Euthanasia in the United States*. Princeton, NJ: Princeton University Press, 2005.

Lee, Patrick, and Robert P. George. "The Nature and Basis of Human Dignity." *Ratio Juris* 12, no. 2 (2008): 173-93.

Levi-Strauss, Claude. *The Raw and the Cooked: Introduction to a Science of Mythology*. New York: Harper and Row, 1969.

Lifton, Robert Jay. *The Nazi Doctors: Medical Killing and the Psychology of Genocide*. New York: Basic Books, 1986; reprinted 2000.

Locke, John. *Two Treatises of Government*. Edited by Peter Laslett. Cambridge: Cambridge University Press, 1988.

Lorberbaum, Yair. "Blood and the Image of God." In *The Concept of Human Dignity in Human Rights Discourse*, edited by David Kretzmer and Eckart Klein, 55-85. The Hague: Kluwer Law International, 2002.

Lyall, Sarah. "Preparing to End her Life, While Protecting Another." *New York Times*, February 28, 2009, A9.

MacKendrick, Paul. *The Philosophical Books of Cicero*. New York: St. Martin's, 1989.

Mackey, John. "The Whole Foods Alternative to ObamaCare." *Wall Street Journal*, August 11, 2009.

Manetti, Gianozzo. *On the Dignity and Excellence of Man*. In *The Italian Philosophers: Selected Readings from Petrarch to Bruno*, edited and translated by Arturo B. Fallico and Herman Shapiro, 65-101. New York: Modern Library, 1967.

May, William E. *Catholic Bioethics and the Gift of Human Life*. 2nd ed. Huntington, IN: Our Sunday Visitor, 2008.

McCoy, Marjorie Casebier. *To Die with Style!* Nashville, TN: Abingdon Press, 1974.

McCrudden, Christopher. "Human Dignity and Judicial Interpretation of Human Rights." *European Journal of International Law* 19, no. 4 (2008): 655-724.

McDermott, Timothy. *Summa Theologiae: A Concise Translation*. Notre Dame, IN: Christian Classics, 1989.

Miles, Murray. "Plato on Suicide (*Phaedo* 60C-63C)." *Phoenix* 55, no. 3-4 (2001): 244-58.

Miller, J. Hillis. *For Derrida*. New York: Fordham University Press, 2009.

Milton, John. *The Riverside Milton*. Edited by Roy Flannagan. Boston: Houghton Mifflin, 1998.

Minois, Georges. *History of Suicide: Voluntary Death in Western Culture*. Translated by Lydia G. Cochrane. Baltimore: Johns Hopkins University Press, 1999.

Montaigne, Michel. *The Complete Essays of Montaigne*. Translated by Donald M. Frame. Stanford, CA: Stanford University Press, 1958.

Morton, James, ed. *The Ancren Riwle*. London: Camden Society, 1853.

Nancy, Jean-Luc. *The Creation of the World: Or Globalization*. Translated by François Raffoul and David Pettigrew. Albany: State University of New York Press, 2007.

Nancy, Jean-Luc. *The Experience of Freedom*. Translated by Bridget McDonald. Stanford: Stanford University Press, 1993.

Nancy, Jean-Luc. *A Finite Thinking*. Stanford, CA: Stanford University Press, 2003.

Nancy, Jean-Luc. "Shattered Love." In *The Inoperative Community*, translated by Lisa Garbus and Simona Sawhney, 82-109. Minneapolis: University of Minnesota Press, 1991.

Nass, Michael. *Derrida from Now On*. New York: Fordham University Press, 2008.

Nixon, Anthony. *The Dignitie of Man*. London, 1612.

Not Dead Yet. Online mission statement. Accessed January 13, 2013. http://notdeadyetnews commentary.blogspot.com/.

Page, Clarence. "'Death Panels' Myth Just Won't Die." *Chicago Tribune*, November 1, 2009.

Palin, Sarah. "Statement on the Current Health Care Debate." Published August 7, 2009. Accessed January 13, 2013. https://www.facebook.com/note.php?note_id=113851103434.

Peeters, Bernoît. *Derrida: A Biography*. Translated by Andrew Brown. Cambridge: Polity, 2013.

Pettigrew, Charles A. "Technology and the Eighth Amendment: The Problem of Supermax Prisons." *North Carolina Journal of Law and Technology* 4 (2002): 191-213.

Pico Project. Università degli Studi di Bologna and Brown University website. Accessed January 13, 2013. http:www.brown.edu/Departments/Italian_Studies/pico/.

Plato. *Phaedo*. Translated by Eva Brann et al. Newburyport, MA: Focus Classical Library, 1998.

Plato. *Phaedo*. Translated by David Gallop. Oxford: Clarendon Press, 1998.

Plato. *Phaedo*. Translated by R. Hackforth. Cambridge: Cambridge University Press, 1955.

Plato. *Phaedo*. Translated by Hugh Tredennick. In *The Collected Dialogues of Plato*, edited by Edith Hamilton and Huntington Cairns, 40–98. Bollingen Series 71. Princeton, NY: Princeton University Press, 1961.

Plato. *Laws*. Translated by Benjamin Jowett, 1892. New York: Cosimo, 2008.

Plato. *Laws*. Translated by A. E. Taylor. In *The Collected Dialogues of Plato*, edited by Edith Hamilton and Huntington Cairns, 1225–516. Bollingen Series 71. Princeton, NY: Princeton University Press, 1961.

Politifact.com. "McCaughey Claims End-of-Life Counseling Will Be Required for Medicare Patients." Published July 23, 2009. Accessed January 13, 2013. http://www.politifact.com/truth-o-meter/statements/2009/jul/23/betsy-mccaughey/mccaughey-claims-end-life-counseling-will-be-requi/.

President's Council on Bioethics. *Human Cloning and Human Dignity*. New York: Public Affairs, 2002.

Privitello, Lucio Angelo. "S/laughter and Animal-lethe." In *Reading Bataille Now*, edited by Shannon Winnubst, 167–96. Bloomington: Indiana University Press, 2007.

Protevi, John. *Political Affect: Connecting the Social and the Somatic*. Minneapolis: University of Minnesota Press, 2009.

Ramsey Colloquium of the Institute on Religion and Public Life. "Always to Care, Never to Kill." First Things website. Published February 1992. Accessed January 13, 2013. http://www.firstthings.com/article/2008/01/006-always-to-care-never-to-kill-36.

Ramsey, Paul. *Ethics at the Edges of Life*. New Haven, CT: Yale University Press, 1978.

Ramsey, Paul. "The Indignity of 'Death with Dignity.'" *Hastings Center Studies* 2, no. 2 (1974): 47–62.

Republican National Committee. "2008 Republican Platform." Accessed January 13, 2013. http://www.gop.com/2008Platform/.

Roberts, Adam, and Richard Guelff. *Documents on the Laws of War*. 3rd ed. Oxford: Oxford University Press, 2003.

Rosen, Michael. *Dignity: Its History and Meaning*. Cambridge, MA: Harvard University Press, 2012.

Rous, Francis. *The booke of Psalmes in English meeter*. London, 1641.

Santner, Eric L. "Terri Schiavo and the State of Exception." University of Chicago Press website. Published March 25, 2005. Accessed January 13, 2013. http://www.press.uchicago.edu/Misc/Chicago/05april_santner.html.

Schiller, Friedrich. "On Dignity and Grace." 1793. Translated by Jane V. Curran. In *Schiller's "On Grace and Dignity" in Its Cultural Context: Essays and a New Translation*, edited by Jane V. Curran and Christophe Fricker, Rochester, NY: Camden House, 2005.

Sensen, Oliver. *Kant on Human Dignity*. Berlin: Walter de Gruyter, 2011.

Shakespeare, William. *The Riverside Shakespeare*. Edited by G. Blakemore Evans. Boston: Houghton Mifflin, 1974.

Shershow, Scott Cutler. "Of Sinking: Marxism and the 'General' Economy." *Critical Inquiry* 27, no. 3 (2001): 486–92.

Shershow, Scott Cutler. "The Time of Sacrifice: Derrida contra Agamben." *Reconstruction: Studies in Contemporary Culture* 11, no. 2 (2011).

Shershow, Scott Cutler. *The Work and the Gift*. Chicago: University of Chicago Press, 2005.

Singer, Peter. *Rethinking Life and Death: The Collapse of Our Traditional Ethics*. New York: St. Martin's, 1996.

Smith, Wesley J. *Culture of Death: The Assault on Medical Ethics in America*. San Francisco, CA: Encounter Books, 2000.

Smith, Wesley J. *Forced Exit: Euthanasia, Assisted Suicide, and the New Duty to* Die. New York: Encounter Books, 1997.

Spenser, Edmund. *The Faerie Queene*. Edited by J. C. Smith. Oxford: Clarendon Press, 1909.

Stern, Paul. *Socratic Rationalism and Political Philosophy: An Interpretation of Plato's* Phaedo. Albany: State University of New York Press, 1993.

Stevenson, Richard W., and Elizabeth Bumiller. "Bush Cites Plan That Would Cut Social Security." *New York Times*, April 20, 2005, A1.

Stock, Gregory. "Go Ahead and Clone." *Reason* website. Published March 18, 2002. Accessed December 23, 2011. http://reason.com/archives/2002/03/18/go-ahead-and-clone.

Strong, James. *The New Strong's Expanded Exhaustive Concordance of the Bible*. Nashville, TN: Thomas Nelson, 2010.

Sullivan, Roger J. *An Introduction to Kant's Ethics*. Cambridge: Cambridge University Press, 1994.

Sypher, Wylie. "The Meanings of Comedy." In *Comedy*, edited by Wylie Sypher, 193-255. Baltimore: Johns Hopkins University Press, 1956.

Terri Schiavo Life and Hope Network. "Letter from Family." n.d. Accessed January 13, 2013. http://www.terrisfight.org/letter-from-family/.

*Trop v. Dulles*. 356 U.S. 86. United States Supreme Court, 1958.

Unitarian Universalist Association of Congregations. "Our Unitarian Universalist Principles." Accessed January 13, 2013. http://www.uua.org/beliefs/principles/index.shtml.

*Vacco v. Quill*. 521 U.S. 793. United States Supreme Court, 1997.

Vine, W. E., Merrill F. Unger, and William White Jr. *Vine's Complete Expository Dictionary of Old and New Testament Words*. Nashville, TN: Thomas Nelson, 1996.

Walsh, P. G., trans. *Cicero: On Obligations*. Oxford: Oxford University Press, 2000.

Warren, James. "Socratic Suicide." *Journal of Hellenic Studies* 121 (2001): 91-106.

Williams, Samuel D. "Euthanasia." In *Essays by Members of the Birmingham Speculative Club*. London, 1870.

Wood, Allen W. *Kantian Ethics*. Cambridge: Cambridge University Press, 2008.

Wood, David, and Robert Bernasconi. *Derrida and Différance*. Evanston, IL: Northwestern University Press, 1988.

Woodward, P. A., ed. *The Doctrine of Double Effect: Philosophers Debate a Controversial Moral Principle*. Notre Dame, IN: University of Notre Dame Press, 2001.

Woodward, P. A. "Introduction." In *The Doctrine of Double Effect: Philosophers Debate a Controversial Moral Principle*, edited by P. A. Woodward, 1-4. Notre Dame, IN: University of Notre Dame Press, 2001.

Yoo, John. *The Powers of War and Peace: The Constitution and Foreign Affairs after 9/11*. Chicago: University of Chicago Press, 2005.

# Index

The letter *f* following a page number denotes an illustration.

abortion, 29, 35, 153

Abraham (Biblical figure), 122

Abrahamic religions, 26-27, 47. *See also* Christian discourse; Judeo-Christian tradition

Abu-Ghraib prison (Iraq), 42

*Accursed Share* (Bataille), ix, xvi, xviii, 173, 177n4, 177n6

achievement, xviii, 34, 69, 96, 152; *a chief venir*, xviii, 34

Adler, Felix, 177n2

advance directives, xiii, 87, 143

*Advancement of Learning, The* (Bacon), 73-74, 76-78

aesthetics, 55-57, 150-51

Agamben, Giorgio, 45, 93, 158-59; and "bare life," xiii, 93, 158-59, 173; *Homo Sacer*, 93, 158-59

*Alice in Wonderland*, 172

Allen, Woody, xiv-xv

Althusser, Louis, 30

"always to care," 92, 94-95, 97, 144, 173

Améry, Jean, *On Suicide*, 100

amputations, 66-67, 113-14, 131-32

anchorites, 62-63

*Ancren Riwle*, 62-63

angels, 33, 48, 70

animals, 33, 36-38; "animal life," 119; and Aquinas, 66-67; as brutes, 59, 70-71; and

Cicero, 59-62; consumption of, 110, 112; and Kant, 82; killing of, 66, 110, 112; and Locke, 110, 112; and Pico, 70-71; and Plato, 110; and sacrifice, 110, 112, 122; and suicide, 110, 112

Annan, Kofi, 51; Nobel Prize lecture, 51

*Anthropology from a Pragmatic Point of View* (Kant), 117-18

aporia, x, 154

appearance. *See* bearing

Aquinas, Thomas, 64-67; Doctrine of Double Effect (DDE), 116, 138; *Summa Theologica*, 64-67; surgical metaphor of, 66-67; and translations, 65-67

arche-trace, 11, 19

aristocratic status, 34; and Cicero, 62-63; and Kant, 78; and Pico, 68; and Shakespeare, 71-72

Aristotle, 64-65, 106

art, works of, 35-36, 150-53

assisted suicide, xii, 29; and Dworkin, 87; in Netherlands, xii; in Oregon, xii, 29; and right-to-die debate, 87-88, 91, 94, 97, 174; Smith's opposition to, 50, 93-94; and sovereignty, 44; in Washington State, xii, 29. *See also* physician-assisted suicide

Atkins, E. M., 54-55, 57-59, 62

*aufhebung*, 14

Augustine, 100, 158

"Ends of Man, The" (Derrida), 6–8
enemy combatants, 41–42
Engels, Friedrich, 84
Esposito, Roberto, 127
esteem, 31, 33–35, 54, 56, 73
ethics, ix, xi, xviii, xix–xx, 33, 35; and Bataille, xviii, 177n6; and Cicero, 56; and cloning, 164, 167–70; and *Cruzan v. Missouri*, 146–47; and "Declaration on Euthanasia," 135; ethical relativism, 2; ethic of care, 97; and eugenic discourse, 131–32; and Kant, xi, 78–79, 83, 88, 109, 112–13, 118–19; and Locke, 112; and Plato, xi, 103; post-Kantian, 69; pure ethics, xix–xx; and right-to-die debate, ix, 86, 92–94, 97, 123–24, 173; and sacrifice, 122, 128, 131–32, 138–40, 152; and slippery slope, 93–94, 123, 164; and suicide, 103, 109, 112–13, 118–19. *See also* bioethics
*Ethics* (Ramsey), 92–93
eugenic discourse, xiv, 123–35, 177nn2–3. *See also* euthanasia; sterilizations
euthanasia, xii–xiv, 177nn2–3; and Binding/ Hoche, 44, 127–33, 180n2; and *Cruzan v. Missouri*, 142, 144; and "Declaration on Euthanasia," 133–36, 138; and Dworkin, 151; and Jost, 44, 127; Nazi programs of, xiv, 44–45, 93, 123–24, 126, 179n1 (chap. 7); and Purdy, 90, 179n1 (chap. 5); and right-to-die debate, 93–95, 97, 123; and sacrifice, 124–34, 137–38, 142, 144, 151; and sanctity of life, 29, 35; Smith's opposition to, 50, 93–94; and sovereignty, 44–45; vexed history of, xii; and Williams, xiii, 36, 124–26
"Euthanasia" (Williams), xiii, 36, 124–26
excellence: and Cicero, 56, 58–59; *excellentia*, 56, 58–59; and Pico, 70; and Shakespeare, 71
*Experience of Freedom* (Nancy), x

factory farms, 112
*Faerie Queene* (Spenser), 72–73
fascism, 18, 124
fate, 115–16
Fathers of English Dominican Province, 65–67
Fazio, Bartolomeo, 69
fear: and Kant, 114–15, 118; and Plato, 103, 110; and right-to-die debate, 94–96; and suicide, 103, 110, 114–15, 118
feeding tubes, 88, 141, 146, 156–57, 160
feminism, 143
fetus, 85

*Final Exit* (Humphrey), 90–91
Final Exit Network, 87; "My Life, My Death, My Choice," 87
financial resources, 90–92, 94, 134–35, 173
*Finite Thinking* (Nancy), 122
force, 14–22, 25; and law, 14–22, 25; as privileged, 16, 19, 21; sovereignty as, 14–17, 21–22, 25; and speech, 16; and structuralist analysis, 16. *See also* sovereignty
"Force and Signification" (Derrida), 16
*Forced Exit* (Smith), 50, 94
"Force of Law" (Derrida), 2–3, 7, 9, 14–22, 27
forgiveness, 25–27; "just forgiveness," 27; pure forgiveness, 27
Foucault, Michel, 30, 44–45, 100
Fournier, Keith, 156
fractal structure, 86
freedom, xii, 8, 23; and Annan, 51; and cloning, 166–68, 170; and Conrad cartoon, 154–55, 155f; and *Cruzan v. Missouri*, 146; free will, 16, 82, 91; and Kant, 78–79, 82–83, 116; and Locke, 110–11; and Pico, 69–71; and Plato, 110; and right-to-die debate, 45, 87–88, 90–92, 165–67; and sacrifice, 140, 146, 154; and self-sovereignty, 76; and suicide, 100, 110–11, 116
*Freedom to Die* (Humphrey), 91
Freud, Sigmund, 12
Frey, R. G., 102
Friedlander, Henry, 126–27
"From Restricted to General Economy" (Derrida), xvi, 3–6, 23
Futurists, 151

Gallop, David, 103–5, 107–10, 179nn2–4 (chap. 6)
gallows humor, 104–5, 129. *See also* comedy, notes of; laughter
Gasché, Rodolphe, 3, 5
gender: and Cicero, 58; and effeminacy, 58, 103; and Plato, 103; and right-to-die debate, 88; and suicide, 103
general economy, ix–x, xv–xviii, 6, 14, 177n6; and right-to-die debate, 173; and Williams, 125
genetic technologies, 166, 168–70
Geneva Conventions, xviii, 41–43, 178n1 (chap. 3); Common Article III, 41–43
"Gentilesse" (Chaucer), 67–68
George, Robert P., 29, 36, 137–38, 147; *The Clash of Orthodoxies*, 36; "Terminal," 137–38